RACISM IN THE CANADIAN UNIVERSITY:
DEMANDING SOCIAL JUSTICE, INCLUSION, AND EQUITY

I0084775

The mission statements and recruitment campaigns for modern Canadian universities promote diverse and enlightened communities. *Racism in the Canadian University* questions this idea by examining the ways in which the institutional culture of the academy privileges Whiteness and Anglo-Eurocentric ways of knowing. Often denied and dismissed in practice as well as policy, the various forms of racism still persist in the academy. This collection, informed by critical theory, personal experience, and empirical research, scrutinizes both historical and contemporary manifestations of racism in Canadian academic institutions, finding in these communities a deep rift between how racism is imagined and how it is lived.

With equal emphasis on scholarship and personal perspectives, *Racism in the Canadian University* is an important look at how racial minority faculty and students continue to engage in a daily struggle for safe, inclusive spaces in classrooms and among peers, colleagues, and administrators.

FRANCES HENRY is a Professor Emerita, York University.

CAROL TATOR is Course Director in the Department of Anthropology at York University.

EDITED BY FRANCES HENRY AND
CAROL TATOR

Racism in the Canadian University

Demanding Social Justice, Inclusion,
and Equity

UNIVERSITY OF TORONTO PRESS
Toronto Buffalo London

© University of Toronto Press 2009
Toronto Buffalo London
utorontopress.com

ISBN 978–0-8020–9981–5 (cloth)
ISBN 978–0-8020–9677–7 (paper)

Library and Archives Canada Cataloguing in Publication

Racism in the Canadian university : demanding social justice,
inclusion and equity / edited by Frances Henry and Carol Tator.

Includes index.
ISBN 978-0-8020-9981-5 (bound). – ISBN 978-0-8020-9677-7 (pbk.)

1. Racism in higher education – Canada.   2. Minorities in higher
education – Canada.   I. Henry, Frances, 1931–   II. Tator, Carol

LB2329.8.C2R33 2009   378.0089′00971   C2009-900988-9

Cover photograph courtesy of Paul Dodson, www.photograph-london.com

University of Toronto Press acknowledges the fi nancial assistance to
its publishing program of the Canada Council for the Arts and the
Ontario Arts Council.

University of Toronto Press acknowledges the financialsupportforits
publishing activities of the Government of Canada through the Book
Publishing Industry Development Program (BPIDP).

This book is dedicated to all those who work towards creating an academy that truly embraces and reflects the knowledge, culture, and values of all of its members.

Contents

RACISM IN THE CANADIAN UNIVERSITY:
DEMANDING SOCIAL JUSTICE, INCLUSION, AND EQUITY

Introduction: Racism in the Canadian University

FRANCES HENRY AND CAROL TATOR

> Our schools, colleges and universities continue to be powerful discursive
> sites through which race knowledge is produced, organized and regulated.
> Marginalized bodies are continually silenced and rendered invisible not
> simply through the failure to take issues of race and social oppression
> seriously but through the constant negation of multiple lived experiences
> and alternative knowledges.
> – G. Dei and A. Calliste, 'Introduction, Mapping the Terrain: Power,
> Knowledge and Anti-Racism Education'

In this collection of essays each author analyses the impact of hegemonic Whiteness and the processes of racialization that continue to function
in the Canadian academy. Drawing upon an extensive body of literature and empirical investigations of racism in Canadian academic institutions, the writers explore how access and equity are often denied to
both racialized faculty and students through the everyday values and
norms, discourses, and practices within a dominant White Anglocentric, Eurocentric, and racialized culture. All of the contributors to this
book believe that the daily struggle to find a safe and inclusive space
for racialized students and faculty within the classroom among peers,
colleagues, and administrators contributes to a sometimes hostile, oppressive, unsafe learning and working environment. Each of the scholars in this collection draws attention to how Whiteness as ideology and
praxis functions in the Canadian academy.

We were drawn to this subject for two main reasons. In the first
instance, our past research and writings have often focused on how
racism and the culture of Whiteness impacts the major institutions of

Canadian society. For example, we surveyed these major institutions in our 1995 book *The Colour of Democracy,* including systems of governance, health and social services, mass media, education, justice, policing, and arts and culture.[1] In researching new material for the fourth edition, in press, we were struck by the increase in the volume of literature on manifestations of racism in the academy, some of it written by often relatively newly hired racialized faculty.

Moreover, Frances Henry spent years in the early seventies struggling to get the right to teach a course on racism and to conduct research on this 'tabooed' and ignored topic; Carol Tator has taught a course for more than a decade related to anti-racism, and through it is exposed to the experiences of racialized students. These experiences have left, and continue to leave, deep impressions on each of us.

Attending and participating in many conferences in almost every province of this country has led both of us to listen to the painful and marginalizing narratives of many Indigenous faculty and faculty of colour. Henry, in writing the report on inequity at Queen's University, had an opportunity to meet with faculty, staff, and administrators to examine the impact of racism and the role of Whiteness in the culture of the university. In 2005, we launched a pilot study to critically analyse the extent to which racism is present in Canadian universities.

All of these factors have added to our involvement with this subject matter, and eventually to this book. As we are deeply committed to critical race theory and its emphasis on experiential voices, it was only natural to invite noted scholars of colour and a highly respected Indigenous scholar to participate in this venture.

Before beginning the discussion of these issues as they play out in the modern Canadian university, the historical and situational site in which these struggles for equity and inclusion takes place needs to be briefly described.

History and Background to the Academy

Universities began in the Western world during the middle ages in Europe, for example, in areas now known as Italy, France, Germany, and England. However, academic institutions that provided advanced and specialist training began earlier in the Arab world. Al-Azhar University in Cairo was founded in 969, centuries before any in Europe. The main areas of concentration in the curriculum were law, medicine, theology, and, later, liberal arts. It was acknowledged even then that the pursuit of knowledge for its own sake was to be one of a university's main objectives.

Since universities are complex institutions with regulations, policies, norms, and values, they fall subject to the changing nature of the society in which they are located. In our globalized world, change is rapid, and one of the principal dynamics of globalization is the increase in the movement of people. Migration has brought peoples from all over the world to Canada, and, as they settle, they or, more commonly, their children begin attending university. The university institution was created and controlled largely by White males of Anglo-Saxon ethnicity who reflected their European origins and experience. On the development of Canadian universities, Dorothy Smith (2002) comments that in the past men took their male-dominated culture in the university as a given, and later both White men and women in institutions of higher learning took for granted the absence of people who could be identified as the 'other' based on the colour of their skin or other physical features:

> Universities in Canada were founded in and were integrated with the ruling apparatus of imperial powers that were implicated in the genocidal treatment of the peoples native to the territory we call Canada, institutions of slavery, the subjugation of other civilizations … Skin colour becomes the present trace of membership in a formerly subjugated people in the context of intellectual and cultural traditions founded in imperialism. (151)

However, as the needs, values, and practices of Canadian society have become more diverse and pluralistic, these anachronistic and monocultural ideological assumptions, policies, and practices, which emphasize Eurocentric dominated learnings, are increasingly being challenged by new voices and different perspectives on knowledge and education. The mission of the university, therefore, needs to adjust to these new challenges. In our globalizing, post-industrial, and democratic society the mission of the university must reflect these current realities:

> The university and society are parties to a social contract. In each era, this social contract must be adapted and renegotiated. Here at the beginning of the twenty-first century, we are renegotiating the social contract between universities and the society which supports them. What should be the mission of the university? What are the essential characteristics of our age

and how should the university adapt to them? What should be the balance between the traditional mission of the university and the changes required of our age? It is widely recognized that, in post-industrial society, the university is important to our economy, to our health care, and to our culture … Universities have a vital role in democratic life with special obligations regarding accessibility and inclusion … University professors have special obligations as critics and conscience of society and to be public intellectuals. (Fallis 2004, 5)

There are three fundamental tenets characteristic of university organization, which have always guided the university's mission. The first is that a liberal education values knowledge for its own sake. This allows for the study of areas and disciplines that appear to have no direct relationship to skills development or career patterns. The second belief is that a liberal education should be a broad education, rather than focused upon a single discipline, and this allows for the evolution of many patterns of learning. The third is that a liberal education creates a free, independent, and thoughtful person.[2]

In this book we maintain that the mission of a university as policy, ideology, and praxis must also change. The academy must identify the sweeping changes made necessary by the movement away from a *relatively* homogeneous social environment to that of a heterogeneous culturally and racially pluralistic society, characterized by values such as equity and access to and inclusion of all of the diverse communities and ideas. Accordingly, these values must be reflected in all aspects of the university structures and systems.

As Canadian society has become increasingly segmented and divided into localized ethno-racial and racialized communities, one of the most important functions of the university should be to provide a training ground for acquiring the necessary knowledge, analytical tools, and critical skills to function effectively in diverse fields such as the arts, education, social work, healthcare, law, and journalism, among many other disciplines, within the context of a multiracial and multicultural society.

One of the most important controversies in regard to the role and function of modern universities is the debate over knowledge and skills training. Community colleges were developed primarily to provide skills training and career development, whereas the university was to remain as the place to gather knowledge. This distinction is to a certain extent breaking down, and both sets of institutions provide both knowledge and skills training. Universities are becoming increasingly commodified production sites that are 'essentially assembly plants for economically useful knowledge, and training facilities for skilled practitioners' (Franklin 2000, 20). As governments cut public funding, educational institutions must rely more and more on corporate funding. The growing dependence on private funding for university research strongly influences what gets studied. There is very limited corporate interest in fields that show little promise of generating profits (Turk 2000). There are significant problems in society that remain unresearched or under-explored because of the lack of recognition and funding. Franklin (2000, 20) makes this point in comparing the lack of funding for peace research in Canadian universities over the past several decades to the increase in the funding of business schools during the same time span and at the same institutions. In the same way, we suggest that racialized and Indigenous scholars have historically found and currently find little support for research that focuses on the racialization of poverty, Aboriginal homelessness, and racism in systems of cultural production, healthcare, and employment systems.

The doctrines of globalization, institutional competition, and market-driven programming are now pushing at the gates of our institutions of higher learning. 'Soft' disciplines such as the social sciences, humanities, and fine arts are losing status in favour of business, technology, the 'hard' sciences, and the professions (Axelrod 1998). A comparison between, for example, enrolments in philosophy courses versus computer technology or some of the applied sciences would demonstrate the point.

These accelerating changes and new developments in the academy, and in the broader society, have come with new questions about identity, belonging, and knowledge organized around complex and contradictory ideas about exclusion and inclusion. As Dei (1996, 250) suggests, 'any agenda of educational and social transformation must be able to deal with these tensions, dilemmas and contradictions.'

We and the contributing authors to this book identify the ways in which traditional models that have guided university life for hundreds of years, based on a social environmant that has focused on White Europeans and their new world descendants, no longer accurately reflect the needs and demands of a racially and culturally pluralistic university and society. Each of the authors believes that the continuance of the traditional patriarchal and monocultural models that support the academy, as well as the more recent phenomenon of market-driven forces, perpetuates an environment characterized by deep ruptures and abiding forms of individual, institutional, and systemic inequity.

As the title, *Racism in the Canadian University: Demanding Social Justice, Inclusion, and Equity,* suggests, the university continues to be a place where various overt and covert forms of racism and other forms of oppression are practised. We strongly believe that the role and effectiveness of education in the twenty-first century in academia depends on very significant shifts in the cultural, structural, epistemological, and pedagogical models and approaches that historically and currently typify the universities.

Following John Dewey, we hold that higher education should provide the conditions for people to involve themselves in the deepest problems of society. Higher education should provide an environment that supports the knowledge, skills, and ethical responsibility necessary for 'reasoned participation in democratically organized publics' (cited in Giroux 2006, 258–9). In the same way, Jacques Derrida argued that if higher education is going to have a future in promoting democracy, it is crucial for educators to take up the 'necessity to rethink the concepts of the possible and impossible' (cited in Simmons and Worth 2001, 5).

The culture of Whiteness is one of the major perspectives that informs the theoretical foundations of this book and a common conceptual framework shared by the authors in this work. Another is the processes of racialization and the constantly mutating forms of racism identified as cultural racism, everyday racism, institutional and systemic racism, democratic racism, epistemological racism, and discursive racism. The theoretical and empirical approaches to the subject of racism in the academy are also informed by critical race theory, critical pedagogy, and the expressiveness of narratology, all of which serve to shape the content of this book.

A Brief History of Racism in the Canadian Academy

Lest it be thought that the Canadian university has been free from charges of sexism, racism, and other examples of systemic discrimination, here are three fairly early examples of charges and allegations made at three separate universities in the country. There have been many other examples of incidences, but at least two of these created a considerable amount of public attention.

1 Sir George Williams University, Montreal 1968

In the spring of 1968, six Black West Indian students accused a biology professor of racism. They complained to the administration but saw little response. By fall of that year, the students made it a public issue. Looking for a quick solution, the school established a Hearing Committee. But the students didn't agree with the choice of representatives. The issue exploded and in late January 1969 more than 200 students occupied the computer centre on the ninth floor of the Hall building and soon expanded to occupy the seventh floor. The school and the protesters negotiated a deal, but there was a misunderstanding: after more than half the protesters left the building, the university reneged on the decision and called the police. Feeling deceived, the students rioted through the building, doing more than $2 million in damages. The computer lab was destroyed, windows were smashed, and computer tapes and punch cards were tossed onto the street below. Police arrested ninety-seven people, sixty-seven of whom were Sir George Williams University students and fifty-five of whom were White.

It was the largest student riot in Canadian history. The riot still stands as the most dramatic and costly student protest in Canadian history. The biology professor was exonerated after an inquiry and continued his career at Sir George Williams and Concordia (Wayland 1995).

2 York University, Toronto 1984

The incidents that sparked an investigation and the subsequent preparation of two reports began in 1981 when Janice Joseph, a teaching assistant and PhD candidate, complained that a neighbour in the graduate residence in which she resided had placed garbage and litter in front of her door. The neighbour, Grant Austin, also taunted her with racist slurs, including: 'They sure didn't make them smart when they made them Black.' 'Hi, girls. How are you, missie?' 'Hi, missie. Take up your garbage.' 'Hi little girl. Did you read my letter, little girl?' 'You didn't understand my letter, little girl. Go and read it again, little girl.' There was also a sign on Austin's door which read 'No Black ... canvassers at this apartment' and the word 'Black' was underlined. A racist letter was also slipped under Joseph's door. As this harassment continued, Ms. Joseph launched a series of complaints. At another time, Austin called the police to the campus saying that three Black students were outside his apartment. Housing and security services at the university did little to intercede in this situation. Ms. Joseph complained to one of her professors who subsequently phoned the housing authority on her behalf.

When the university finally convened a hearing, it consisted almost entirely of White authorities and administrators. Its findings were equivocal and 'reflect a failure to call racism by its name, to understand its particular offensiveness, and to identify its perpetrators' (see York University 1984). It did not charge Grant Austin with racist conduct but convicted him of acting towards the complainant 'in a harassing and insulting manner.' The penalty against Austin was that he not be allowed to live in residence on campus. In April 1983, the then president of the university convened a Special Review Committee on Charges of Racial and Sexual Harassment at York University. The committee published two reports, one written by the majority of the committee and one by the minority. The Minority Report called for stronger punitive measures against racism at the university. Even the Majority Report condemned the actions of the university:

> Our committee ... [h]ave all expressed our profound dissatisfaction with the verdict and the penalty and have formally asked the President to review this decision and impose the penalty of expulsion which is commensurate with the seriousness of the offence. We construe the presidential statement against racial and religious intolerance to mean that such intolerance, when it is no longer a private state of mind but expressed in overt acts of harassment, has absolutely no place in this University. (1984a, 36)

A few years later and partly as a result of the Joseph incident, the university established a 'race relations' office.

These events took place more than twenty-five years ago and apparently little real progress in identifying, defining, and challenging racism has been made. As this book was nearing completion, sometime during the evening of January 22 and the morning of January 23, 2008, less than twelve hours after Martin Luther King Jr. Day, shocked members of the York University community found racist graffiti in the form of anti-Black statements defacing the doors of the York University Black Student Association (YUBSA) office, the nearby washroom, as well as in other spaces on campus. Phrases such as 'All niggers must die,' 'Niggas go back to Africa,' and 'White = right/black = jail' were written. Although the university responded by sending York security and a representative of the Office of the Ombudsperson and Centre for Human Rights to the sites, President Mamdouh Shoukri did not make a public statement condemning the incident until twenty-four hours later, only after numerous emails and phone calls, and a student outcry.

This incident resulted in two large protests. York University students continue to speak out against racism and the anti-Black graffiti that have recently threatened students' safety on campus. After some criticism of the president's failure to immediately respond to the York community and particularly the Black students and faculty, President Shoukri acknowledged that the administration could have acted a little faster. He also expressed surprise at 'the level of mistrust that is out there.' At the second protest, the president of YUBSA, Zannalyn Robest, raised a number of rhetorical questions such as: 'Where are the Black faculty members in science? Why are there not more Black students being taken as grad students? Where are the Black TAs?' (*Excalibur* January 30, 2008).

3 University of British Columbia, Political Science Department 1992–1995

In 1992, a group of graduate students in the political science department at UBC expressed their concerns about the department to an associate dean. Among their many complaints were 'practices, classroom dynamics, curricular offerings, and interactions with faculty which they considered sexist, racist, or both' (McIntyre 2000). Asked to put their concerns in writing, they produced a document that included allegations of 'denigration of women's academic abilities and interests; discouragement of classroom participation by women; marginalization of, or intolerance towards, critical race and feminist theory; the use of racist metaphors and remarks in the classroom; unequal funding of women and men graduate students; and instances of sexual harassment of women of colour' (148). The chair of the department expressed surprise at the complaints and deplored their 'inflammatory' language. Little attention was paid to the student complaints and later that year the department underwent a program review in which it was praised and lauded for its productivity. The report also noted that the faculty was largely White and male and that many of their approaches were outdated and that graduate students expressed a high level of discontent. The review committee's final report, however, omitted many of their concerns and this was the version widely distributed.

The following year another group of students issued another memo to the dean of graduate studies criticizing the department's response to their earlier memo and expanding their list of grievances. The dean eventually replied, noting that 'nothing in my experience suggests to me that the characterization of this department as pervaded by gender bias or racism and ethnocentrism is accurate' (McIntyre 2000, 151).[3] At the same time, three individual students raised individual grievances against the department, including the telling of a racist and sexist joke by a professor against a woman of colour. Another listed a number of sexist and racist incidents she experienced in interacting with White faculty members in the department. The university finally hired an outside consultant to probe into the allegations and write a report of her findings. After an exhaustive study, the author's report concluded that there were at least nine serious issues facing this department and that there was cause for the allegations of racism and sexism. She recommended that the department be closed to further student admissions until all students received education equity (McEwen 1995). The report and the subsequent suspension of admissions polarized the university community and led to considerable unease and discontent at all levels of this organization. Finally in 1995, the suspension was lifted. Three years later, the department was identified as the wronged party and an apology by the president of the university was issued.

Sheila McIntyre (2000), among others, was profoundly disturbed by this result. In writing about racism and sexism at the university, she cited the incident at UBC and stated:

> Its conclusions shocked me. To my knowledge, no Canadian 'chilly climate' report has ever before culminated in so outright a reaction and so publicly and authoritatively declared a defeat for those who attempted to name and curb manifestations of systemic inequality within the university setting ... no previous campus struggle resulted in so shocking a triumph for studied ignorance and so outrageous an assertion of privileged innocence. In my view, willful blindness on many levels was required to account for the conclusion of the Department of Political Science affair at UBC. (158)

These are only three early examples. There is a significant body of scholarship written largely by racialized and Aboriginal faculty in the early and mid-nineties in which the racism and oppression at university level is clearly documented. These include, for example, *Unsettling Relations: The University as a Site of Feminist Struggles* (Bannerji et al. 1991). Speaking from different social locations and their own personal experiences in the academy, each of the five authors, Carty, Bannerji, Dehli, Heald, and McKenna, identify how gender, race, ethnicity, and sexual orientation reinforce marginalization within the dominant White culture of the university.

As Carty comments, universities were perpetuating society's racism and oppression: 'there is little difference between what we experience on the streets as Black women and the experiences we have inside the university ... the university's commonsense appeal to reason and science may take the rough edges off or sediment the particular behaviour, but the impact is no less severe' (1991, 15). Racialized faculty were unsupported. Bannerji, referring to her teaching experience in a Canadian university, states: 'The perception of the students is not neutral – it calls for response from them and even decisions. I am an exception in the universities ... I am meant for another kind of work – but nonetheless I am in the classroom ... I am authority' (1991). These individual narratives of everyday racism, which are found throughout this book, are also valuable as they signal not just individual manifestations of racism, but also point to the ways in which pervasive institutionalized and systemic forms of racialized oppression operate in the academy.

One of the first and most substantive investigations of 'race relations' took place in 1991 at Queen's University, Kingston, Ontario, under the guidance of a widely regarded specialist in the field of intergroup relations, psychology professor John Berry. The report (Queen's University 1991) identified a significant number of vital curriculum issues that needed to be addressed including:

- the existence of course names that do not reflect their content [e.g., 'The History of Political Thought' should be renamed 'The History of *Western* Political Thought'];
- the prevalence of core courses [those required for particular degrees] that include only Eurocentric issues;
- the need to hire faculty who can teach courses that do not have a Eurocentric focus;
- the lack of anti-racist courses in the curriculum and the need to make these mandatory in some curricula;
- the need to introduce more interdisciplinary studies, such as Black studies and Native studies;
- the need to review science curricula to make the important point that even science is not value-free;

- the need to develop supplementary programs for minority students that would help them meet academic standards.

The report also pointed to the need for recruitment and selection procedures for new faculty to make the university more representative (Queen's University 1991). Thirteen years later in 2003, another study and report was commissioned by Queen's, authored by Frances Henry. The research revealed that there had been a lack of any real progress. The culture of Whiteness continued to dominate the values, norms, and philosophy of the university (Henry 2003).

As will be demonstrated throughout this book, there is a lengthy history of racialized incidents and racialized processes taking place at Canadian universities. Writing now, several decades after the racial crisis at Sir George Williams University and a multiplicity of other manifestations of racism in the academy, we find we are still deeply mired in the systems and structures of racial inequities.

The discourse of denial is still largely evident in universities where allegations of racism have become public knowledge. The 'it can't happen here' response is still very much the discursive approach, despite the huge body of evidence that diverse forms of marginalization, exclusion, and oppression are pervasive and systemic in the Canadian academy. One of the main reasons for the lack of change on Canadian university campuses today is that, over the years, the administration has made nothing more than cosmetic changes to its overall structure. A serious effort to combat racism in all its guises at university has not been undertaken. What we have instead are a series of minor approaches – tokens – which have led to little improvement in lives of racialized students and faculty.

We found only two structural changes. Almost all universities declare a commitment to anti-racism, diversity, and equity in their mission statements; however, mission statements and policies in themselves have little to do with implementing substantive change. And, most universities have established some sort of 'race relations,' equity, or diversity office.[4] Some universities have appointed a 'special advisor' on race relations to the president, at least for temporary periods. The office is invariably headed by a person of colour either appointed from within faculty ranks or recruited from outside the university. In either event, many of the appointed individuals have had limited knowledge and background in the practice of managing a 'race relations' or 'human rights' office, and most important, lack the necessary knowledge, skills, and *power* to address the institutional and structural barriers to access and equity.

Another serious deficiency in their work is that their mandate almost always includes only the hearing and possible investigation of complaints brought in by students and, in some instances, staff and faculty. Their investigatory resources are extremely limited and they have virtually no authority to decide on penalties. As a result, even if their limited investigation revealed discriminatory behaviour, little more than an apology could be recommended in their reports. These are powerless, almost completely marginalized offices that have virtually no ability to promote or activate institutional or systemic changes related to racism.

Some universities, in addition to or in place of a diversity office, have created a position of special advisor to the president on these matters. However, while the incumbent might, at least in theory, have the ear of the president, achieving structural change remains another matter entirely. Often, all the president is required to do is to take the matter 'under advisement.' From there, it is let to quietly die.

A more recent development has further eroded the power to effect anti-racist change at the university. Following the fashion of the intellectual and political times of the last ten years, the human rights paradigm and diversity model has been heralded as the prominent symbol of a commitment to social transformation. This paradigm includes a commitment to human rights for all, thereby incorporating all issues that deal with social justice and equity, including gender, disability, race, ethnicity, religion, sexual orientation, and others defined by human rights codes. Subsuming 'race' in this generic model means even less emphasis is placed on racial oppression, especially as it is extraordinarily difficult to substantiate or 'prove.' Thus, whatever attempts are made to stimulate systemic change for all of the marginalized groups within the academy, and however laudable such efforts are, the overall effect is that 'race' issues often get lost in the process. As well, this model, based as it is on provincial and federal human rights commissions' approach to addressing racial discrimination, works on a case by case attempt at individual resolution. It is not linked to initiating, developing, or creating systemic or structural change.

Diana Relke's (1998) satiric analysis of how a university manages 'diversity' is an excellent example of how the academy stifles any kind of structural or substantive change, while at the same time claiming a strong commitment to diversity. Relke asks: 'How does the University in which so many are committed to diversity manage to achieve so little on its behalf?' and notes:

> The institution has a way of saying No to diversity while appearing to say Yes. [For example:]
> - The University has nothing whatsoever against diversity, as long as it doesn't interfere with the white masculine status quo. Or, to put it another way, the University has nothing against multiculturalism, as long as it remains peripheral to monoculturalism.
> - The University has nothing against requiring that every College on campus produce an equity policy on hiring, as long as no College is actually required to implement it.
> - The University doesn't mind adding a few more women and Aboriginal scholars to the faculty, as long as it's implicitly understood that what we are really hiring are equity tokens.
> - The University doesn't complain that the percentage of visible minorities on the faculty is four times the goal established by the Human Rights Commission, as long as 87 percent of that category of faculty is male.
> - The University doesn't mind establishing an office of President's Advisor on the Status of Women, as long as the position can be slashed before the Advisor's work can properly begin.
> - The University has no objection to establishing interdisciplinary departments of Native Studies and Women's Studies, as long as they make do with three or four faculty so that the monodisciplinary departments can continue to operate with fifteen or thirty.
> - The University has nothing against requiring yet another committee to produce yet another report on our questionable equity record, as long as we are free to ignore the report's most important recommendations. (3–4)

Thus, it can be argued that it is not only the snail's pace of introducing change into a system that impedes the development of anti-racist and other measures designed to reduce individual, institutional, and structural forms of oppression found in Canadian universities. Perhaps, more importantly, it is the inability or unwillingness to change the fundamental values and norms on which academia has traditionally been based that is at the heart of the continued disadvantage of racialized and Aboriginal students and faculty. Each of the authors of *Racism in the Canadian University: Demanding Social Justice, Inclusion, and*

Equity believes that there is an urgent need confronting our universities in the new millennium. At every level, our universities must become *responsible, accountable,* and *answerable* to the diverse constituencies within its walls, as well as the racialized and Indigenous communities within Canadian society. We believe it is time to move beyond studies, task forces, and inquiries related to racism. Action is needed *now* to address the direct and indirect structural and systemic barriers deeply embedded in the White culture of the Canadian academy.

Outline of the Book

In chapter 1 the editors, Frances Henry and Carol Tator, explore some of the common theoretical perspectives that inform the analysis of all the contributors to the book. Drawing from an extensive body of literature, as well as empirical evidence based on data drawn from our interviews and a survey with Canadian academics across the country, we explore how racism is manifested in the academy. In this conceptual framework we map how the contours and processes of Whiteness and racialization intersect in the academy and impact upon racialized and Aboriginal faculty, as well as Aboriginal academics and students of colour. We probe the diverse ways in which both overt and covert forms of racism are manifested in what counts as knowledge and scholarship and how Eurocentric standards impact upon hiring, promotion, and tenure decisions. The narratives of racialized academics and students that are included in this book are characterized by self-doubt, apprehension, frustration, and disappointment. Despite over two decades of scholarship documenting the problem of racism in our universities, and endless recommendations, there remains huge resistance to change.

Chapter 2, written by Audrey Kobayashi, focuses on how women of colour in Canadian academia are notable for being *un*seen. Androcentric and Eurocentric values, supported by the power of 'old white boys' networks, have kept women of colour out of the academy. Even when women of colour are present in the academy, they experience the effects of racism through the practice of Whiteness. A Whiteness lens makes it very difficult for the majority to see or understand the experiences of women of colour. The impacts of Whiteness that define the experiences of women of colour are identified as denigration, deflection, exotification, and guilt. Kobayashi draws upon examples from her own experience to demonstrate that we cannot really understand systemic effects of racism without a recognition that normalized patterns of racialization are acted out through individual bodies. She argues that social institutions, such as the university, need to acknowledge the 'adverse effects' of racialization. Effects such as the scarcity of bodies of colour on almost all Canadian university campuses and the overwhelming culture of Whiteness lead in turn to deeply personal experiences of exclusion.

Patricia Monture in chapter 3 reflects on the many lessons of survival she has learned since she began her university teaching in 1989. Monture suggests that the collective experience of Aboriginal people in universities is still about lived oppression of Indigenous ways of being and knowing. She describes, in some detail, how her positioning as an Indigenous scholar in the university was often seen as problematic. Her analysis indicates how the rules and traditions governing promotion and tenure decisions were used against her in ways that led to a denigration of her experience and her research. Monture states that the processes of tenure and promotion largely depend on counting refereed papers and books, whereas for her and most Aboriginal scholars the emphasis should be on publishing in venues that are accessible to Aboriginal people. She argues that in the university there is an unwillingness to place an individual's accomplishments in the context of a recognition of gender, race/culture, and class, and then taking account of these identities and experiences.

In chapter 4 Camille Hernandez-Ramdwar turns attention to racialized students, in this case, those from the Caribbean, and their experiences in the university. Her interviews with undergraduate and graduate students who have migrated from the Caribbean and those who are second generation (born in Canada to migrants) identify some of the factors that impact on academic performance. She found that graduate students had the most to say on the subject of racism in the academy and identified the lack of mentoring and lack of support as key barriers. Racialized students felt that they had to work harder and continually prove themselves to their professors. Her interviews revealed the powerful impact of family problems, as well as the burden students carry for financial problems in the home and in the costs associated with being a university student. Caribbean students also indicated their feelings of marginalization in the Eurocentric environment of the university. For many of them, the increasing violence in Caribbean communities, family obligations, and family expectations are all factors that affect their academic performance.

In chapter 5 Carl James focuses on policies designed to create change in the university and the many impediments to their implementation.

He argues that in so far as the universities are formed by Western European middle-class patriarchal ideologies, expectations, and traditions, the norms, values, and principles by which they operate are not raceless, colour-blind, neutral, or fair and objective, despite claims that they are. Therefore, the assumptions that potential job applicants are able to access positions 'if they are qualified' ignores the systemic ways in which identities such as race and ethnicity function in enabling access to university faculty positions. James identifies some of the issues that impact upon racialized applicants for faculty positions and promotions including such factors as cultural differences and race of candidates in the hiring process; and the struggle over terms such as 'excellence,' 'demonstratively superior,' 'equally qualified,' and 'a good fit.' James argues that racially diversifying the university means acknowledging race and racial differences as salient to individuals' experiences and knowledge. He suggests that racial minority faculty members are not mere bodies 'representing' the various racial groups that exist in society but, rather, should be seen as offering colleagues and students new alternative insights and knowledge based on their scholarship, experiences, and pedagogical approach.

In chapter 6 Enakshi Dua continues the analysis of university policies and praxis in her discussion of the findings of a recent preliminary investigation on the extent to which universities in Canada have developed anti-racist policies and practices. She raises the question as to how effective such policies and practices have been in addressing the many forms of individual and systemic racism. Her analysis is informed by reviewing policies and mission statements of thirty-seven Canadian universities, as well as telephone interviews with a number of directors of human rights and equity offices in these universities. Her study demonstrates the difficulties in creating and implementing policies designed to develop structural change. She found that most Canadian universities have developed some form of policies to address racism within the academy, including employment equity, anti-harassment policies and clauses, and anti-racism workshops. Most universities surveyed had structures within the university which validated the *need* to address racism. However, from the perspectives of human rights and equity officers that she interviewed, these policies and interventions had a limited effect on actually addressing racism. Dua identifies a number of limitations in the construction of and implementation of these policies. The most powerful barrier is the unwillingness of senior administrators to address systemic and structural racism.

The various perspectives offered by each of the contributors of this book are linked to a strong commitment to the notion that teaching and learning are deeply political practices and that our universities must ensure protection of the rights of all Indigenous and racialized students and faculty to find a safe, inclusive, and intellectual home in our universities.

NOTES

1 See, e.g., Henry and Tator 1998, 2002; Tator and Henry 2006.
2 However, as Goldberg (1993) states, liberalism also 'plays a formative role in the process of normalizing and naturalizing racial dynamics and exclusions. It serves to legitimize ideologically and to rationalize politically and economically pervasive forms of racialized conditions and racist practices.'
3 See also Dean Patricia Marchak's book on the controversial events (1996).
4 The terms 'race relations' and 'diversity' are highly contested. On the term 'race relations,' see Stephen Steinberg (2001); on 'diversity,' see Diana Relke (1998), and Himani Bannerji (ch. 1, 2000).

REFERENCES

Axelrod, P. 1998. 'The Uncertain Future of the Liberal Education.' *Historical Studies in Education* 10(1–2):1–19.
Bannerji, H. 2000. *The Dark Side of the Nation: Essays on Multiculturalism, Nationalism, and Gender.* Toronto: Canadian Scholars' Press.
Bannerji, H., L. Carty, K. Dehli, S. Heald, and K. McKenna. 1991. *Unsettling Relations: The University as a Site of Feminist Struggles.* Toronto: Women's Press.
Carty, L. 1991. 'Black Women in Academia: A Statement from the Periphery.' In H. Bannerji, L. Carty, K. Dehli, S. Heald, and K. McKenna, *Unsettling Relations: The University as a Site of Feminist Struggles,* 6–15. Toronto: Women's Press.
Dei, G. 1996. 'Critical Perspectives in Antiracism: An Introduction.' *Canadian Review of Sociology and Anthropology* 33(3):247–67.
Dei, G., and A. Calliste. 2000. 'Introduction, Mapping the Terrain: Power, Knowledge and Anti-Racism Education.' In G. Dei and A. Calliste, eds., *Power, Knowledge and Anti-Racism Education: A Critical Reader,* 11–22. Halifax: Fernwood.
Fallis, G. 2004. 'The Mission of the University.' A Discussion Paper prepared for the Post Secondary Review chaired by Bob Rae, Oct.
Franklin, U. 2000. 'What Is at Stake? Universities in Context.' In J. Turk, ed.,

The Corporate Campus: Commercialization and the Dangers to Canada's Colleges and Universities, 17–22. Toronto: James Lorimer, CAUT Series.

Giroux, H. 2006. *The Giroux Reader: Cultural Politics and the Promise of Democracy.* London: Paradigm.

Goldberg, D. 1993. *Racist Culture: Philosophy and Politics of Meaning.* Oxford, UK and Cambridge, MA: Blackwell.

Henry, F. 2003. *Systemic Racism Towards Faculty of Colour and Aboriginal Faculty.* Queen's University. Also known as The Henry Report. http://www.queensu.ca/secretariat/senate/Mar30_06/SEECHenryRpt.pdf.

Henry, F., and C. Tator. 1998. *Challenging Racism in the Arts: Case Studies of Controversy and Conflict.* Toronto: University of Toronto Press.

– 2002. *Discourses of Domination: Racial Bias in the Canadian English-Language Press.* Toronto: University of Toronto Press.

Marchak, P. 1996. *Racism, Sexism, and the University: The Political Science Affair at the University of British Columbia.* Montreal and Kingston: McGill-Queen's University Press.

McEwen, J. 1995. *Report in Respect of the Political Science Department of the University of British Columbia, Vancouver,* June 15.

McIntyre, S. 2000. 'Studied Ignorance and Privileged Innocence: Keeping Equity Academic.' *Canadian Journal of Women and the Law* 12:147–96.

Queen's University. 1991. *Towards Diversity and Equity at Queen's: A Strategy for Change.* A Report of the Principal's Advisory Committee.

Relke, D. 1998. 'Doubletalk and Other Languages of Diversity at the People's University.' http://www.usask.ca/wgst/faculty/relke.htm.

Simmons, L., and H. Worth, eds. 2001. *Derrida Downunder.* Auckland, NZ: Dunmore Press.

Smith, D. 2002. 'Regulation or Dialogue.' In S. Kahn and D. Pavlich, eds., *Academic Freedom and the Inclusive University,* 150–7. Vancouver: University of British Columbia Press.

Steinberg, S. 2001. '"Race Relations": The Problem with the Wrong Name.' *New Politics* 8(2).

Tator, C., and F. Henry. 2006. *Racial Profiling in Canada: Challenging the Myth of 'A Few Bad Apples.'* Toronto: University of Toronto Press.

Turk, J. 2000. 'Introduction: What Commercialization Means for Education.' In L. Turk, ed., *Corporate Campus: Commercialization and the Dangers to Canada's Colleges and Universities,* 1–13. Toronto: James Lorimer, CAUT Series.

Wayland, S. 1995. 'Immigrants into Citizens: Political Mobilization in France and Canada.' PhD Dissertation to Faculty of Graduate Scholarship at the University of Maryland.

York University. 1984. Majority Report and Minority Report. Special Review Committee on Charges of Racial and Sexual Harassment at York University.

1 Theoretical Perspectives and Manifestations of Racism in the Academy

FRANCES HENRY AND CAROL TATOR

Introduction

Over the last two decades racialized and Indigenous faculty, along with their anti-racism colleagues, have engaged in the process of critically analysing the role of theory and theorizing in the social sciences and in other disciplines. They have interrogated the ways in which the culture of Whiteness impacts upon their lives inside the academy and in the wider society. Students and professors of colour are searching for safe spaces in which they can individually and collectively articulate their opposition to the traditional processes of theorizing that have either consciously or inadvertently ignored or omitted the voices, knowledge, and perspectives of racialized people. They are seeking to critique and change the hegemony of White culture that is embedded in everyday interactions in classrooms and in the institutionalized spaces where power is exercised. Racialized and Indigenous academics and students across the country are raising critical questions such as: Whose knowledge counts and whose knowledge is discounted? Whose voice is heard and who is ignored?

When analysing these and many other questions, it becomes clear that the knowledge and status of Indigenous and racialized faculty in the academy today is commonly not judged to be commensurate with that of their White colleagues. These forms of inequity that are manifestations of racism in the academy constitute the subject matter of this book.

Theoretical Perspectives

As research on racism in Canadian society in general and in the university in particular has expanded rapidly in the last two decades, so too have the various theoretical perspectives that seek to analyse and explain this phenomenon in its various institutional guises. However, as it is often the case in Canada, scholarship has been relatively slow in catching up to theoretical developments in the study of racism and anti-racism that have already occurred elsewhere. This is especially true in comparison with the United States and the United Kingdom where critical race theory perspectives took hold many years ago, but have only recently gained prominence in Canada. The main reason for this time lag is that it is only in the last decade or so that racialized faculty have begun to find a place, however limited, in Canadian universities.

Anti-racism and anti-oppression theories as applied to the university structure and its 'culture of whiteness' have been particularly useful in not only explaining the persistence of racism, but also in showing how social justice and educational equity in our universities and Canadian society can be attained. Thus, critical race perspectives such as racialization, Whiteness studies, and various constructs of racism such as everyday, institutional, and epistemological are useful to frame and explain the issues raised by ourselves and the contributors to this book. The following establish the key theoretical perspectives that inform these goals.

Racialization

Many scholars today (Murji and Solomos 2005; Small 1999) have moved away from the use of race and instead focus on the processes of racialization. The classic definition of racialization refers to 'those instances where social relations between people have been structured by the signification of human biological characteristics in such a way as to define and construct differentiated social collectivities' (Miles 1989, 70). Racialization also refers to the broad social processes, including colonialism and cultural privileging, through which racialized 'others' are constructed, differentiated, stigmatized, and excluded (Anthias 1998). To say that society is racialized suggests that it is systematically arranged around beliefs about race, and that the distribution of power, resources, images, and ideas closely corresponds with membership in racialized groups. Furthermore, focus on the processes of racialization moves scholarship away from the discredited biological construct of race to the sociologically more powerful notion of a racialized ideology or ideological process.

Although the concept has recently been problematized (Murji and Solomos 2005), and important scholars such as Goldberg (1993) maintain that 'racism' carries more weight than racialization as an analytic concept because it has empirical referents in specific behaviours, actions, and events, there is still general agreement among many other scholars that it is useful in describing events and social relationships in which biological constants influence social interactions. Whiteness studies have become an important adjunct to racialization processes, as it is now recognized that being White also constitutes a biological referent.

The processes of racialization in the academy and elsewhere do not operate in isolation from other forms of oppression. Although racism is the primary focus of our analysis in this book about racial inequity within the academy, we also stress that the processes of racialization intersect with other forms of subjugation. The matrix of domination operates along a series of socially constructed axes that include race, gender, class, ethnicity, language, religion, sexual orientation, and different abilities (Collins 1991). This interlocking framework is important in understanding how power and powerlessness operate in the spaces of the academy. While there are many instances where these oppressions overlap and interlock with one another, the saliency of race and racism in education remains at the centre of our analysis, as Dei and Calliste observe:

> A genuine anti-racist project demands space for race to be analyzed outside of class and gender – so that race is reduced to neither class or gender. Distinguishing race, class and gender as separate analytical categories (albeit interconnected) is an important step in unraveling the ideological effects of specific racialized material processes and structures. (2000, 15)

Whiteness Studies

Frankenberg's (1993) seminal work *White Women, Race Matters: The Social Construction of Whiteness* succinctly defined the field of Whiteness studies across three interlinked dimensions. She said it is: 'a location of structural advantage ... it is a standpoint or place from which white people look at ourselves, at others and at society ... and it refers to a set of cultural practices that are usually unmarked and unnamed' (447).

Toni Morrison (1992) further advances the understanding of the complex meanings of Whiteness and racialization processes by placing the onus of responsibility on the 'racial subject,' namely White people. 'My project is an effort to avert the critical gaze from the racial object to the racial subject; from the described and imagined to the describers and imaginers; from the serving to the served' (90). This shifts the onus in studies of cultural, epistemological, institutional, and systemic racism from the racialized communities of colour to those who are White and privileged. This approach emerges from the widely accepted view that White perspectives are considered natural, normative, and essentially raceless.

Whiteness studies reverse the focus on 'Blackness,' 'Aboriginalness,' 'Muslimness,' and other forms of 'Othering' to critically examine the role of Whiteness in preserving and reinforcing cultural hegemony, racial bias, and exclusion. Whiteness studies offer the possibility of destabilizing Whiteness as an identity and an ideology in order to advance a different vision of society (Visano 2002). This approach analyses the link between White skin and the position of privilege operating in most societies, including those that have been subjected to European colonialism. White privilege confers benefits in almost all sectors of society, whereas racialized peoples are often disadvantaged, marginalized, and excluded because of their skin colour and its associated stereotypic beliefs.

Whiteness contests the often held view of colour-blindness – the notion that one does not see skin colour (I never noticed the colour of his skin) – as untrue and inaccurate. Whites see the 'colour' in others in the same manner as they are seen as 'white.' Most White people do not, however, recognize themselves as a racial category and their self-identification rarely includes the descriptor 'white.' Such people are often not even aware of being White and, without that essential self-recognition, find difficulty in recognizing and accepting their role as perpetrators of racial discrimination and exclusion. It is important to emphasize that 'Whiteness' and 'colour' or 'Blackness' are essentially social constructs applied to human beings rather than veritable truths that have universal validity. The power of Whiteness, however, is manifested by the ways in which racialized Whiteness becomes transformed into intellectual, social, cultural, political, and economic behaviour. White culture, norms, and values in all these areas become normative and natural. They become the standard against which all other cultures, groups, and individuals are measured and usually found to be inferior. Whiteness comes to mean normality, knowledge, superiority, merit, motivation, knowledge, truth, neutrality, and objectivity. '*Rarely, however, is it acknowledged that whiteness demands and constitutes hierarchies, exclusion, and deprivation*' (emphasis in original, Fine et al. 1997, viii).

Although Whiteness theory and research has become a popular perspective in social science, largely because it involves a critical perspective, a number of important disclaimers in regard to this perspective must be made. First, we emphasize that we are not suggesting that all White people are equally advantaged. Whiteness is almost always mitigated by other manifestations of social identity such as class, gender, sexuality, ethnicity, religion, and so on.

In recent work Brander-Rasmussen et al. (2001) attempt to further redefine Whiteness as an analytic concept. It is now understood that different individuals relate to their Whiteness as an identity and social position. Whiteness is not a monolithic status; rather it is fluid, situational, and sometimes related to its local geographical context. The power of Whiteness and its strong link to racialization and racism is stressed throughout the book, but we also take note that all groups including White people experience a wide range of complex identities and ideologies. It is therefore important not to over-emphasize essentialism in constructing Whiteness.

Gabriel (1998) underscores this point by asserting that not all White ethnicities are dominant and not all Whites are privileged. Just as Blackness defies definition in terms of a fixed set of ethnic/racial attributes, so too should Whiteness be viewed as heterogeneous, fluid, and hybrid. Thus, we accept the view that not all Whites consider themselves raceless, and in our particular study of the university we and our contributing authors also support the position that not all White members of the academy consider themselves to be invisibly White.

However, it should also be emphasized that Whiteness takes place within academic institutions. As such, organizational cultures have developed in which values and norms based on Eurocentrism and Whiteness have defined knowledge, merit, and what should be included in the curriculum. Thus, our primary concern is with how the culture of Whiteness operates within the academy and, more specifically, the ways in which the learning and workplace culture is characterized by invisibility, marginalization, and oppression.

It is against this background that critical race scholars of Whiteness[1] and each of our contributing authors, Audrey Kobayashi, Carl James, Patricia Monture, Enakshi Dua, and Camille Hernandez-Ramdwar, provide powerful insights and perspectives into these dynamics, with the ultimate aim of exposing the power of Whiteness in order to dismantle some of its overwhelming hegemony over those who are 'non-White.'

The challenge for Whites, especially White academics, is to redefine themselves as racialized social actors in a shared quest to build a common social domain marked with and beyond identity (Levine-Rasky 2002, 5). To do this, as an initial step, would entail defining Whiteness not as an attribute of identity adhering to a White body, 'or a constantly shifting location upon complex maps of social, economic, and political power' (Ellsworth 1997, cited in Levine-Rasky 2002, 5). Such an approach to the analyses of the processes that produce Whiteness, racialization, and the systemic injustice of racism could help reduce the unproductive thoughts and feelings related to individualistic culpability, which commonly lead to the discourses of denial, colour-blindness, political correctness, reverse racism, and so on (Henry and Tator 2002).

Constructs of Racism

Racism in universities manifests itself in many ways including:

> through the formal and 'hidden' curricula (such as climate and tone of the campus, university calendars and recruitment materials); through racial/ethnic slurs, jokes and stereotyping; and through racial harassment of Aboriginal and racialized/ethnicized minorities; through the exclusion of these groups from positive representation; and through the so-called 'objective' interpretations and explanations that actually represent the dominant racial/ethnic groups' interests. (Calliste 2000, 149)

EVERYDAY RACISM

Everyday racism in the academy, as well as across a wide range of interlocking institutional and discursive spaces,[2] involves the many and sometimes small ways in which racism is experienced by racialized people in their interactions with the members of the dominant White culture. It expresses itself in behaviours; anecdotes; sexualized, ethnicized, and racialized jokes; inappropriate glares and glances; gestures; and forms of speech. Often it is not consciously experienced by its perpetrators, but it is immediately and painfully felt by its victims. The everyday racism in the academy heightens one's sense of vulnerability and affects one's sense of self-esteem and personal self-confidence. It can have a powerful impact on racialized people's physical and mental health.

Anthony Stewart articulates an example of everyday racism experienced by racialized professors:

It is one thing to be called a name from a passing car, or have your car spat on as you sit in the driver's seat ... But it is something else altogether when the offence is subtler. When, for instance, a professor whom I did not know compared me to Ben Johnson, as I stood in a hallway during the year of my Masters degree ... he wasn't calling me a nigger outright or saying that we all look alike, or was he? (Stewart 2004, 35)

In describing the battle to resist internalizing the racist experience of the university, Patti Doyle-Bedwell suggests:

It takes incredible courage to stand up in front of a class where no matter what I say, it is Mi'kmaq dribble. It takes incredible courage to say I am a law professor. Who do I think I am? That, I do not know. Why do I do the Indian thing and believe in their perception that I am incompetent as a teacher? I am frozen for many weeks. I am scared to even cry, for fear that I will never stop. (Doyle-Bedwell 1997)

It is important to note that from a research perspective, these incidents of everyday racism are difficult to quantify because they are only revealed in the thoughts, feelings, and articulations of victims. As Essed states:

It is very difficult to determine 'objectively' the nature of everyday interaction between whites and blacks ... [A] variety of studies have shown that those who are discriminated against appear to have more insight into discrimination mechanisms than those who discriminate. ... blacks have a certain amount of expertise about racism through extensive experience with whites. The latter, conversely, are often hardly aware of the racism in their own attitudes and behaviour. (Essed 1990)

Everyday racism incorporates the myriad ways in which racialized ideas are reinforced in ordinary everyday actions, language, and beliefs. It is part of the normative fabric that is often unnoticed and thus serves to reinforce racialized ideology often expressed very subtly and spontaneously. Racialized people know when they experience everyday racism because it is repetitive and consistent with past experience. However, White people often do not see it or recognize it, even in their own words and actions. Underpinning this denial is the liberal notion that intent counts more than impact.

This creates one of the main problems at universities because White university administrators and non-racialized faculty often don't realize that discrimination is a matter of impact and not intent. Thus, one frequently hears the argument that it is not our intention to discriminate against anybody. What is not realized in this simplistic understanding of how discrimination operates is that traditional rules and practices have unintentional consequences in denying equity and equality to faculty of colour and Indigenous faculty and scholars. This commonly held view, that discrimination or racism was not intended, often plays a significant role in the anger and sense of betrayal experienced by institutional power-holders when those who experience discrimination in the universities speak out against racism. A further aspect of the denial is the view that racism is either present or it is not, which leads to the discourse of 'blame the victim.' Dominant members of the faculty or administration often devalue claims that curriculum or pedagogy is racially insensitive or not inclusive of racialized peoples, Aboriginals, or women. Instead, these concerns are seen as personal attacks, which serve to threaten professors' careers (Prentice 2000). This pattern operates across individual, institutional, and systemic forms of racism.

INSTITUTIONAL AND SYSTEMIC FORMS OF RACISM

Institutional racism is manifested in the policies, practices, and procedures of various institutions that may, directly or indirectly, consciously or unwittingly, promote, sustain, or entrench differential advantage or privilege for people of certain races. Peggy McIntosh (1989) observes: 'I was taught to see racism only in individual acts of meanness, not in invisible systems conferring dominance on my group.' She goes on to say that as Whites we have been taught not to recognize the power and privilege that comes with all Whiteness. White privilege is like an invisible, weightless knapsack of special provisions, maps, passports, codebooks, tools, and resources (1).

Institutional racism generally encompasses overt individual acts of racism to which there is no serious organizational response, such as discriminatory hiring decisions based on the generalized bias of a department. It also includes organizational policies and practices that, regardless of intent, are directly or indirectly disadvantageous to racial minorities, such as the lack of recognition of foreign credentials or the imposition of inflated educational requirements for a position. Institutional racism can be defined as those established laws, customs, and practices which systematically reflect and produce racial inequalities in Canadian society. If racist consequences come about as a result of institutional policies, customs, or practices, the institution is manifesting elements of racial inequality, whether or not the individuals maintaining those practices have racialized intentions or not.

As is clearly demonstrated in the literature on racism in universities and also in empirical research findings, the tenure process is seen as one of the most powerful examples of institutionalized racism, whereby individuals are punished or rewarded based on their adherence to obsolete rules and standards designed to ensure conformity to Whiteness and maleness. Commonly, racialized academics have found that their own personal experiences are not valued in the tenure review process.

In addressing the subject of Indigenizing the academy, Taiaiake Alfred (2007) notes:

> Being an Indigenous academic is a more serious matter that goes beyond glorifying one's bloodline or tokenizing one's status as an 'aboriginal Canadian.' Indigeneity is a struggle not a label. And for those who work in academia, accepting one's Indigeneity means a constant fight to remain connected to our communities, to live our culture, and to defend our homelands, all the while fulfilling our professional duties inside what is, essentially, a central institution of colonial domination. (22)

Systemic racism, although similar to institutional racism, refers more broadly to the laws, rules, and norms woven into the social system that result in an unequal distribution of economic, political, and social resources and rewards among various racial groups. It is the denial of access, participation, and equity to racial minorities for services such as education, employment, and housing. An example of systemic racism that is manifested in academe is viewing epistemology as operating in a neutral space. In reality, however, production of knowledge contributions, curricular decision making, and allocation of funds within the academy are always related to power and who holds it. Thus:

> Under conditions of systemic sexual, racial, and economic inequality and pervasive ablism, heterosexism, and colonialism, we are *all* gendered, raced, and classed ... Under conditions of systemic inequality, dominant groups, their world views, and their interests are entrenched ... and normalized as unstated standards against which Otherness – that is, non-

whiteness, nonmaleness, nonhetereosexuality … and non-Western origin and culture – is (re)marked as different. (italics in original, McIntyre 2000, 162)

The various manifestations of racism can be isolated for discussion purposes, but in reality they form a complex dynamic of interrelated attitudes, feelings, beliefs, and behaviours that are linked to the collective belief system and are expressed in individual, institutional, and systemic policies and practices, and at even deeper levels of culture and civilization.

DEMOCRATIC RACISM

The conflict between the ideology of democratic liberalism and the racialized ideology present in the collective belief system of the dominant culture is reflected in the racialized discourse that operates in all of our institutions including universities. Many scholars have pointed to the deep relationship between power, knowledge, discourse, and 'truth.' In his seminal work *Power/Knowledge* (1980), Foucault argued that knowledge is a product of discourse and power relations. In his view, statements about the social, political, or moral world are rarely simply true or false, and the language used to describe alleged facts often interferes with the process of categorically defining what is true or false: 'The question of whether discourse is true or false is less important than whether it is effective in practice. When it is effective – organizing and regulating relations of power – it is called a "regime of truth"' (131). Foucault sees all knowledge, including historical knowledge, through the prism of discursive formations.

The everyday discourses that take place in curricular decision making, in clashes in the classroom, and in department meetings convey deep social meanings. Language can never be 'neutral' because it bridges our personal and social worlds (van Dijk 1988). It can never be 'objective' or 'detached' because it draws on myth and illusion.

Over and over in the literature and in the lived experiences of racialized and Indigenous scholars and educators it is evident that 'new' forms of racism are discursive and that these expressions of racism are articulated through a wide spectrum of expressions and representations, including a nation's recorded history; biological and scientific explanations of racial difference; economic, legal, and bureaucratic doctrines; and cultural representations in the form of national narratives, images, and symbols (Goldberg 1993; Dei, Karumanchery, and

Karumanchery-Luik 2004). Racialized discourse refers to the way that society gives voice to racism.

The discourses of dominance associated with Whiteness include the myths, explanations, codes of meaning, and rationalizations that establish, sustain, and reinforce the status quo. This discourse is contextualized within humanistic, democratic, and liberal values. However, the central values of liberal ideologies carry different meanings and connotations depending on the context.

The mainstay of liberal philosophy is the emphasis on individual rights and equality of opportunity. It also includes freedom of speech, expression, and ideas (particularly important in the university context), as well as a deep commitment to the rule of law. Limiting the power of government and maintaining its transparancy are also hallmarks of liberal thought. Classic liberal thought places great emphasis on individual freedom and the need to control any forces, traditional, religious, or institutional, that would control individual thought and action. While clearly developing rules, practices, and procedures necessary to govern any institution, universities have been identified as bastions for the maintenance of individual expression, while always attempting to contain dominance and repression.

Tolerance, equality, and freedom of expression – central concepts in liberal discourse, especially in the context of the academic institution – have immensely flexible meanings. These liberal principles often become the ideological framework and discourse through which racialized beliefs and exclusions are enabled, reinforced, and defended (see Moosa-Mitha 2005; Mackey 2002; Goldberg 1993). This flexibility of meaning has important consequences for racialized scholars and students because it creates the moral tension inherent in an institution characterized by an ethos of democratic racism. While, on the one hand, democratic liberal values form the foundation of the academy, racialized discourse, thought, and practice are allowed to continue unabated, impinging on the education and the very lives of racialized members of the academy.

Universities, like other systems such as structures of governance, mass media, policing, justice, and human services, are discursive spaces. Within these spaces, largely controlled by the dominant White culture, there exists a constant moral tension: there are the everyday experiences and lived reality of racialized students and faculty, and, juxtaposed against this, are the perceptions and responses of those who have the power to redefine that reality, that is, White educators and administrators in the academy. To acknowledge that ethno-racial differences and racism makes a difference in the lives of people is to concede that Euro-Canadian hegemony continues to organize the structures within the policies, programs, and practices of university life. In these discursive spaces there is a persistent tension relating to how racism is imagined, internalized, and acted upon by those with White skin privilege and those whose skin colour marks them with a racialized identity of 'otherness' (Yon 2000).

In the same way, Dei and Calliste (2000) suggest that 'colonial and imperial discourses and practices heavily influence how learners come to know race today. Racialized tropes deployed in the social construction of racialized identities and the representation of marginalized bodies as racial "others" are heavily encoded in prevailing ideologies that maintain the validity of conventional academic knowledge' (11).

However, obfuscations and justifications are employed to demonstrate continuing faith in egalitarian ideals. Henry and Tator (2006) have framed these tensions as part of the theoretical framework of democratic racism. Democratic racism is an ideology in which two conflicting sets of values are made congruent to each other. Commitments to democratic principles such as equality, fairness, and justice *conflict* with, but also *coexist* with, negative feelings about racialized individuals and groups and discrimination against them. One of the consequences of this conflict is a lack of support for policies and practices that might improve the relatively low status of racialized communities. Efforts to combat racism require substantive interventions in order to change the cultural, social, economic, and political systems. However, there is a strong opposition to any change to the status quo. There is a strong resistance to seeing racism as anything but the aberrant behaviour of a small number of individuals. More important, efforts to dismantle racialized systems and structures lack legitimacy according to the egalitarian principles of liberal democracy.

Liberal values expressed in liberal discourses include the primacy of individual rights over collective rights, freedom of expression, equality opportunity, and so on. But liberalism is full of paradoxes and contradictions depending on one's social location and angle of vision (Hall 1986; Goldberg 1993). Commonly articulated discourses in the 'liberal' spaces of the academy are strongly influenced by traditional liberal theories and assumptions as they relate to issues of race, racism, and other forms of oppression. The coded language of liberalism within the academy incorporates the ideologies and discourses of 'universalism,' 'colour-blindness,' 'diversity,' 'objectivity,' 'neutrality,' 'merit,' 'standards,' and 'equal opportunity.' One of the most powerful of all these discourses is the categorical denial that racism exists, with the commonly voiced exception referred to in the context of isolated and individual acts of overt prejudice by a relatively few atypical persons.

In the academy, the discourse of 'political correctness' is commanding and pervasive. Demands for inclusion, representation, and equity are deflected, resisted, and dismissed as authoritarian, repressive, and a threat to academic freedom. Green (2002) observes that political correctness has become the clarion call echoing across North American campuses: 'those of us who name and object to our oppression, or who stand in solidarity with marginalized others, are transformed by our stance into the oppressors of those whose privilege we challenge ... Institutional intransigence and colleagues' hostility and derision freeze many of us out of the academy' (88). Making a similar point Sarita Srivastava states: 'Political correctness discourse has amplified the already controversial challenges of representation, equity and racism in social movements, universities, schools, and government agencies. Antiracist and equity battles in academia have been increasing as political correctness discourse is re-signified to implicate universities' (1996, 291).

An oppositional view is taken by those who argue that people who call for inclusion of different voices and stories should stand accused of supporting Orwellian armies of thought police moving across campuses in North America. John Fekete (1994) identifies the pressures of political correctness, or 'pc,' gripping the nation as a form of 'primitivism which promotes self-identification through groups defined by categories like race or sex' (22), arguing that 'biopolitics' – a regressive 'anti-politics' – is 'fast becoming deeply integrated into the central practices of public policy and administration' (25). He goes on to state that 'this tendency has endangered the very cornerstones of liberal democracy – i.e. freedom of expression and due process.' In the contestation over racism and sexism in the Political Science Department of the University of British Columbia, the discourse of political correctness was employed as a powerful 'ideological code' (see Smith 1999; McIntyre 2000; Bishop 2005). Each of these rhetorical strategies or dominant discourses as discussed in this section can be deconstructed to reveal the power and accumulated capital of Whiteness in all aspects of university life.

EPISTEMOLOGICAL RACISM

In an analysis of the categories or levels of racism, Scheurich and Young (1997) contend that attempts to define racism in the academy must go beyond the individual, institutional, and societal manifestations to also incorporate the epistemological and ontological constructs of racism. The authors assert that epistemological racism is drawn from the broad civilizational structures, that is, 'the level that encompasses the deepest assumptions about the nature of reality (ontology), the ways of know-ing that reality (epistemology), and (axiology) ... presumptions about the real, the true and the good' (6). These assumptions also include the notion that 'the search for the "truth" of the Western canon of "Great Works" is actually based on the epistemological error that presumes there exists a language of primordial Being and Truth' (McLaren 1994, 50).

Assumptions are different for different civilizations, and not all peo-ple 'know' in the same way. Large and complex civilizations commonly include a powerful, dominant culture, as well as subordinate cultures, races, and groups who have different civilizational assumptions and distinctive epistemologies or theories of knowledge (Collins 1991). That knowledge reflects the values and interests of its producers and that all knowledge is relative to the cultural context in which it is produced is axiomatic in the social sciences. Critical race scholar Ladson-Billings (2000) observes:

> How one views the world is influenced by what knowledge one possesses, and what knowledge one is capable of possessing is influenced deeply by one's world view ... The process of developing a world view that differs from the dominant world view requires active intellectual work on the part of the knower, because schools, society, and the structure and produc-tion of knowledge are designed to create individuals who internalize the dominant world view and knowledge production and acquisition. (258; see also Ladson-Billings and Tate 1995)

Expanding on this view of knowledge, Strega (2005) points out that the defining characteristics of modernism include the view that

> knowledge can be objective, impartial, innocent in intention and effect, and neutrally discovered; that there is one true method by which knowledge is acquired; and that knowledge can be discovered by a rational subject who

is distanced from its object and investigation and who can separate her-self or himself from emotions, personal self-interests and political values in creating innocent knowledge. Information gathered by other methods and by researchers who socially and politically locate themselves, fails to attain the status accorded to knowledge. (204)

Strega emphasizes that these are not abstract philosophical issues, but rather that the foundation of the epistemic method prescribes what 'good research involves, justifies why research is done, gives a value base to research and provides ethical principles for conducting re-search' (211). In the academy, dominant discourses of knowledge are articulated through traditional forms of curricula, pedagogy, research priorities, tenure decisions, and recruitment procedures. Clearly the most obvious example of dominant discourses of knowledge is em-bedded in the teaching of the canon of an Anglocentric Eurocentric curriculum.

One of the foci of anti-racism and anti-oppression research is that the ownership of knowledge no longer exclusively resides in the dominant group but also includes those who experience marginality and exclu-sion. Writing specifically in regard to Aboriginal forms of knowledge production, Joyce Green (2005) notes:

The knowledge producers, universities, construct and replicate forms of knowledge that they also have the power to determine; and in so do-ing, they mostly legitimate forms of knowledge that are alien to and hostile to Aboriginal forms and to critical contestation. Universities are overwhelmingly populated by those who know little or nothing about Aboriginal peoples and issues, and teach to student bodies that have only a few Aboriginal members. Thus, in both the knowledge presented and recruited, the ivory towers remain white, and the graduating elites carry with them this white-preferential way of seeing and organizing the world. (9)

Anti-racism and anti-oppression curricula and pedagogy are based on the recognition that knowledge is socially constructed, embedded in people and the power relations between subordinated communi-ties and the dominant culture. Anti-racist and anti-oppression scholars and educators recognize that knowledge is political; it is created in the power differences between people.

The Role of Narrative Inquiry in Academic Research, Pedagogy, and Curricula

Each of the contributors to this book strongly supports the view that narrative inquiry can illuminate social, political, ethical, and moral dimensions of life and experience that other research approaches cannot. The telling of documented stories can serve as primary data in academic research, as well as a powerful educating and organizing tool. The stories uncovered in our literature review and the stories shared in our face-to-face and telephone interviews with racialized and White academics, and the narratives articulated by each of the contributing authors, are contextualized in personal/individual experiences.

Forms of narratives communicate broader cultural assumptions, beliefs, and habits of thinking that transcend the individual (Bourdieu 1999). In this way, stories create a link between individual experience and broader societal systemic patterns. The role of the counter-narrative is to challenge dominant discourses that are intended to orchestrate the appearance of unanimity among the dominant group and consent among subordinated groups. The hegemonic dominant narrative acts as a meta-code that shapes the 'mindset' from which the dominant group, that is Whites, observe, interpret, and understand the world (see Williams 1991; Ewick and Silbey 1995). These codes exclude or silence other possible interpretations, thereby providing a justification for the maintenance and preservation of existing social hierarchies that are based on socially constructed categories of racial differences. Dominant narratives of Whiteness and racialization include liberalism and equal opportunity, political correctness and merit, and neutrality and objectivity. Each of these narratives requires constant repetition and reiteration to maintain its power.

Stories that reflect the dominant White culture in institutions of higher learning, as well as in other systems such as justice and media, are used strategically to reinforce White culture's identity in relation to out-groups and to portray itself in a favourable light and confirm its superior position as natural (Razack 1998). Counter or oppositional narratives present both a critique and challenge to the assumptions, beliefs, myths, and misconceptions embedded in the dominant narrative or transcript. These stories serve to 'break the silence' and 'bear witness' to the histories and lived experience of people of colour and other minorities in the face of a hegemonic culture that distorts, stereotypes, and marginalizes that reality (see Bell 2003). The counter-narratives that describe the common psychological understandings of racialized communities cut across the boundaries of race, class, gender, and sexual orientation. In the postmodernist deconstruction of the dominant narratives, there is a sense of 'yearning' that 'wells in the hearts and minds of those whom such narratives have silenced in the longing for critical voice' (hooks 1990, 9).

We are well aware, however, of the critique of counter-narrative stories as research data that has been severely criticized by social science 'hard liners' who subscribe to positivist approaches and a commitment to the power of science and scientific methodology (Wallace 2000). Science or scientific materialism is based on the Newtonian model of the universe which maintains that if something cannot be measured objectively, it does not exist. Critics of the counter-narrative approach such as Rosen maintain that 'in its most radical form, the storytelling movement is a direct assault ... on the possibility of objectivity.' Rosen also argues the use of personal narratives is incompatible with rational analysis because 'narrative is fictional or quasi-fictional, and therefore at best anecdotal, at worst a tissue of lies – not the stuff of reasoned argument that stories merely tell of subjectively defined events' (cited in Nunan 1999). Thus, the old dichotomy between objectivism and subjectivity emerges once again in this dialogue. The main argument is that subjective phenomena cannot be analysed scientifically and cannot therefore be replicated by other scientists. According to this perspective, subjective experiential data is unscientific and deserves to be ignored. We take the position, however, that narratology is a useful methodology that results in a powerful form of knowledge.

Critical Race Theory

One field that has used narratives successfully and has strongly argued for this approach is critical legal theory, which applies to the law and the justice system. Critical race theorists such as Aylward (2000), Delgado (1995), D. Bell (1987), and Williams (1991) have written extensively about the use of narrative stories in law and have effectively created scenarios to argue legal issues.

In the same way, scholars in critical race theory, such as Ladson-Billings, have incorporated this theoretical framework into an analysis of the barriers in curricula and pedagogical practices. Ladson-Billings (1995) chooses to select an epistemology that reflects 'who I am, what I believe, what experiences I have had,' as it relates to her membership in a marginalized racial/cultural group (470).

Critical race theory's axiology is composed of two fundamental elements: equity and democracy. This perspective identifies the immense systemic racial inequities in education as well as in such social systems as law, justice, and employment. Critical race theory describes and critiques not a world of bad actors, wronged victims, and innocent spectators, but rather, a world in which all of us are more or less complicit in socio-legal webs of domination and subordination (Romero 2002). Critical race theory rejects the notion that racism is perpetuated by isolated and aberrant individuals and argues that racism is an endemic aspect of life in our society and that neutrality, objectivity, colour blindness, and meritocracy are all questionable constructs.

It has long been standard practice for the dominant hegemonic decision makers and institutional authorities in universities and other institutional sites to dismiss counter-narratives of racialized individuals and communities. Thus, we have chosen to discuss at length our reasons for using personal narratives throughout our collective analysis of racism in the university. We view narrative analysis as an important methodological tool for understanding the experiences of racialized peoples, who must deal with their myriad exclusions and expressions of marginalization in their everyday lives. Critical race theorists argue that counter-narratives reveal truths about the social world that are often hidden or silenced by more traditional methods of social science and legal scholarship (Delgado 1995; Crenshaw et al. 1995). Storytelling is viewed in this context as a form of cultural activism; it allows those who have been oppressed and silenced 'to name and reclaim over and over, the connections we are taught to ignore, the dynamics we are told do not exist' (Morales 1998, 5).

Critical Pedagogy

Critical pedagogy is an analytical tool that provides critical educators with a vehicle for challenging exclusionary practices in the classroom and outside of it. In Giroux's view, radical educators should be able to allow students to rewrite differences by crossing over 'into cultural borders that offer narratives, languages and experiences that provide a resource for thinking the relationship between the centre and margins of power as well as between themselves and others' (Giroux 1992, 229). Giroux refers to this kind of approach to difference as 'border pedagogy.' It is a pedagogy that goes beyond the opening of diverse cultural and historical spaces. It challenges the notion that classroom teaching is a neutral and objective process, removed from the issues of power, hegemony, and domination.

In the same way, Freire (1970) believes that education is neither neutral nor does it take place in a vacuum. Both educator and students bring into the classroom their cultural beliefs, their experiences of privilege or discrimination. The purpose of education should be human liberation. A learner is not an empty vessel or an object of education. Learners have agency and their learning is enhanced through the process of dialogue in which educators, students, administrators, and community are co-learners. The goal of dialogue in the classroom and beyond the walls of academia is critical consciousness. Critical awareness begins with perceiving the root causes of one's place in society. Critical thinking must go beyond perception to action and reaction. Dialogue in education is the practice of freedom. Freire argues that knowledge develops the interaction of reflection and action (praxis) and occurs 'when human beings participate in a transforming act' (1985). However, as many Canadian scholars point out, the incorporation of critical pedagogy in the classroom has been problematic and challenging.

Hoodfar (1992) citing Ellsworth (1989) identifies some of the risks of critical teaching, such as the presence of a multiplicity of experiences and knowledge that students and educators bring into the learning environment and the assumption that these differences can be captured, understood, and shared by others. Hoodfar points to the particular difficulties faced by racialized teachers who attempt to engage in critical pedagogy:

> As a 'token' outgroup teacher, I face different reactions than do most mainstream teachers. The legitimacy of my occupying the powerful position of teacher in a classroom is, at best, shaky. As a rule, most minority teachers, particularly those in the early stages of their career, have to invest much energy in establishing themselves as *bona fide* teachers, both in the eyes of their students and in the eyes of colleagues. (Hoodfar 1992, 310)

Razack (1998) suggests the need to critically analyse our multiple identities and be aware of 'how we hear and how we speak; on the choices we make about which voice to use and when to use it; and, most important of all, on developing pedagogical practices that enable us to pose these questions and use the various answers to guide those concrete moral choices we are constantly being called upon to make' (54; see also Boyce 1996).

Tastsoglou (2000) contrasts traditional liberal curricula and pedagogical methods with critical, feminist, and anti-racist pedagogies that claim to 'disrupt' the canon of the academy to bring about social change. She goes on to state that 'such pedagogies highlight "subjugated knowledges" (Foucault 1972, 81–2) and "alternative histories" (Mohanty 1990, 185) as well as ways of knowing that have traditionally been invalidated, for example experiential knowing or knowing arising from socially marginalized positions' (104). However, education liberates when it challenges dominant ideology, teaches critical literacy, and how to learn. A critical pedagogical praxis links liberatory education to acts of resistance in order to bring about political change and social transformation (Freire 1970). The way to influence social change is to recognize in the classroom the presence of a multiplicity of knowledges, resulting from the way differences have been used to structure social relations inside and outside the classroom (Ellsworth 1989, 321).

Thus, many anti-racism scholars and critical pedagogues, across disciplines, identify a multiplicity of challenges as related to everyday teaching practices in the university, as well as schools. The challenges of moving towards racial and other forms of social justice demands a critical examination of whose 'stories are told, by whom, and to what ends.' Critical pedagogy requires educators to consider how we can connect institutional norms and individual agency related to access, power, and resources in the context of race and racism in the academy and in the world (Cooks and Simpson 2007).

Rather than standing apart from students, educators should create collaborative partnerships, becoming a 'guide on the side, not a sage on the stage' (Freire 1970, 31). Critical approaches to education in the context of anti-racism and anti-oppression require 'teaching against the grain.' The role of the critical teacher is to 'emphasize the historical inequality that [has] been deeply embedded in social structures and to facilitate the radicalization of students' (Ng, Staton, and Scane 1995).

Manifestations of Racism in the Academy

Moving from a discussion of some of the theoretical issues that frame and inform our approach to the issue of racism in the academy, the second part of this chapter draws on the results of our empirical research. Our small pilot study used a number of data-gathering techniques, including face-to-face interviews with academics in a small sample of universities and disciplines, telephone interviews with academics, and questions emailed to interested academics across the country. In total, there were over sixty respondents in our study. In addition, we incorporated some of the significant body of literature that addresses the manifestations of racism in the academy.

Under-representation of Racialized Faculty

A deep and abiding problem at universities in Canada and elsewhere is the under-representation of racialized faculty even in pluralistic urban centres with very mixed populations.[3] Although many universities, particularly those in major cities, now have a very diverse student body, diversity is poorly reflected at the level of faculty, especially in social science and humanities disciplines.[4] This leads to many significant problems, not the least of which is that it limits their influence and impact on the curriculum since too few faculty are available to teach courses that deal with the issues and concerns of racialized peoples. It also means that such faculty commonly must take on an extra workload, as they are often called upon to sit on university committees, thus ensuring that their department is demonstrating 'representation.' Minelle Mahtani, drawing from her research interviews with racialized faculty, found that 'many women of colour professors are expected to take on gargantuan tasks simply because they were seen as being a "two-fer," both a woman and a woman of colour. This in turn results in greater isolation and exhaustion and some even choose to abandon the academy' (2006, 23).

Faculty of colour commonly serve as mentors to racialized and Indigenous students who seek them out as role models. Thus, when their research and publication record is analysed during promotion and tenure reviews, all too often it is deemed insufficient. Their increased workload is not seriously considered in these reviews.

A recent report released by the Canadian Association of University Teachers (CAUT 2007) underlines the problem by noting that 'when members of equity-seeking groups are under-represented, the diversity of pedagogical techniques used, research subjects explored, questions posed, and methodologies employed may also be limited' (1).

As there is little quantitative research that reveals the actual numbers of racialized and Aboriginal faculty, figures, such as they exist, must be gathered from employment equity and other reports published by individual universities. As well, census data, although very incomplete, can also be used. The CAUT report states:

> Aboriginal Canadians are seriously under-represented within the academic world [see table 1.1]. In 2001, the most recent year for which data are available, just 0.7 per cent of all persons self-reporting to be university teachers identified themselves as Aboriginal, up only marginally from 0.5 per cent in 1996. By contrast, Aboriginal Canadians comprised 2.3 per cent of the total labour force aged 25 and older in 2001. Of all university teachers, 12.4 per cent self-identified as visible minorities in the 2001 Census, up slightly from 11.7 per cent in 1996. This generally reflects the composition of the labour force as a whole in 2001 when visible minorities represented 12.7 per cent of all workers 25 and older.

These figures are based only on those who described themselves as 'university teachers' on the census. These data were also cross-tabulated with income, and results indicate that racial minority university teachers make substantially less income than do others. This disparity, however, is due to the numbers of contract, part-time, and junior faculty among the racialized.

In a separate study, Nakhaie (2004) researched the ethno-racial origins of Canadian university administrators including presidents, vice-presidents, and deans from 1951 to 2001. He notes that there

> is a gross under-representation of visible minority and/or non-European origins among those who control Canadian universities. There has not been even one visible minority president and only recently have a few become deans or vice-presidents. Only 3.6 of the vice-presidents in 2001 and approximately 5 percent of the deans in 1991 and 2001 could be classified as visible minority and/or non-European. (95)

Furthermore, it has been pointed out that racialized women hold 18.7 per cent of doctoral degrees in Canada, and yet constitute an average of only 10.3 per cent of faculty positions nationwide (Kobayashi 2002). Thus, racialized faculty are under-represented at all levels of the university structure.

Henry and Tator Pilot Study Survey Findings

Responses from interviews and a survey questionnaire demonstrate strong dissatisfaction with recruitment and selection processes at Ca-

Table 1.1
Racial identification of university teachers, 1996 and 2001

	1996	2001
Aboriginal	0.5	0.7
White	83.9	82.4
South Asian	3.6	3.4
Chinese	2.9	3.6
Arab/West Asian	2.0	1.9
Black	1.5	1.6
Latin American	0.6	0.6
Japanese	0.6	0.5
Korean	0.3	0.3
Southeast Asian	0.3	0.3
Filipino	0.2	0.2
Other	0.3	0.3

Source: Statistics Canada, Census 1996 and 2001.

nadian universities. With only one exception, respondents agreed that recruitment and selection processes are inadequate to meet the challenge of establishing a pluralistic and inclusive faculty. The commitment to equity hiring is often very low. Our survey respondents were fairly unanimous in stating that recruitment policies and practices have not substantially changed.

A White faculty in a medium-sized university in a major city in Canada noted such policies are 'woefully inadequate: as far as I know there is no systematic training of administrators and hiring and promotion committees on this issue.'

Another White faculty in a large major university noted:

The university does not meet diversity hiring quotas, nor does it track these matters, so there's no accountability structure in this area. In some technical disciplines, there is a great deal of hiring from minority groups and from international universities, while in the social sciences and humanities there is much less. The major status positions – endowed chairs, Canadian Research Chairs, honorific titles such as 'University Professor' – are mostly held by White faculty.

A voice from one of the western province universities said:

The University includes the standard statement that 'applications are welcomed by women, visible minorities, aboriginals, and individuals with physical or mental challenges.' However, in my opinion, there is a need for the University ... to aggressively recruit racialized faculty members. Second, in examining senior administration, it is clearly populated by members of the dominant group.

In a very forthright statement, a faculty of colour in one of the major urban centres of the country notes that 'there has been some progress as evidenced by the outcomes of recent competitions but the employment polices, practices and processes remain uneven, arbitrary and the outcomes reflect that. Efforts to increase the level of transparency and to democratize the process, and possibly infuse it with equity principles, have been met with hostility.' Another member of an urban-based university commented that 'XX has an equity plan but it hasn't been adequately explained to faculty. All members of faculty hiring committees were required to take a day-long session in hiring, but equity was only mentioned tangentially.' And from a smaller university located in a smaller city, 'I am unaware of any formal University policy on visible minority hiring except for gender equity issues.' A western provincial university faculty member reports: 'Although a new position for Aboriginal study is in plan, no preference is given to visible minority. So, we only have one Chinese, one Latina, and 1.5 First Nations faculty out of 24 people.'

Very few respondents provided positive responses on the question of recruitment and selection. For example: 'At University A ... there are very clear, robust and transparent policies for hiring and selection ... At University B the contrast could not be more significant and one of the reasons why I departed.' One of the only positive statements came from a White faculty in a professional faculty whose university is located in a major city:

> Increasing the number of racialized and Aboriginal faculty has been the top priority. 6 of the last 10 positions went to Aboriginal or racialized women and men, one of whom has a visible disability. As well, the current administration has been equity-oriented in appointing part-time contract staff, such that the part-time ranks also include a number of racialized faculty from the government or NGO sectors.

Racialized Graduate Students

Faculty representation is closely allied to the numbers of students in graduate schools, some of whom are preparing themselves for academic teaching and research. Unfortunately, data of numbers of racial-

Table 1.2
York University Aboriginal/racialized graduate students and contract faculty: actual
numbers making up 5 per cent of total

	Contract Faculty	Graduate Students (1075)	MBA Students
Aboriginal		1	
Chinese	3	10	34
Black	3	4	2
South Asian	3	5	11
Latin American		3	5
All Other Racialized Groups	16	17	16

Source: Michael Ornstein, 2005, *Graduate Students, Contract Faculty Members and
Equity at York University*. Report to CUPE 3903. Institute of Social Research, Oct.

ized graduate students and specifically those studying for the PhD are
difficult to come by. One important exception is a study conducted at
York University which included graduate students, MBA students, and
contract faculty. Overall, 25 per cent of contract faculty, 39 per cent of
graduate students, and 67 per cent of MBA students considered themselves to be Aboriginal or students of colour.

Eurocentric Curricula

Another systemic barrier identified by our empirical findings is the
curricula, which represents a critical manifestation of marginalization
and exclusion. One of the most important symbolic messages commu-
nicated by the curriculum is that only particular kinds of knowledge
are validated and valued. Eurocentric frameworks, standards, and content are often not only given more resources and curriculum space, but
also more dominance and status especially when it comes to hiring and
promotion/tenure decisions. Many racialized and Aboriginal faculty
have argued that only specific types of knowledge continue to be recognized as legitimate, thereby excluding other forms that diverge from
the Eurocentric norm (see Wagner 2005; Calliste 2000). Furthermore, it
is argued that this ideological framework also influences choice of curriculum materials, such as required course readings, organization of
workshops and seminars, as well as decisions about visiting lecturers,
and even who should receive honorary degrees. Struggles to recentre
Aboriginal history, philosophy, and culture, and the incorporation of

anti-racism models of knowledge, are often met with resistance and hostility from White students, and a lack of support from White colleagues and administration.

Efforts to introduce more critical forms of pedagogy are also challenged. In the last decade or more, anti-racist feminist writers have critiqued the traditional pedagogical paradigms and canons of many disciplines, and attempted to modify the ideological frameworks through which racism is constructed and reproduced. Concern and disappointment has been particularly strong in relation to women's studies programs that have, to some extent, failed to incorporate a focus on the intersection of race and gender into their theoretical and methodological models. The majority of our survey respondents agreed that there were major problems with respect to curriculum. For example, 'Curriculum issues relating to equity based pedagogy have been a source of significant contention, and tension.' Another respondent added a disclaimer to his comment: [there are] 'courses on social inequality in general – but nothing specific on racism – usually tacked on as part of a wide range of issues (class, sexualities etc.).'

In a few departments, such as social work (e.g., Ryerson School of Social Work and University of Victoria Faculty of Social Work), respondents indicated that courses on aspects of racism are now part of the core or mainstream curriculum. However, the majority of responses from other departments of social work indicated that such courses are not considered an essential component of the core curriculum.

These brief comments indicate the level of marginalization that appears to exist in many departments. Two respondents representing cultural studies departments, however, indicated not only a wide range of equity and racism related courses but also those on many other aspects of oppression. However, it should be noted that the interdisciplinary field of cultural studies was essentially founded by critical theorists and in most instances its emphasis is on studies of oppression.

With rare exceptions courses on oppression and/or equity related issues are taught by racialized faculty. There were a few exceptions noted. These occurred when racialized faculty were on leave and their courses taught by White faculty. In another case, one course was co-taught by a White and a faculty of colour.

We also asked respondents to describe students who take equity related courses. One factor influencing the make-up of the student body was, of course, location of the university. The majority of the student body in non-urban smaller universities is still largely White. However, in the urban contexts, most respondents indicated that at least half or more of their students came from many different backgrounds and were racialized. No one indicated that more than about 30 per cent of their students were White. This suggests that courses on racism, anti-racism, and other equity related issues largely attract racialized and Aboriginal students. At the same time, it also suggests that the percentage of White students taking such courses is relatively low.

Concern with curriculum issues also characterizes the feelings of racialized students. Briefly, the main area of concern identified by respondents is the lack of attention to diversity and Aboriginal issues within the curriculum. Students also noted that many courses were taught from a Eurocentric perspective and that there were few courses on racism related issues. One person noted:

> The list is huge. The main issues concern the fact that many professors simply do not recognize that racism is an issue. They have a normative concept of curriculum, and often dismiss concerns of students of colour. It's easy to say, 'but that's not what this course is about.' Students who write papers on topics concerning racism often come to me because they feel their work has been misunderstood. An example, nearly all of the students have had some exposure to the work of Immanuel Kant, but virtually never to the extremely racist things that he wrote. When I introduce Kant from a different perspective in my course, they are very upset.

Another said: 'Many students of colour have told me that they are the only ones who typically bring up issues of race and racism in their courses, and that they often face denial or backlash in doing so, usually in subtle forms. This is within a program that tries to address racism and diversity issues directly in a number of ways.'

Students of colour are also very aware of context, and there are situations where they do not feel comfortable in raising concerns about racism. They note the insensitivity of some faculty members and students from the dominant group towards them. For example, 'racialized and other outsider students mostly comment on the contrast between contexts in which they feel free to speak openly about systemic inequality and those where they don't. The distinction is wholly a product of the instructor's course design, content and requirements and of the language adopted to discuss or avoid inequality-related materials.'

Survey respondents were also asked to comment on whether their courses are sufficient to prepare students to live and work in a multicultural and multiracial society. Most found this question difficult to answer. A very few felt confident that their curriculum was sufficient. However, these were specialty schools or faculties. Most doubted whether their work was enough to prepare students for societal realties. Some said that not enough of their faculty members were critically engaged in these ideas or processes to influence students.

While there is a relatively small body of literature about the feelings and experiences of racialized students of colour in their interaction with peers and professors (see Samuel 2005), an article by Michelle LaFlamme (2003) captures the essence of the processes of racialization. She writes that as a graduate student in English literature at a major western Canadian university she experienced the mind-numbing effects of Eurocentrism in the curriculum, which rarely included the literature of racialized people. At the interpersonal level LaFlamme experienced hostility from fellow students for speaking up about racism and colonialism and was angrily put down by a professor:

> As a graduate student I was, for the most part, 'the brown one' in every seminar. This meant that when I addressed issues of power and privilege that related to representations of race within a given text, I was met with a number of responses ranging from blank stares from the class, hostility from the professor who felt holes were being identified in his (usually a white male) curriculum, theoretical underpinnings or worst yet, his person. (1)
>
> … Another time I found myself in my First Nations literature class. One day, a Professor was challenged by the tiny core of Native students who felt that her perspective was too Eurocentric in its focus and was missing much of the symbolism. Instead of looking at this as an amazing learning opportunity for herself and the students, she became arrogant and suggested that when and *if* a First Nations person appeared with a Ph.D. she would gladly turn over the class to her. We all smoldered at the ways in which this comment was loaded with ramifications of class, power, privilege and the 'r' word. She became defensive and this shut down class discussions. (emphasis in original, 2)
>
> … We talk of Postcolonialism in literature classes but the word race is never mentioned. (4)

Observation and discussions with graduate students over years of teaching and attending conferences suggest that the experiences LaFlamme writes about are commonplace in Canadian universities.

Tenure and Promotion Processes

One of the most significant issues that face racialized faculty is the traditional ways in which tenure and promotion decisions are made. Most racialized faculty who are hired into tenure stream positions (as opposed to contractually limited terms) must face mandatory promotion and eventual tenure decisions. These decisions are initially made by a departmental committee, sometimes augmented by outside members, as well as a representative of the dean of the relevant faculty. The membership of these committees reflects the dominant profile of tenured faculty and is therefore largely White and often male.

The criteria used by such committees are time worn and traditional. There is always a heavy emphasis on research and publications. Thus, single authored books published by reputable publishers that rely on peer review to make their selections are heavily favoured. Within this category, university presses are favoured over smaller more progressive publishers. Multiple authored books and edited books usually follow. Many departments, especially in disciplines where peer reviewed journal articles are more highly regarded than books, place these first in their considerations. Even in social sciences, where books are more likely to be valued, committees place great stress on the peer review, and articles published in smaller, sometimes regional or community based journals, such as those in which racialized faculty are more likely to publish, are given little credence in the review process. The number, size, and granting institution of research grants are also critically important in the review process. Even the prestige of the granting institution is evaluated. Thus, in social science, the Social Sciences and Humanities Research Council of Canada (SSHRC) is more highly regarded than a smaller, less prestigious organization. Equally in science, National Science Foundation (NSF) grants have higher prestige than more localized agencies. With respect to teaching, student and peer evaluations are taken into account by promotion and tenure committees.

Of considerable importance in the review process are the letters of reference and support gathered in support of candidates. It is important to note that not only the content of the letters, but the prestige and the university affiliation of the letter writers is often a major consideration. Someone who is very well known in the field to members of the committee and who teaches at a prestigious university is more highly regarded than an academic little known to them or teaching at a small undergraduate university.

At every point in this complex process, faculty of colour and Aboriginal faculty are disadvantaged. The many demands placed on their time often prevent the publication of books and peer reviewed journal articles in appropriate numbers until later in their careers. The regions of the world in which they often specialize are not as well known to traditional scholars who sit on their review committees. The smaller and often regional journals in which racialized faculty publish are often not known to the committee members and sometimes not given sufficient weight. The length of time it normally takes to publish in larger mainstream journals works against racialized faculty who cannot wait two to three years for a submitted article to be accepted. Moreover, they often prefer to publish their findings in publications more receptive to their areas and theoretical perspectives.

Chilly Climate Issues: Backlash

Other manifestations of racism in the academy are clearly seen in the contestation over the 'chilly climate' reports, which many universities have produced in recent years.[5] Universities across Canada have produced numerous reports that document the evidence of racial and gender discrimination and offer a series of recommendations to address these inequities. Challenging these findings are reports, articles, and books written by White administrators, professors, and others that dispute both the diagnosis and the prescription for action (Resnick 1999; Marchak 1996; Fuerdy 1997; Fekete 1994). In this 'hyperbolic atmosphere, equity-seekers who point to systemic discrimination in higher education are vilified, and their institutional critiques are reframed as personalized attacks' (Prentice 2000, 200–1).

An example of the contestation over racial and sexual discrimination at the Department of Political Science at the University of British Columbia is by a highly resistant professor emeritus of this department, who argued that institutional measures to redress sexism and racism in his university's Political Science Department inflicted 'public disgrace' and 'public humiliation' on scholars in the department (Durrant, *Globe and Mail*, letter to the editor, August 8, 1995, cited in Prentice 2000, 90).

Razack (1998) provides an insightful analysis of how liberal educational norms manifest and fuel this form of hubris:

[P]luralistic models of inclusion assume that we have long ago banished the stereotypes from our heads. These models suggest that with a little practice and the right information, we can all be innocent subjects, standing outside hierarchical social relations, who are not accountable for the past or implicated in the present. It is not our ableism, racism, sexism, or heterosexism that gets in the way of communicating across differences, but *their* disability, *their* culture, *their* biology, or *their* lifestyle ... the cultural differences approach reinforces an important epistemological cornerstone of imperialism: the colonized possess a series of knowable characteristics and can be studied, known, and managed accordingly by the colonizers whose own complicity remains masked. (emphasis in original, 10)

Conclusion

This overview of the theory and praxis in the academy is best concluded by citing a recent statement written and distributed by a coalition of racialized academics:

Statement from a Coalition of Academics of Colour
Racism and discriminatory hiring practices continue to exist in Canadian universities. In the February 2007 issue of *Academic Matters* (Ontario Confederation of University Faculty Associations' [OCUFA] publication), Frances Henry and Carol Tator highlight the under-representation of Aboriginals and people of colour in academia. CAUT's Almanac of Post-secondary Education 2007 statistics show Canadian University Teachers by Visible Minority Status were 10.3% in 1996 and 11.1% in 2001. However, there is no indication how many of these faculty are contract faculty, untenured and when tenured, how many are at the rank of Assistant, Associate and Full Professor.

Systemic racism exists by privileging white dominant interpretations of 'standards.' Teaching Evaluations, the criteria and process by which tenure and promotion are granted, the type of publications that are recognized as being refereed as well as the criteria by which research and teaching excellence are measured are some of the ways in which universities systemically recreate the status quo in academia. The lack of support from colleagues, chairs of departments and deans reinforces, to varying degrees, this social marginalization, and, in some cases, social exclusion.

Despite research documenting racism in academia by established scholars and several individual cases of faculty being 'pushed' out of academia, there seems to be no oversight body that is taking up these issues in any substantive way. Many faculty of colour are currently experiencing a hostile and alienating work environment. Several are being systematically marginalized and/or excluded from this workplace. Many more are engaged in exploitative working conditions as contract faculty. In their Academic Matters article, Frances Henry and Carol Tator conclude: 'The experiences of racialized students, faculty of colour, and Aboriginal academics across this country reflect the failure of administrative policies, programs, and everyday practices to address racism, to create a more equitable learning and working environment, and, above all, to vigorously challenge the "culture of whiteness" still so dominant at most Canadian universities.'

We call on CAUT, OCUFA, and the Canadian Federation for the Humanities and the Social Sciences to put these issues on the political agenda. Analysis of the results of the Federal Employment Equity Act and the Federal Contractors' Compliance Programme is overdue: it is also timely in relation to post-secondary education's capacity to renew itself. As Canadian scholars, we call for accountability and justice.[6]

NOTES

1 Critical race scholars include Richard Delgado (1995), Patricia Williams (1991), Ruth Frankenberg (1993), Elizabeth Ellsworth (1997), Carol Aylward, (2000), Razack (1998), Levine-Rasky (2002).

2 The interlocking web of everyday racism crosses all sectors in Canadian society including systems of governance and lawmaking, law enforcement, justice, immigration, mass media, education, and employment systems. See David Goldberg (1993).

3 Under-representation is not only evident in Canada. In the United States, for example, faculty of colour are at most 14 per cent of total faculty. There are also many accounts and descriptions of ethnic and racial bias written by scholars of colour (see Turner 2003). Turner also cites figures to show that 5 per cent of full-time faculty are African American, 2.4 per cent are Hispanic, 5.1 per cent are Asian American, and only 0.4 per cent are 'Native American.' Faculty of colour in the United States have almost exclusively and until very recently been employed in Black colleges and community colleges rather than mainstream universities and colleges.

4 We use the label 'diversity' because it is so often used in the literature and in the media but acknowledge that it is a contested term that we, as most critical race scholars, deplore.

5 See an analysis of some of these documents in The Chilly Climate Collective 1995; Sheila McIntyre 2000; Susan Prentice 2000; Anne Bishop 2005.

6 This call was originally circulated at the Canadian Federation for the Humanities and Social Sciences (CFHSS) sponsored panel 'Glass Ceilings and Trap Doors: Anti-Racist Equity Hiring, Retention, and Accountability in Canadian Universities,' co-organized by vice-presidents, Equity Issues (CFHSS) Dr. Donna Pennee and Dr. Malinda S. Smith, University of Alberta, May 30, 2007.

REFERENCES

Alfred, T. 2007. 'Indigenizing the Academy? An Argument Against.' *Academic Matters* Feb.:22–3.
Anthias, F. 1998. 'Rethinking Social Division: Some Notes towards a Theoretical Framework.' *Sociological Review* 63:505–33.
Aylward, C. 2000. *Canadian Critical Race Theory: Racism and the Law.* Halifax: Fernwood.
Bell, D. 1987. *We Are Not Saved: The Elusive Quest for Social Justice.* New York: Basic Books.
Bell, L.A. 2003. 'Telling Tales: What Stories Teach Us about Racism.' *Race, Ethnicity and Education* 6(1):1–18.
Bishop, A. 2005. *Beyond Token Change: Breaking the Cycle of Oppression in Institutions.* Halifax, NS: Fernwood.
Bourdieu, P. 1999. 'Language and Symbolic Power.' In A. Jaworski and N. Coupland, eds., *The Discourse Reader,* 502–13. London: Routledge.
Boyce, M. 1996. 'Teaching Critical as Act Praxis and Resistance.' *EJROT (The Electronic Journal of Radical Organizational Theory),* Sept. 22.
Brander-Rasmussen, B., E. Klinenberg, I. Nexica, and M. Wrag, eds. 2001. *The Making and Unmaking of Whiteness.* Durham, NC: Duke University Press.
Calliste, A. 2000. 'Anti-Racist Organizing and Resistance in Academia.' In G. Dei and A. Calliste, eds., *Power, Knowledge and Anti-Racism Education,* 142–61. Halifax: Fernwood.
Carty, L. 1991. 'Black Women in Academia: A Statement from the Periphery.' In H. Bannerji, L. Carty, K. Dehli, S. Heald, and K. McKenna, *Unsettling Relations: The University as a Site of Feminist Struggles,* 13–44. Toronto: Women's Press.
CAUT (Canadian Association of University Teachers). 2007. Equity Review Report. http://www.caut.ca/en/publications/equityreview/ Nov.:1–6.
Chilly Climate Collective. 1995. *Breaking Anonymity: Chilly Climate for Women Faculty.* Waterloo, ON: Wilfrid Laurier University Press.
Collins, P. 1991. *Black Feminist Thought: Knowledge, Consciousness and the Politics of Empowerment.* New York: Routledge.

Cooks, L., and J. Simpson. 2007. *Whiteness, Pedagogy, Performance: Displacing.* Lanham: Lexington Books.

Crenshaw, K., N. Gotanda, and K. Thomas, eds. 1995. *Critical Race Theory: The Key Writings that Informed the Movement.* New York: The New Press.

Dei, G., and A. Calliste, eds. 2000. *Power, Knowledge and Anti-Racism Education.* Halifax: Fernwood.

Dei, G., L. Karumanchery, and N. Karumanchery-Luik. 2004. *Playing the Race Card: Exposing White Power and Privilege.* New York: Peter Lang.

Delgado, R. 1995. 'Legal Storytelling: Storytelling for Oppositionists and Others: A Plea for the Narrative.' In R. Delgado, ed., *Critical Race Theory: The Cutting Edge,* 64–74. Philadelphia: Temple University Press.

Doyle-Bedwell, P. 1997. 'Justice and Healing: A Teach Journal.' *Status of Women Supplement of the CAUT Bulletin* 44(4) April.

Ellsworth, E. 1989. 'Why Doesn't Think Feel Empowering? Working Through the Repressive Myths of Critical Pedagogy.' *Harvard Educational Review* 59(3) August:297–324.

– 1997. 'Teaching Positions: Difference, Pedagogy and the Power of Address.' New York: Teachers College Press.

Essed, P. 1990. *Everyday Racism: Reports from Women of Two Cultures.* Claremont, CA: Hunter House.

Ewick, P., and S. Silbey. 1995. 'Subversive Stories and Hegemonic Tales: Towards of Narrative.' *Law and Society Review* 29:197–226.

Fekete, J. 1994. *Moral Panic: Biopolitics Rising.* Montreal: Robert Davies.

Fine, M., L. Weiss, L. Powell, and L. Mung Wong. 1997. *Off White: Readings on Race, Power, and Society.* London: Routledge.

Foucault, M. 1980. 'Two Lectures.' In *Power/Knowledge: Selected Interviews and Other Writings.* New York: Pantheon.

Frankenberg, R. 1993. *White Women, Race Matters: The Social Construction of Whiteness.* Minneapolis: University of Minneapolis Press.

Freire, P. 1970. *Pedagogy of the Oppressed.* New York: Seabury.

– 1985. *The Politics of Education.* South Hadley, MA: Bergin and Garvey.

Fuerdy, J. 1997. 'Academic Freedom vs. the Velvet Totalitarian Culture of Comfort on Current Canadian Campuses: Some Fundamental Terms and Distinctions.' *Interchange* 28:331–50.

Gabriel, J. 1998. *Whitewash: Racialized Politics and the Media.* London: Routledge.

Giroux, H. 1992. *Border Crossings: Cultural Workers and the Politics of Education.* New York and London: Routledge.

Goldberg, D. 1993. *Racist Culture: Philosophy and Politics of Meaning.* Oxford, UK and Cambridge, MA: Blackwell.

Green, J. 2002. 'Transforming at the Margins of the Academy.' In E. Hannah, L. Paul, and S. Vethamany, eds., *Women in the Canadian Tundra: Challenging the Chilly Climate*, 85–91. Montreal and Kingston: McGill-Queen's University Press.

– 2005. *From Stonechild to Social Cohesion: Anti-Racism Challenges for Saskatchewan*. Presentation to the Canadian Political Sciences Association, 'Theory, Policy, and Pedagogy or Decolonization,' 1–24. University of Western Ontario, June 2–4.

Hall, S. 1986. 'Variants on Liberalism.' In S. Hall and S. Donald, eds., *Politics and Ideology*, 34–69. Milton Keynes: Open University Press.

Henry, F., and C. Tator. 2002. *Discourses of Domination: Racial Bias in the Canadian English-Language Press*. Toronto: University of Toronto Press.

– 2006. *The Colour of Democracy: Racism in Canadian Society* (3rd ed.). Toronto: Nelson Thomson.

Hoodfar, H. 1992. 'Feminist Anthropology and Critical Pedagogy: The Anthropology of Classrooms' Excluded Voices.' *Canadian Journal of Education* 17: 303–20.

hooks, b. 1990. *Yearning: Race, Gender and Cultural Politics*. Boston, MA: South End Press.

Kobayashi, A. 2002. 'Now You See Them, How You See Them: Women of Colour in Canadian Academia.' In S. Herald, ed., *Feminist Issues: Selected Papers from the WIN Symposia, 2000–2001*, 44–54. Ottawa: Humanities and Social Sciences Federation of Canada.

Levine-Rasky, C., ed. 2002. *Working Through: Whiteness International Perspectives*. Albany: Albany State University Press.

Ladson-Billings, G. 1995. 'Toward a Theory of Culturally Relevant Pedagogy.' *American Educational Research Journal* 35:465–91.

– 2000. 'Racialized Discourses and Ethnic Epistemologies.' In N. Denzin and Y. Lincoln, eds., *Handbook of Qualitative Research*, 2nd ed. Thousand Oaks, CA: Sage.

Ladson-Billings, G., and W. Tate. 1995. 'Towards a Critical Race Theory of Education.' *Teachers College Record* 97:47–68.

LaFlamme, M. 2003. 'An Uppity Memoir and Some Cheeky Tips ... ' http://www.thirdspace.ca/articles/laflamm2.htm.

Mackey, E. 2002. *House of Difference: Cultural Politics and National Identity in Canada*. Toronto: University of Toronto Press.

Mahtani, Minelle. 2006. 'Challenging the Ivory Tower: Proposing Anti-Racism Geography within the Academy.' *Gender, Place, and Culture* 13(1):21–5.

Marchak, P. 1996. *Racism, Sexism, and the University: The Political Science Affair at the University of British Columbia*. Montreal and Kingston: McGill-Queen's University Press.

McIntosh, P. 1989. 'White Privilege: Unpacking the Invisible Knapsack.' *Bimonthly Journal of Women's International League for Peace and Freedom,* July/August:1–6.

McIntyre, S. 2000. 'Studied Ignorance and Privileged Innocence: Keeping Equity Academic.' *Canadian Journal of Women and the Law* 12:147–96.

McLaren, P. 1994. 'White Terror and Oppositional Agency: Towards a Critical Multiculturalism.' In D. Goldberg, ed., *Multiculturalism: A Critical Reader,* 45–74. Oxford, UK and Cambridge, MA: Blackwell.

Miles, R. 1989. *Racism.* London: Routledge.

Mohanty, C.T. 1990. 'On Race and Voice: Challenges for Liberal Education in the 1990s.' *Cultural Critique* Winter:170–208.

Moosa-Mitha, M. 2005. 'Situating Anti-Oppressive Theories within Critical and Difference-Centered Perspectives.' In L. Brown and S. Strega, eds., *Research as Resistance: Critical, Indigenous, and Anti-Oppressive Approaches,* 37–72. Toronto: Canadian Scholars' Press.

Morales, A. 1998. *Medicine Stories: History, Culture and the Politics of Integrity.* Cambridge, MA: South End Press.

Morrison, T. 1992. *Playing in the Dark: Whiteness and the Literary Imagination.* Cambridge, MA: Harvard University Press.

Murji, K., and S. Solomos, eds. 2005. *Racialization: Studies in Theory and Practice.* New York: Anchor.

Nakhaie, R. 2004. 'Who Controls Canadian Universities? Ethno-racial Origins of Canadian University Administrators and Faculty's Perception of Mistreatment.' *Canadian Ethnic Studies* 36(1):95.

Ng, R., P. Staton, and J. Scane, eds. 1995. *Anti-Racism, Feminism and Critical Approaches to Education.* Toronto: Ontario Institute for Studies in Education.

Nunan, R. 1999. 'Critical Race Theory. Part III. CRT's Narrative Soul.' *Newsletter on Philosophy, Law and the Black Experience* 98(2):1–18.

Ornstein, M. 2005. 'Graduate Students, Contract Faculty Members and Equity at York University. Report to CUPE 3903.' Institute of Social Research, York University.

Potts, K., and L. Brown. 2005. 'Becoming an Anti-oppressive Researcher.' In L. Brown and S. Strega, eds., *Research as Resistance: Critical, Indigenous, and Anti-Oppressive Approaches.* Toronto: Canadian Scholars' Press.

Prentice, S. 2000. 'The Conceptual Politics of Chilly Climate Controversies.' *Gender and Education* 12(2) June:195–207.

Razack, S. 1998. *Looking White People in the Eye: Gender, Race, and Culture in Courtrooms and Classrooms.* Toronto: University of Toronto Press.

Resnick, Philip. 1999. 'Why PC? Why B.C.?' In Cyril Levitt, Scott Davies, and Neil McLaughlin, eds., *Mistaken Identities: The Second Wave of Controversy over 'Political Correctness.'* New York: Peter Lang.

Romero, V. 2002. 'Critical Race Theory in Three Acts: Racial Profiling, Affirmative Action, and the Diversity Visa Lottery.' *Albany Law Review* 66(Winter 2):375–88.

Samuel, E. 2005. *Integrative Antiracism: South Asians in Canadian Academe.* Toronto: University of Toronto Press.

Scheurich, J.J., and M.D. Young. 1997. 'Coloring Epistemologies: Are Our Research Epistemologies Racially Biased?' *Educational Researcher* 26(4):4–16.

Small, S. 1999. 'The Contours of Racialization: Private Structures, Representations and Resistance in the U.S.' In R. Torres, J. Inda, and L. Miron, eds., *Race, Identity, and Citizenship: A Reader.* Malden, MA: Blackwell.

Smith, D.E. 1999. 'Politically Correct: An Organizer of Public Discourse.' In S. Richler and I. Weir, eds., *Writing the Social: Critique, Theory, and Investigation,* 23–50. Toronto: University of Toronto Press.

Srivastava, S. 1996. 'Song and Dance? The Performance of Antiracist Workshops.' *Canadian Review of Sociology and Anthropology* 33(3):291–315.

Strega, S. 2005. 'The View from the Poststructural Margins: Epistemology and Methodology Reconsidered.' In L. Brown and S. Strega, eds., *Research as Resistance: Critical, Indigenous, and Anti-oppressive Approaches,* 199–254. Toronto: Canadian Scholars' Press.

Stewart, A. 2004. 'Penn and Teller Magic: Self, Racial Devaluation and the Canadian Academy.' In C. Nelson and C. Nelson, eds., *Racism, Eh?: A Critical Inter-Disciplinary Anthology of Race and Racism,* 33–40. Concord, ON: Cactus Press.

Tastsoglou, E. 2000. 'Mapping the Unknowable: The Challenges and Rewards of Cultural and Pedagogical Border Crossings.' In G. Dei and A. Calliste, eds., *Power, Knowledge and Anti-Racism: A Critical Reader,* 98–120. Halifax: Fernwood.

Turner, C. 2003. 'Incorporation and Marginalization in the Academy: From Border Toward Centre for Faculty of Color?' *Journal of Black Studies* 34(Sept., 1):112–25.

van Dijk, T. 1998. 'How They Hit the Headlines: Ethnic Minorities in the Press.' In G. Smitherman-Donaldson and T. van Dijk, *Discourse and Domination.* Detroit: Wayne State University Press.

Visano, L. 2002. 'The Impact of Whiteness on the Culture of Law: From Theory and Practice.' In C. Levine-Rasky, ed., *Working Through Whiteness: International Perspectives.* Albany: Albany State University Press.

Wagner, A. 2005. 'Unsettling the Academe: Working Through the Challenges of Anti-Racist Pedagogy.' *Race, Ethnicity and Education* 8(Sept., 3):261–75.

Wallace, B. 2000. *The Taboo of Subjectivity: Towards a New Science of Consciousness.* New York: Oxford University Press.

Williams, P. 1991. *The Alchemy of Race and Rights*. Cambridge, MA: Harvard University Press.

Yon, D. 2000. *Elusive Culture: Schooling, Race, and Identity in Global Times*. Albany: SUNY Press.

2 Now You See Them, How You See Them: Women of Colour in Canadian Academia

AUDREY KOBAYASHI

Now You See Them . . .

Women of colour in Canadian academia are notable for being *un*seen. Members of 'visible minority' groups hold 18.7 per cent of the PhDs in Canada, yet make up on average about 12 per cent of university faculties across the country. Visible minority women are much more poorly represented than their male counterparts, who tend to be disproportionately represented in the sciences and health-related disciplines.[1] In contrast, the numbers of visible minority students in Canadian universities have risen sharply in recent years, approaching or even exceeding 50 per cent of the total student bodies of several institutions, including the University of Toronto, York University, the University of British Columbia, and the University of Calgary.

Only recently has it been recognized that the lack of representation of people of colour in the academy is what the law terms an 'adverse effect' of systemic discrimination. Androcentric and Eurocentric values, supported by the power of 'old white boys' networks, have kept women of colour out of the academy very effectively. Recent commitments to equitable hiring practices on the part of most Canadian universities, and proactive employment equity policies in some cases, may have resulted in some increase in the rate of hiring, but progress is slow both because it takes a long time to change attitudes, and because adverse effects work throughout the system. The university has long been, and remains, a zone of white privilege.

When you *do* see them, however, women academics of colour do not necessarily face an easy professional road. Henry and Tator (1994) outline the effects of systemic discrimination in universities as:

- Overwhelming power on the part of White academicians to define the content and standards of university education and research, and to control who has access to positions;
- Strong resistance on the part of those in power to recognizing that problems of racism exist, bolstered by moral superiority, complacency, and insensitivity;
- Lack of institutional procedures to combat systemic racism towards current or potential faculty members;
- Retreat into excuses based on dominant concepts of academic excellence;
- Eurocentric curricula;
- Inadequate or inappropriate supervision for graduate students who either wish to pursue research topics related to racism or who, as students of colour, require supervisors that are understanding of their circumstances;
- A higher burden of counselling and advising of students of colour by under-represented faculty of colour;
- Inadequate recognition, or denigration, of the work of faculty in consideration for tenure, promotion, research grants, or other forms of achievement recognition;
- Overt racism in the form of direct discrimination, harassment, or assault;
- The creation of a hostile environment for faculty of colour;
- Overwork and burn-out for faculty of colour working on issues of racism in the institutional environment, exacerbated by the fact that such faculty members are often exposed to hostility, lack of cooperation, and marginalizing behaviour on the part of their colleagues.

With the exception of overt racism, these effects are now generally viewed as systemic, because they can arise, not only from deliberate racist actions or attitudes on the part of identifiable individuals, but also as a result of the ordinary ways in which university business is conducted. Systemic racism is a normative aspect of Canadian ways of doing things, and deeply entrenched within university culture.

The concept of systemic discrimination, especially in the field of employment, received legal recognition in the case of *Action Travail des Femmes*,[2] in which the Supreme Court of Canada provided the following definition of systemic discrimination:

[S]ystemic discrimination in an employment context is discrimination that results from the simple operation of established procedures of recruitment, hiring and promotion, none of which is necessarily designed to promote discrimination. The discrimination is then reinforced by the very exclusion of the disadvantaged group because the exclusion fosters the belief, both within and outside the group, that the exclusion was the result of 'natural' forces, for example, that women 'just can't do the job' ... To combat systemic discrimination, it is essential to create a climate in which both negative practices and negative attitudes can be challenged and discouraged. (209–13)

This case has created a range of precedents for systemic discrimination cases, especially those involving gender, but has also informed the conceptual framework in which increasing attention has been placed on systemic racism, the concern of this chapter. A small but growing number of voices have been raised within the academy to signal that all is not well for academics of colour.[3] Systemic racism in Canadian universities has recently received wider recognition through several unfortunate, high profile cases over the past decade. At the University of British Columbia, a Human Rights complaint on the part of graduate students in the Department of Political Science resulted in commissioning a private consultant's report, subsequent sanctions towards the department, and a later retraction of those sanctions and an apology to Political Science from the president of the university, who determined in retrospect that the complaints were groundless. Whatever the merits of the particular case, however, the events occurred in an atmosphere that was highly racially charged and where there was a general lack of recognition that systemic effects cannot be understood or changed according to established ways of seeing.

At the University of Toronto, in the case of Kin-Yip Chun, the Canadian Association of University Teachers (CAUT) undertook an independent review of Dr. Chun's allegation that he had been treated unfairly by being denied a tenure-track position on several occasions. The report found that Dr. Chun had been the victim of systemic discrimination, and requested an Ontario Human Rights Commission tribunal investigation.

According to the Report:

Canadian law recognizes three forms of discrimination. Direct discrimination encompasses intentional acts and is evidenced by behaviour such as racial slurs. Adverse effect discrimination occurs when ostensibly neutral rules have an unintended discriminatory impact (for example, compulsory work attendance on a Sabbath). Systemic discrimination arises from the unintentional and even unconscious operation of long established practices and procedures that tend to exclude or discriminate against certain groups within society. (CAUT 1999, 97–8)

The Human Rights Commission subsequently refused to hear the case. This refusal is neither a rejection nor a support of the charges of discrimination, but rather a statement about the system in place at the commission, which hears a small minority of the cases brought before it based on limited grounds and specific kinds of evidence. The University of Toronto nonetheless made a settlement with Dr. Chun, which reinstated him in the Physics Department and included the possibility that he will in future become eligible for consideration for tenure. The case has focused huge attention on issues of racialization[4] in the academy. Like other cases, it shows a general unwillingness to confront problems of racism, a tendency to view problems as *anything but* racism, and an overwhelming unwillingness to shift the perspective from that of the white majority to that of the minority.

At Queen's, my own university, a report (widely known as the 'Henry Report') on systemic racism toward faculty of colour and Aboriginal faculty undertaken by Frances Henry drew strong criticism, including overt and hostile racist comments from alumni, when it suggested that the university fosters a 'culture of Whiteness' (Henry 2003). What was most striking about the environment in which the report was received was that, despite the fact that the report was taken seriously by many, there were loud and numerous voices raised in denial, especially over the fact that the emphasis was placed on the culture of the majority rather than on the experience of the few.

In this chapter, I wish to subject to greater scrutiny what has become the prevailing wisdom concerning systemic racism as unintentional. While I agree that racism in the academy is produced and reproduced systemically, and that individuals are often not directly reflective of their complicity in the process, it is also important to recognize that women of colour experience the effects as individuals in relation to other individuals. In the complex human interactions that make up the daily life of the institution, the attitudes, assumptions, and beliefs that perpetuate racism are held or implemented by some *body*. The pain, shame, and frustration that all women of colour feel at different points in their careers are usually associated with some *body*. If relations among social bodies are to change, that change must involve changing the behaviour of individuals, or the programs to combat systemic racism currently being undertaken by many university administrations will be for nought.

This is a difficult assertion to make because it brings under scrutiny the very emotional qualities of interpersonal relations. It makes it impossible for individuals to hide behind assertions that the remedies can only be undertaken at a systemic level, and requires, instead, that they make personal commitments to understand the hurt, pain, and marginalization that their colleagues of colour have undergone. It demands that all of our colleagues become involved in the process, rather than leaving it to those either directly involved in specific human rights cases, or those with a direct administrative responsibility to promote workplace equity. It is also a difficult assertion to make because it requires a commitment on my own part to examine some of the experiences that have made my own academic life at times uncomfortable. In this chapter, I enter that zone of discomfort to address some of my own experiences. I contend that while the situation in which academics of colour such as myself find ourselves may be systemically produced, it is lived through at the level of the individual. Therefore, future work needs to address the relationship between individual and systemic effects as an integrated whole rather than as separate processes.

Stages of Seeing

While racialization has always been a dominant feature of Canadian social relations, the specific actions and the forms of social relations through which racialization occurs have varied significantly over time and in different Canadian places. Casting back over my own professional career, I can identify stages of racialization, no doubt strongly related to my personal development and my understanding of the process. I relate them here not to personalize the process, but to illustrate the experiences of many academic women of colour. The stages of my life also represent significant social stages, from the 1950s to the present day, during which bodies of colour have been made visible on the social landscape in significantly different ways.

I am the child of an interracial marriage between a Japanese Canadian father and an English Canadian mother. Their marriage in the 1940s was an extremely rare event, and they paid a severe cost for their actions (another story entirely). I was brought up in a low-income, blue-collar setting. Looking back, I can see the various ways in which I and my best school friend, who was Aboriginal, were marginalized by our classmates, but at the time I had virtually no understanding of the concept of 'race.' It is only in retrospect that I realize that students of colour and Aboriginal students were seen by their peers as 'different' and treated as such. I compensated by excelling at my school work, until the late 1960s when I blossomed as a flower child suddenly endowed with the caché of the exotic breed. In the heady early days of the human rights movement, Black and Asian bodies were re-viewed in popular culture under the general slogan that 'Black is beautiful.' As an undergraduate, however, I was bemused, and often amused, at the lengths that my fellow students would go to let me know that they carried no prejudices. But not for a moment would they let go of the notion that I was 'different.' From the perspective of many years and an acquired academic analysis I now realize that what I experienced is well documented under the concept of Orientalism.

Graduate school was another story. Here, the processes of socialization were strong indeed. Throughout the 1970s, there was a gradual awakening in social science disciplines of the significance of class and gender, but issues of 'race' were virtually ignored, except for the occasional foray into the urban ghettoes of the United States, actually dubbed by some geographers as exploratory 'expeditions.' Aside from my MA advisor—who advised that I would be better off studying Japanese Canadians than the Maya of the Yucatan, thus setting me on the trajectory that leads to the present day – my graduate school mentors treated me as white, and used examples of white culture in their teaching. In the sophisticated world of the university where white male privilege was still relatively sacrosanct, I actually never noticed that I was the only person of colour in my MA cohort at the University of British Columbia. In my PhD cohort at the University of California at (multicultural, racialized, ghettoized) Los Angeles, there was one Chicano man among our class of approximately thirty. Outside of the classroom, however, I was increasingly involved in community politics, part of the third generation of Asian Americans and Canadians suddenly awakened to their heritage. In Canada, I became involved in the fight for redress for the uprooting and dispossession of our community during the 1940s. It was a schizophrenic existence, however, where the world of community activism had little connection with that of the academy.

Today, we often hear reference to the term 'colour-blindness' to refer to the 'progressive' developments of the 1970s through which members of our society began to believe that colour is not a meaningful way of distinguishing human beings, or that colour *'makes no difference.'* Such an interpretation would have been fine in a world in which colour had no meaning and was not used as a marker for discrimination. But such was not the case; it was, rather, an *in-difference* to the effects of racialization throughout our society, and a failure (or refusal) to see the need for social scientists either to study the effects of racialization or to become activists for change. It was also a denial of the need either for affirmative action practices to increase the number of students of colour, or for mentoring practices to help them to adjust to a racialized academy. The result of the apparently progressive attitudes to 'race' – as well as to gender, to disability, and to other forms of marginalization – is a situation in which most Canadian universities today provide programs and prescriptive messages about equality and accessibility (often disguised in the language of 'diversity'), while the members of those institutions are unable to see that marginalized groups remain marginalized.

How are we to understand the ways in which this briefly sketched history affects women of colour in the academy today? First, we all bring our past histories to our present lives; they define us to ourselves and to others. Members of racialized minority groups bring those histories to academic institutions and classrooms. While they are not, and should not be, the only ones who can teach about racism, they can teach about the racism experienced in their own communities in very particular and powerful ways. Second, in our personal lives and in our relations with colleagues our past lives, and theirs, inform – and at times deform – everyday human relations, producing and reproducing racialized practices. Our histories cannot be whitened, nor can they be set aside. We and others need to learn to live with them. That process is also one of learning to see differently.

I took my first faculty position at McGill University in the early 1980s, still operating under the assumption that my life as a member of a community of colour and my life as an academic were not especially connected. That all changed when I was asked to negotiate with the federal government on behalf of Japanese Canadians seeking redress for the effects of the uprooting of the 1940s. It was a profound experience in many ways. From that point onward, I would see academic scholarship and anti-racist activism as, for me, a single project.

It was also at this time, however, that I became aware of how deeply racialized is the university environment. To my students, I was known – sometimes with affection, sometimes with contempt, and sometimes with dread – as 'The Dragon Lady.' I spent a lot of time developing pedagogic techniques to gain and inspire their confidence and to help them to think critically about cultural constructions. For some of the most open students, I was able to use the dragon lady construction as a heuristic device for understanding the process of racialization.

With my colleagues, most of whom were male, the eighties decade was a constant struggle over gender issues. Like other feminists, I learned a variety of techniques: cajoling, persuading, paralysing with logic and, occasionally, confrontation. But, whereas it was difficult for them to ignore the presence of a feminist in their midst, 'race' didn't seem to be an issue. They were not very interested in my research or in its connection to community activism, until, that is, it came time for my tenure decision. The application was strongly supported at the departmental level, but members of the faculty committee challenged it on grounds that my work was too political and that I had devoted too much effort to writing for the community instead of for international academics. It passed nonetheless, and a progressive dean even made a complimentary comment about my community contributions in his official letter. The trauma of having my tenure application challenged on such a basis, however, remains a vivid memory after nearly twenty years, not only because it was emotionally difficult. The experience showed me that one makes a choice, even about what might seem to be a straightforward racial identity. One can act white, follow the white rules, and people will go out of their way to be accepting according to their rules; to challenge whiteness,[5] however, is to embark upon a perilous journey.

When I arrived at my current university in 1994, it was with the celebratory sense that I was actually hired *because of* my established reputation as an activist. Although I was hired primarily into an administrative position, my teaching was entirely in the areas of 'race' and gender. It seemed like academic heaven.

But I was in for a number of rude surprises. As a woman, let alone a woman of colour, in my first administrative post, I faced a very steep learning curve, and the university provided very little support or recognition of the circumstances that I and others in similar circumstances faced. While on the one hand I had a great deal to learn about effective administration, on the other, I was trying to apply feminist principles of inclusion and equality in an institutional setting not at all accustomed to such practices. Even more disturbing was the cool reception on the part of many of my new feminist colleagues. I struggled to develop a way of gaining their trust. It was a genuine shock to realize that for years I had been building my own connections among anti-racist feminists whose academic culture was very different from that of the white feminist culture to which I was now introduced. I had read different things. I had different theoretical and methodological perspectives. I was engaged in different forms of activism. I found, like many before me, that the close connection I had assumed between issues of racism and gender was not necessarily recognized in a setting where some saw the introduction of 'race' issues as a threat to their long battle for gender equality and where others simply viewed the two as synonymous. To make matters worse, the first time I walked into a large first-year class and stared out into that sea of white faces, so very different from the diversity I was accustomed to on big-city campuses, I teetered behind the podium in genuine consternation. I have never in my life felt so alone as I did in those first days.

I also faced many students who complained to us at the prospect of studying 'race' in addition to gender, or who were so overcome with white guilt that they became emotionally unable to act effectively. These particular problems mean that special pedagogic and counselling techniques have to be developed for dealing with students in an anti-racist classroom, a challenge that has hardly begun to be met in most Canadian universities.

Since that time, nearly fifteen years ago, both the number of students and the number of faculty of colour have increased; over five years, one or two were hired each year, so I went from being the only woman of colour in the social sciences and humanities to being one of several. But increasing numbers did not break down the barriers between white academic culture and the cultures of otherness. Even as I learned more and more about how to provide support and safety for students of colour, and how to teach anti-racism effectively to white students, I was more and more confused by my inability to gain the trust of my white colleagues. It seemed impossible to achieve frank and open discussions. Gossip was rife, and much occurred behind closed doors. Ironically, although I was recognized outside my own university as an expert in issues that include not only anti-racism but also employment equity, I was stymied in my attempts to achieve equity in my own surroundings.

This is a complex story with many facets. I do not need to develop the details here. But this story is not unique, which is why it is important. Since that time, I have discovered that it is the same story, with different details, told over and over again by women of colour in Canadian universities. They find themselves most marginalized not by those who practise overt racism, but by the majority of white faculty who simply cannot see, feel, or understand the ways in which Others are marginalized. As Philomena Essed points out in her analysis of everyday racism, it is only from the perspective of the individual who experiences the subtle effects of marginalization that the normative actions of the majority can be understood (1991). The subjective process of understanding oneself as racialized, then, is a significant part. It needs to be told over and over to make the point – that it is not sufficient simply to hire more minority faculty. The institutional culture has to change in order to break down the processes of racialization. The basis of that culture, however, needs to be understood from the perspective of the marginalized individuals.

Changing the Culture

I began this chapter with the assertion that social processes of racialization have changed over recent decades to reflect larger changes in dominant social attitudes. It speaks to the power of racism that it is so readily transformed, that it adapts to the contours of the social times, naturalizing and normalizing, so that it becomes difficult to recognize and therefore all the more powerful. Older forms of overt racism, such as name calling, physical abuse, restriction from jobs and social venues, and hate crime, still occur at troublingly high levels in Canadian society; but they are so much easier to name, and therefore to confront, than the new racisms of the twenty-first century that involve backlash effects, cultural marginalization, and personal politics. These are the characteristics of an academy that suffers from the pervasion of whiteness, a form of discrimination in which people use 'colour-blindness' and public ideology of opposing the old forms of racism as foils for actions that are, in their own ways, just as damaging for academics of colour.

In other words, at the same time that universities are giving (what I view as largely) lip service to the importance of overcoming systemic discrimination, those who make up the university community continue to *act* in ways that marginalize and, therefore, discriminate. Understanding how this process occurs is difficult, because the actions to which I refer are normative, and therefore tend to be naturalized. As such, they are very difficult for those who practise them to see, and the process of seeing differently is often painful. In the balance of this chapter, therefore, I explore patterns of whiteness in an attempt to expose that unseen and unacknowledged dimension of academic life that most academics of colour experience.

By 'whiteness' I do not mean simply the fact of being 'white.' I mean the construction of dominant discourses and the mobilization of power according to standards set within a white cultural framework. Whiteness is not necessarily malevolent: it often takes forms that are benevolent, patronizing, or condescending. It is not always direct discrimination, but the creation of difference by subtle cultural means that are every bit as excluding as restrictive covenants. Whiteness ranges from speech patterns to body language, from social distance to etiquette, and from friendship to collective action. Below I outline four of the major ways in which academic women of colour experience whiteness.

Whiteness as Denigration

Whiteness as denigration is the dominant form of academic racialization. It denigrates the work of academics of colour not directly, but by valuing the Eurocentric. It operates according to a powerful logic by which, for example, studies of Asian Canadians (almost non-existent on Canadian campuses) are seen as the domain of 'Asian Studies' rather than Canadian Studies; by which studies of Aboriginal women are seen as the domain of 'Aboriginal Studies' rather than Women's Studies; and by which studies based on Eurocentric standards are given more space, more prestige, more resources, and more dominance, and other areas, such as Islamic Studies, are completely missing. Such may be the case even in the critical areas of postcolonial studies that privilege the Other. It denigrates the work of academics of colour by failing to challenge gate-keeping practices in ostensibly international journals and by failing to recognize that anti-racist work is often more effective when placed in venues accessible to communities of colour. It denigrates the work of academics of colour in a myriad of small, often barely hinted, comments about standards of scholarship, and in more vicious ways when anti-racist work comes under the scrutiny of promotion and tenure committees, often clothed in the terms of 'merit.' In more benign ways, it denigrates the work of academics of colour in the ordinary expression of scholarship: through the development of curricula, choice of readings, organization of seminars and workshops, and choices over who should receive invitations to give guest lectures or to receive honorary degrees. Whiteness by denigration is systemic because it occurs through established and ordinary practices, oblivious of the racialized effects; but when challenged, it often reacts with offence or in defence of the status quo.

Whiteness as Deflection

Whiteness as deflection is the style of the progressive university of the twenty-first century, where people want to be seen as unprejudiced. It relegates overt racism to the realm of the deviant, to be dealt with by grievance boards and human rights procedures. It therefore perpetuates the myth that racism is taken care of, yet it can still express great indignation and outrage when rare cases of extreme racism are discovered. It is inclusive and treats everyone as equal – that is, as white. Instead of racism, it speaks of valuing diversity. Instead of anti-racist training, it propounds cross-cultural understanding, as though we all begin at the same starting gate and need only to understand one another to get along. In its worst manifestations, instead of racial slurs, it engages in personality assassination. It is ambitious, smug, self-serving, and insidious.

Whiteness as Exotification

Whiteness as exotification is the domain of the critical and the culturally hip. This form of whiteness can be rooted in genuine if ill conceived commitment to social change, but its practitioners are often too smug and too set in their own ways to recognize that they may actually impede change. Whiteness as exotification places a high premium on difference, engages in sophisticated theoretical analysis, and constructs ideological positions with great care. But it often fails to engage in meaningful or sincere ways with real people of colour. It treats them as too fragile or too sensitive to deserve sincerity. It is over-protective to the point of patronizing. It collects people of colour as testaments to its openness, resulting in a new form of domination and cultural appropriation. It engages in a kind of reverse valuing of skin colour – the darker the better – but fails to recognize that in so doing it is engaging in yet another form of differencing by skin colour. People of colour know whiteness by exotification when they see it.

Whiteness as Guilt

No expression of whiteness is more difficult to deal with than white guilt. I confront it every year, about a month into my course on racism, among students who come to me in tears because they cannot deal with the racism that goes on in their families or their home towns or their student residences. Their tears are the result of genuine anguish, care, and a desire to learn and to change. I confront similar attitudes among my colleagues and I am similarly gratified by their concern. But those who experience white guilt need to learn three things: 1) People of colour are generally not moved by their tears, and may even see those tears as a self-indulgent expression of white privilege. It is after all a great privilege to be able to express one's emotions openly and to be confident that one is in a cultural context where one's feelings will be understood. 2) Guilt is paralysing. It serves no purpose; it does no good. It is not a substitute for activism. 3) White guilt is often patronizing if it leads to pity for those of colour. Pity gets in the way of sincere and meaningful human relationships, and it forestalls the frankness that meaningful relationships demand. White guilt will not change the racialized environment; it will only make the guilty feel better.

Conclusion

Today's universities have equity offices and human rights offices. Collective agreements and other official policies and documents contain equity clauses. But academics of colour still feel marginalized, and universities are struggling both to increase numbers and to create safe and comfortable environments. The reason is twofold: because such policies still remain in the control of predominantly white scholars and administrators who have defined the bounds of racism according to their own terms; and because relations of whiteness prevail in the everyday setting. The result is a terrible smugness on most campuses, even claims of zero tolerance for racism, but yet a failure to see that it is whiteness, not overt racism, which is the dominant problem of the twenty-first century. The examples I have raised, while not representing the full range of ways in which racialization occurs, describe how whiteness works in everyday personal relations as one of the systemic ways in which academics of colour are marginalized.

I have also used examples from my own experience to show that whereas the effects of racialization are certainly systemic, in that they are built into established institutional practices, their effects are not always intended, and they occur at levels that seem to supersede the agency of individual actors. We cannot understand systemic effects without a recognition that the normalized patterns of racialization are acted out by and through individual bodies. We need therefore to address the actions through which racialized bodies are made visible in particular social institutions such as the university. We need to acknowledge that the 'adverse effects' of racialization range from the scarcity of bodies of colour on virtually all Canadian campuses, to deeply personal experiences of exclusion.

Academics of colour are in general discouraged, disillusioned, sceptical, and distrustful. They need the support of their white colleagues, but not if that support is patronizing, burdened by white guilt, or insincere. To bring about cultural change in these circumstances will take so much more than policies and equity offices. It will require that academics take on anti-racism as a personal project, addressing not only the 'system' but their own actions. It will require that they look beyond the systemic to the personal, that they reach out to others, that they talk to one another, that they engage in the very educational processes that it is our job to provide. It will require that they give up whiteness.

NOTES

1 Data submitted by universities to the Federal Contractors Program do not provide a breakdown by gender. No reliable estimate of the numbers of women of colour faculty is therefore available. A recent report by the CAUT (2007) similarly fails to provide the breakdown. I attempted to obtain more detailed information for my own discipline, geography, to find that when broken down by gender the figures indicated that women of colour faculty made up just 2 per cent of the discipline (Kobayashi 2002, 245–8).

2 *Action Travail des Femmes v. Canadian National Railway et al.* (1987), pp. 209–13. See Webb (1996).

3 There is now a significant literature, internationally, on this topic. See especially Dua and Lawrence (2000); Essed (1994); Essed (2000); Bannerji et al. (1991); Ng (1994); also the entire special issue of *Canadian Woman Studies* 14(2).

4 I use the term 'racialization' to refer to the process according to which the socially constructed concept of 'race' is invoked to create raced bodies. The term refers to the entire system of social relations/discourses through which

racism has become a dominant feature, in particular, of Western society. See Guillaumin (1995); Miles (1989).

5 The concept of whiteness refers to the cultural process of normalizing patterns of human relations based in a Eurocentric tradition. The practice extends from the level of personal relations to that of state power, but recent literature has stressed the significance of whiteness in everyday relations. This literature is now very extensive, but see, for example, Eisenstein (1994); Frankenberg (1993); Ignatiev and Garvey (1996); Razack (1998).

REFERENCES

Action Travail des Femmes v. Canadian National Railway et al. (1987), 40 D.L.R. (4th) 193 (S.C.C.) per Dickson, C.J.C., pp. 209–13.

Bannerji, H., L. Carty, K. Dehli, S. Heald, and K. McKenna. 1991. *Unsettling Relations: The University as a Site of Feminist Struggles*. Toronto: Women's Press.

Canadian Woman Studies. Special Issue 14(2).

CAUT (Canadian Association of University Teachers). 1999. *Report of the Academic Freedom & Tenure Committee into the matter of Dr. Kin-Yip Chun*. http://www.utoronto.ca/acc/chun/caut/aftreport.htm#summary.

– 2007. Equity Review Report. http://www.caut.ca/en/publications/equityreview/.

Dua, E., and B. Lawrence. 2000. 'Challenging White Hegemony in University Classrooms: Whose Canada Is It?' *Atlantis* 24(2):105–22.

Eisenstein, Z.R. 1994. *The Color of Gender: Reimagining Democracy*. Berkeley and Los Angeles: University of California Press.

Essed, P. 1991. *Understanding Everyday Racism: An Interdisciplinary Theory*. Newbury Park: Sage.

– 1994. 'Making and Breaking Ethnic Boundaries: Women's Studies, Diversity and Racism.' *Women's Studies Quarterly* 22:232–49.

– 2000. 'Dilemmas in Leadership: Women of Colour in the Academy.' *Ethnic and Racial Studies* 23(5):888–904.

Frankenberg, R. 1993, *White Women, Race Matters: The Social Construction of Whiteness*. Minneapolis: University of Minnesota Press.

Guillaumin, C. 1995. *Racism, Sexism, Power and Ideology*. London and New York: Routledge.

Henry, F. 2003. *Systemic Racism Towards Faculty of Colour and Aboriginal Faculty*. Queen's University. Also known as The Henry Report. http://www.queensu.ca/secretariat/senate/Mar30_06/SEECHenryRpt.pdf.

Henry, F., and C. Tator. 1994. 'Racism and the University.' *Canadian Ethnic Studies* 26(3):74–90.

Ignatiev, N., and J. Garvey. 1996. *Race Traitor*. London: Routledge.

Kobayashi, A. 2002. '20 Years Later and Still Two Percent: Women of Colour in Canadian Geography.' *The Canadian Geographer/Le géographe canadien* 46(3):245–8.

Miles, R. 1989. *Racism*. London and New York: Routledge.

Ng, R. 1994. 'Sexism and Racism in the University: Analyzing a Personal Experience.' *Canadian Woman Studies* 14(2):41–6.

Razack, S. 1998. *Looking White People in the Eye: Gender, Race and Culture in Courtrooms and Classrooms*. Toronto: University of Toronto Press.

Webb, M. 1996. 'The Law: What Is Discrimination and How Can It Be Proven?' *Status of Women Supplement of the CAUT Bulletin* (April).

3 'Doing Academia Differently': Confronting 'Whiteness' in the University

PATRICIA MONTURE

I come from a people, the Haudenosaunee, who value peace. It is a, if not *the,* core value that organizes our society. As a result of these teachings, I have learned to be committed in my life and therefore in my scholarship to the consideration of peaceful relations. I turn to a traditional teacher and university professor, the late John Mohawk (Seneca), for a broader glimpse of the intellectual practices of the Haudenosaunee:

> The text of our thinking (that is the way of peace) is found in the converse of the argument. If you do not believe in the rational nature of the human being, you cannot believe that you can negotiate with him. If you do not believe that rational people ultimately desire peace, you cannot negotiate confidently with him toward goals you and he can share. If you cannot negotiate with him, you are powerless to create peace. If you cannot organize around these beliefs, the principles cannot move from the minds of men into the actions of society. (1989, 221)[1]

From this brief quotation, it is clear that Haudenosaunee knowledge systems are rational, peace-based ways of locating 'man' in society. This I take to be my starting point. Rationality requires the ability to think clearly, sensibly, and logically. In my traditions, we have ceremonies that ensure the people are maintaining these abilities. Rationality moves the thinker beyond emotion, reaction, and prejudice. Rationality is the way to peace. Living in peace recognizes the world beyond us. It requires us to be able to live at peace, which also requires being reconciled with the self.

'Living at peace' and 'living in peace' are the standards I am now adopting to examine my university experiences. This process of reflection may sound crazy to some people. I work in a White institution (the university) that has little, if any, real understanding of the tenets of First Nations ways of life including our knowledge systems. It may appear to be contradictory to others. After all, the academy has its own rigorous standards and accepted practices. However, in the stories I am about to tell, turning the standards inside out (that is, holding White practices accountable to First Nations standards) seems important as a strategy to expose the multiple ways in which I experience the power of the institution, my profession, and the imposition of its standards as something I am often 'othered' against. Within the institution, there is an expectation that we will all be functionally 'White' and have all become so because of our years of education and the simple act of our employment.

The consequences for a person who is othered are quite devastating and totally contradictory to a commitment to living one's life in and at peace. Warren Crichlow explains the traps that being presented as a role model rather than a colleague and faculty member entail:

> In performing the authorized role, however, the 'model' can come perilously close to losing his or her sense of identity and individuality. That is, both are subject to displacement by irresistible illusions of institutional power, authority, legitimacy, and job mobility. Vested with normative institutional identifications, expectations of 'role' conformity consequently structure university and classroom protocol in forced and often alienating ways. The results are usually disastrous for the process of teaching and learning, both for the subjected student and the person who carries the burden of perfect model expectation. (2001, 147–8)

If we are not learning to reflect and resist – knowing resistance is only one possible choice of action – then the structures and practices at the university will consume us. Every act of an othered person in an institution like a university is an act of power (conscious or not). We are giving power up or taking it.

Even with each struggle that one decides to stand up against, the position of the othered or racialized faculty member is diminished in the university. There is a roller coaster effect in the relationship between faculty member and institution; some days, weeks, or years may pass in relative comfort and then the bottom falls out again and a new lesson is learned about the way compliance is held in the hands of those who possess patriarchal or the racialized power of Whiteness. Because the relationship is complex and varied, both for individuals and across individuals, it means that it is hard to identify. Therefore, it is difficult to reflect on. It is hard to identify because of the often embedded and hence invisible nature of power and White privilege. Sometimes, in the moment, we are left only with emotional reaction; we should return to those moments later to digest them, as emotional reaction diminishes our status in the institution. The work that othered faculty members must invest to just stay in the institution is significant, and the process of staying itself often becomes exhausting.

A word or two about Whiteness seems essential as I start the journey this chapter takes. Whiteness, as experienced in the university, is always a gendered term. Implicit in its use is maleness and the power with which being male privileges you. White privilege, as Peggy McIntosh explains, means being able to count on certain conditions during the course of daily life. It is a system of benefits, advantages, and opportunities compared to racism, which is a system of negatives – detriments, disadvantages, and denials. White privilege means you go shopping without worrying if you will be followed or harassed; that when the teacher talks to you about 'civilization' the group represented share your skin colour; that you can challenge a situation without being called a credit to your race; or that you can take a job without being accused of being the affirmative action hire (1990, 31–3).[2]

It is my view that we should focus more on neutralizing the power of Whiteness than on creating equality for the racialized or otherwise excluded other. It is privilege in persons and institutions that is invisible, not the racial hatred directed at certain individuals. As teachers, in our classrooms, we can make sure that we are dismantling the privilege of Whiteness. And privilege is not about linear relationships. There are times when racialized faculty members hold less power than their White students. When discussing 'starlight tours'[3] – the police practice, which made national headlines in 2001, of dropping Aboriginal men on the outskirts of town on freezing cold nights – several students (usually white and male) retaliate against the idea that this is a racialized attack on Aboriginal persons (Tator and Henry 2006). Aboriginal students are yet more vulnerable in university classrooms. For example, in classes about Aboriginal people in the Canadian criminal justice system, we can acknowledge for Aboriginal students in the classroom that this is the stuff they and their families might have survived. Grading options should then include the opportunity to journal about those experiences, rather than write distant third person essays where if you cannot assume that position, your grade is compromised.

This chapter is organized in two parts. In the first part, I present an edited version of an earlier article about the challenges of securing tenure when one is othered and working in a hostile environment. It is based on a talk that was given in 1999 at Carleton University and a paper that was subsequently written from the transcripts of that talk and published by the Canadian Research Institute for the Advancement of Women (CRIAW) in 2003. In early 2008, my experiences of race, gender, and their intersectionality in the university have increased, and my perceptions have changed a little. For this reason, I offer a conclusion that is based on my experiences of the university since that time.

Part 1: The Tenure 'Wars' and Their Legacy

Within the details of my own struggle to secure tenure are a number of lessons for those who are coming along behind me. My experience and these details also offer an opportunity to others to reflect on the institution through experiences that might be different than their own. My tenure story is not unique. As Rashmi Luther, Elizabeth Whitmore, and Bernice Moreau explain:

> Much of what we do is invisible (to the university and to most colleagues), especially the ongoing support and encouragement of students of colour and Aboriginal students that is absolutely crucial to their attraction, retention and successful completion of university programs. Yet, as faculty of colour and Aboriginal faculty, we are rewarded with tenure and promotion only for traditional activities, especially for acquiring a Ph.D. and publishing in mainstream journals. (2003, 11)

This is another reason why it is so important to allow our stories of tenure struggle to be told. If we do not address the differences in our lives in the academy, then standards we are held up against for tenure and promotion will never reflect that realities of our experiences. This means that aspects of the tenure and promotion processes are not individual, nor is it just about merit. The tenure and promotion processes contain systemic and structural barriers to building an inclusive, respectful, and peaceful environment for all. The result of these barriers is that to be rewarded in the same way as those who are privileged in the institution we are required to do much more work. Our silence, then, only compounds our oppression. Yet the choice to speak is also fraught with danger as the potential for backlash always exists (Montoya 2002, 247).

The lessons, in the traditions of my people, are important to share with those who are coming along behind me. I wish to share these lessons in the hope that through sharing stories we can build community. In many places, Aboriginal scholars and racialized faculty work in isolation. This makes it very difficult to share amongst ourselves what we have survived and how we have survived it. At least, those coming along will have the opportunity through the sharing of written stories to not be blind-sided by tenure events such as the one I survived. Perhaps this is naïve and the best that can be offered is an opportunity to share ways of protecting oneself in the academy. This desire to share with others is part of my desire to live in the way of peace. And perhaps those who force conformity in the name of merit or institutional order can also learn from this sharing. It is not only a way to make peace with what happened, but to be at peace.

I have learned many lessons of survival since I began my university teaching career in July of 1989. In the fall of 1997, while employed in my third academic post, I applied for tenure and encountered some difficulties along the way. I am not sure that the specific details of who did what is as important as a sharing of the issues from the struggle that I fondly call the 'tenure wars.' Focusing on who did what operates to reinforce the personal nature of the struggle and thus denies the systemic nature of what happened. When I consider the experiences of my struggle to secure tenure, the nature of the omissions is as revealing as an analysis of who did what, when. Mentorship is but one example of the gaps I have experienced. Most junior faculty members when they are young White men have mentors (senior White male faculty) that guide them through the maze of university rules, conventions, and practices. They share where the important places to publish are and include the new scholars they mentor in their grant applications. Often these conventions and practices are not written and are therefore not accessible to those of us who do not have such guides to show us through the maze. This is especially problematic if the head of your department does not take his or her role in the tenure process seriously. This gap was not fully transparent to me until I applied for promotion to full professor in the fall of 1988, which, quite calculatedly, I did the year after the tenure wars. The two tenured members of my departmental (both White males) resigned from my promotion committee. Consequently, a chair of the department committee was appointed from another department. This man provided detailed explanations of both the process and what was required, including the preparation of a teaching dossier (I had never heard of this requirement before).[4]

The difficulty, lacking a mentor in the university,[5] has been an experience of race/culture and gender. In general, I experience the university as a 'chilly' place. The lack of a guide to lend assistance in clearing the maze of unnecessary obstacles is just one of the processes by which women and racialized persons are, at worst, covertly excluded from the ranks, or more often merely managed within those ranks (that is, being tokenized). There was never a time before these applications where I had felt that my lack of a mentor was an issue greater than loneliness and isolation (that is, another experience of Whiteness). I now understand this failure to share with new colleagues the importance of investing in and maintaining mentorship relationships to be a covert strategy that operates to deny success to 'outsiders' (most broadly defined as anyone who is not a White male or is chosen by them usually for the way they mimic Whiteness).

Most of the choices I have made in my professional life are grounded in a single value: what is 'good' for 'Indian' people. This means I saw (and continue to see) myself located in my community more than I saw myself located in the university. This is a consequence of university experiences that left me othered, as well as a personal choice to stand in my community. One example is my scholarship. I had never really considered that peer reviewed journal articles are an essential element of the phrase 'publish or perish.' I had not understood, until more recent experiences on the college committee that reviews tenure and promotion decisions, that there are 'the' journals in each discipline, and tenure is most easily secured if publication in those journals has been gained. But publication in these journals denies access to my work to many Aboriginal peoples as they have no access or knowledge of university libraries. Not only did I not consider this, but also no one shared this wisdom with me and certainly not in a timely fashion (such as shortly after hiring) that could have made a difference to tenure decisions. Without this information, I had chosen to publish in venues that are accessible to Aboriginal people, the people I write for.

In the first decade of my career, I had published in a number of peer reviewed law journals, but since coming to the University of Saskatchewan, my focus shifted.[6] There are several structural reasons for this. If I had wanted to write in peer reviewed journals, I could have done so.[7] As Native studies is a relatively new discipline (then, about twenty years old in Canada) there are significant gaps in the scholarly literature. This gap also has some specific contours. Very little scholarship has been available for course materials written by Aboriginal people. That Aboriginal voice must be brought to Native studies, and this is another principle that influenced my choice of both what and where to publish. Consequently, in the years immediately prior to tenure, I had chosen to contribute to particular books, many of which were intended to be used as textbooks for Native studies classes.

At the time of the tenure wars, the Native studies department I taught in was manned (gender pun intended) by non-Aboriginal (that is White) professors (an anthropologist, a historian, and a geographer).[8] An opportunity had not been created by the Department of Native Studies to consider the space that could be occupied by Indigenous knowledges and Indigenous scholars. There was no recognition of the choices Indigenous scholars are left to make between scholarship driven by commitments to Indigenous people and/or to academic canons. And making the choice to practise within an Indigenous knowledge system, a system that also has rigorous criteria, should not preclude the opportunity to secure tenure or to secure it only after struggle and resistance.

Although not all Native studies departments in the country are the same, this problem does not exist only at the University of Saskatchewan.[9] There are a number of ways this concern about space (both intellectual and physical) can be demonstrated. For example, the structure of many Native studies departments' curriculum reflects non-Indigenous ideologies and ideas about people (and even a variety of colonial biases).[10] Why is confederation considered an important historical marker in Indigenous history classes? What is the distinction between Canada and the United States and why is it relevant? After all, some of our nations, such as the Mohawk, Blackfoot, and Mi'kmaq, straddle that border. As a result of these questions and their answers, it was necessary for me to create several new courses over the first five years that I was at the university. This need for new courses and the collateral demand on a professor's time overlaps with the challenge of finding materials when organizing and teaching courses. Often creating these new courses is a necessity of our hiring and not an individual faculty member's choice. And the time required to develop new classes certainly limits the time available for other scholarly tasks such as research and writing.

University calendars are useful tools for understanding the nature of any department. Particularly for Native studies, the structure of the curriculum reveals both the beliefs and biases of the department's faculty. It is easy to determine how many courses are historical, anthropological, or about 'issues.' Is the curriculum built on a study of colonization or on decolonization? Are the courses overly general, looking at broad issues like literature, history, or governance? What specializations does the curriculum reveal? For example, there was a three-credit course (one semester, three hours of lecture per week) on Native women. The course was called 'Native Women in Canada' and was the only class on this topic offered by the small department. This second-year course purports to cover in thirty-nine hours of classroom teaching: 'Examination of the position of women in traditional, pre-contact Native society, the changes to that position wrought by contact with Europeans, and contemporary issues of concern to Native women' (University of Saskatchewan Calendar 1999–2000, 113).

For anyone who understands the diversity of Aboriginal peoples, the impossible teaching obligation of this course is readily apparent. However, this is only the most obvious issue. All the 'time markers' in the course are colonial and reflect a Western way of viewing the world.[11] Aboriginal nations have a history on this continent for at least 10,000 years. This recognition must contextualize the mere 500-year history we have with Europeans and their descendants. Yet, the important date in the structure of this course is contact with Europeans. Equally, when Canada is seen as a colonial construct, the artificial boundary surrounding the state can be understood as drawing lines through many Indian nations including the Haudenosaunee. Most disturbing is the more subtle deference in this course description, which goes like this: Native women were traditional prior to contact. European contact changed Aboriginal women. Aboriginal women did not change Europeans.[12] And as time has gone on Native women have become less 'traditional' as a result of European influence and impact. It is the ever popular myth that Indians, or at least 'Indian-ness,' will some day disappear. In the end, Native women are left with 'contemporary concerns.' This denies the vibrant roles that Native women have played (and still do play) in their communities. Women are central forces in the structure of our governments and legal systems (see, for example, Monture 1999a and Yazzie 2005).

Rather than waiting to be asked to teach this second-year women's class, and having to articulate my concerns about the inappropriate structure of the course description, I volunteered to create a new fourth-year course, 'First Nations Women and the Law.'[13] This allowed me to avoid challenging the inappropriate and colonial structure of the existing second-year course in a public way at a department meeting where teaching assignments were being discussed. This strategy allowed me to avoid the immediate controversy and conflict that would have resulted from being asked to teach the course and refusing. However, the strategy is not without its consequences. Developing a new course, including a reading package, is a significant amount of work.

The curriculum issues are multifaceted and are not always clearly gender-based as is the previous example. My other area of 'expertise' is justice. In my new department there was one course on Aboriginal people and the Canadian criminal justice system. Despite the fact that I created one upper year justice course focusing on women, there were still gaps in the justice curriculum.[14] There was still no course on Aboriginal children and the impact on them of the Canadian criminal justice system. There was no course in the department on treaties, and many treaties address criminal law powers. Although creating new courses was an effective strategy to insulate myself against teaching courses that forced me into an unconscionable choice between ethical chaos and peace in the department, this strategy will not always work. This strategy depends on a department head who welcomes new course proposals; in a small department with resources already stressed to the limit, it will not always be a viable choice. Chronic under-resourcing, particularly in a department like Native studies, is an ongoing issue at the University of Saskatchewan.[15] The curriculum difficulties do not only exist in the areas that I teach. For example, the department did not, even though we are situated in the middle of the prairies, have a treaty course. Sixty-seven per cent of the courses in the department were history courses at the time of my tenure application (and thus contributed to the view that Indians are indeed vanishing). The remainder are issues courses. This led me to wonder: 'What am I? An artifact or an issue?'[16]

In hindsight, I have wondered if I would have accepted the employment offer of the University of Saskatchewan to teach in the Native Studies Department if I had understood what was the ideological structure and 'faith' of the department. As I already held a tenure-stream job at another Canadian university, I had been very candid during the interview process about my desire to continue to move toward bringing to campus the dream of Aboriginal people of meaningful educational experiences.[17] As I had received an offer after my job talk, I assumed that my dream for an inclusive place for Aboriginal people in the university was shared by others in this department.

There was indeed an ideological difference between the department and myself. It was not a personal problem between the Department of Native Studies and myself. It was not that I had chosen to theoretically situate myself differentially from other members of the department. It was not a conflict between different theoretical schools of thought that can be academically debated. It was that, as an 'Indian' woman, I was differentially situated. It was more than being different, as it was not about individual preference but about power and space. I was not willing (nor am I now) to assume the role of Native informant; it sacrifices my relationship with my communities (Cook-Lynn 1997). The problem was really, therefore, a structural issue much larger than the personalities involved. As an 'Indian' woman I cannot and do not access White privilege. I do not value 'Whiteness.' Further, the conflict was too easily and too often characterized as personal, because the definition of what constitutes sound scholarship that includes Indigenous knowledges and persons had not been recognized as a necessary debate.

Any ambiguity in the disciplinary framework of Native studies creates the potential to victimize and isolate those of us (usually but not always the traditional First Nations scholars) who refuse to toe the conventional line and follow university protocols in a way that does not challenge. And I do not believe this phenomenon is an accidental one. It privileges the academic status quo and disenfranchises the 'outsider' (that is, the non-White, non-male). As Russell Thornton has pointed out about the discipline of Native studies:

> In the late 1980s, Annette Jaimes of the University of Colorado called it a structurally and conceptually rudderless discipline, generally isolated both within the academic environment and from its own cultural roots, and functioning all too often as a career ladder for those who wish to 'work with Indians' rather than as an intellectual enterprise for Indians themselves. A decade later, Elizabeth Cook-Lynn, professor emeritus of Eastern Washington University, asserted, 'Native American Studies in American universities has not been nurtured in appropriate ways nor has it been actualized since its inception in the way that other epistemologies have been, Feminism, for example, or Black Studies which has produced major African-American intellectuals speaking out on all manner of national issues.' (1998, 97)

This structural issue of what is good for Native studies scholarship, measured in conventional academic terms, was clearly an issue that made possible the kind of challenge that was brought against my tenure application. Historically, Indigenous systems of knowledge have been excluded from the university. As a result, the definition of good scholarship, even from within a department such as Native studies, remains embedded in those conventional academic terms and measured by the number of books you have published and articles you have written. Further, the articles are believed to be more significant if they have been published in peer reviewed journals.[18] This unfortunately extends (or reproduces) the exclusion of Indigenous knowledge in the university. The choice individual professors are left with is whether to conform to these embedded structural pressures or to risk their continued employment in the university by remaining true to their training in Indigenous knowledge systems.

The exclusion of Indigenous knowledge from the university (and specifically the knowledge held and produced by Aboriginal people) is a fairly simple task to accomplish. Most people who have been trained in the structure, content, and production of Indigenous knowledge do not hold university degrees, and particularly, they do not hold advanced university degrees. Until very recently, the knowledge of Aboriginal people, cultures, and traditions that has been available in the university classroom has been either appropriated from our communities or placed in an intellectual framework that does not do justice to the full extent of the knowledge borrowed. The material is, at best, incomplete, and is often incorrect.

There are many examples of my concerns with the scholarship produced by non-Aboriginal people (and Aboriginal people who no longer or have never maintained a connection to their community). A Canadian criminal justice text (and I will not name it) goes as far as to say in the introduction that the lack of scholarship written by Aboriginal people is both a gap and a problem. Therefore, the authors decided to include newspaper clippings, most written by Aboriginal people! How do scholarly standards justify such a decision? Therefore, as I was aware of these gaps, instead of writing scholarly journal articles, I have madly been writing chapters for books that are being published for use as course materials. During my tenure struggles, the university chose to judge my scholarship without clearly understanding the context in which I, as an Aboriginal scholar, publish. This is tantamount to holding me individually responsible for the structural shortcomings in the academy because of the historic exclusion of Aboriginal persons.[19]

Part 2: The Years after Tenure

Since securing tenure in 1998 and being promoted to a full professor in 1999, the knowledge I have gained about the university has continued to grow. At times, I joke about being a reverse anthropologist, studying the culture of the university and the habits of the White professorial tribe. This endeavour has been made possible by identifying White scholars who can operate as 'my informants,'[20] explaining to me the university culture when it bewilders me. That I feel like a participant observer, on many days, in the institution is a troubling realization, as I have earned the title and rank of tenured full professor but often not the privileges that flow to others (White men) from the same earning. As such, it is a realization that challenges my ability to be at peace and living in peace at the university.[21]

An analysis of the position that I (and others like me) occupy in the university also exposes another contradiction. Before I put fingers to the computer keyboard, everything I write has been solicited. As a result of watching and paying attention to my senior colleagues and the conversations they have in the hallways at the university, I have learned that this is very unusual. Yet, I see nowhere in the structure of assessing a professor's scholarship any recognition that one might grow beyond submitting articles for publication and writing articles and book chapters that are solicited. Surely the soliciting of scholarship for inclusion in both journals and books is a form of academic refereeing, or at least honouring.

There is another way my scholarship differs from the work of other scholars; like many other Aboriginal scholars, my work often crosses disciplinary borders (this might be considered interdisciplinary; I prefer to think of it as transdisciplinary). I have published in law, Native studies, English, political studies, women's studies, and most recently in sociology. If considerations used to evaluate scholarship were broadened to include the kinds of factors I have just described, rather than just counting peer reviewed journal articles, it would harmonize both the tenure and promotion processes for people who have found ways to mediate their othering by the institution. The result would be the opportunity to have tenure and promotion processes that reflect the reality of the lives of many racialized scholars.

The problem as I see it, and as I most frequently encounter it, is a failure to take account of individuals and what some would call 'difference.' This is about understanding the context in which scholars work and live. It is the unwillingness, or perhaps the inability, of institutions to place an individual's accomplishments in the context of their actual achievements. This, at a minimum, means recognizing gender, race/culture, sexual orientation, disability, and class, and then taking account of these experiences. After the account taking, the most important thing institutions need to do is to respond positively to what they have learned about 'difference.' This means they must do equity – and doing probably requires changing. Equality should not be something you talk about. It must be something you do.

I can best demonstrate what I see as a responsibility to take account by sharing my experiences. When I got the news that there was a problem with my tenure application, I was sitting at home in front of the computer. I was preparing a paper for a plenary panel at a conference being held at Yale Law School.[22] I work a lot at home and it surprises me that my absences from the university have never become an issue. I worked a lot at home because I then lived on what is referred to as an 'Indian reserve.' My children's father's community is three hours northwest of Saskatoon. I did this huge commute, back and forth all the time, in order that my children could be raised in a First Nations community with access to culture, language, and ceremony; equally, I wanted to protect them from issues of racism that many Aboriginal people were facing, and continue to face, in the urban public school system.[23]

In my mind, location is an equity issue. Most Aboriginal people who come to the university are forced to leave their communities. There is no choice that you are going to get to go to a university in your hometown, because your hometown is probably a 'reserve' and there you cannot complete more than a few, if any, university courses. Access to post-secondary education requires the willingness to leave your community, your people, your way of life, and all that feels comfortable to you. That the reserve is home and comfortable for First Nations citizens should not be lost under the knowledge of the poverty or violence that exists in some of our communities; the reserve is the place where you are in sync with the world and culture around you. You fit. Many other non-Aboriginal students are required to leave small towns and rural communities to go to university, too; however, that leaving is not as total (or systemic) as it is for a First Nations person leaving the reserve, as non-First Nations do not necessarily leave behind their culture, their language, their ceremonies, and their traditions.

Given all the losses that First Nations experience as a result of a commitment to pursue post-secondary education, and despite the fact that most post-secondary institutions now have equity entrance policies for students,[24] I have yet to see a policy that truly reflects the contours and reality of my own life as a First Nations citizen. I have noted elsewhere (see Monture-Angus 1999b) that I think universities are equity literate (at least the ones I have experienced), meaning that they can write equity down but still struggle to practise or live equity. This does not come as a full surprise, despite the disappointment, because universities are places of writing, not doing. Equity, then, requires us to teach faculty and administrators to think and do differently.

One of the most poignant personal examples I have of the denial of a lived experience of equity is the position I was cast into as a result of my application for tenure. After the acting associate dean called to say the College Review Committee had turned down my tenure application, the very first place I went, after the shock and sucking in my breath, was 'I guess I am really a stupid "Indian" after all.' It was probably one of the most painful moments of my life; I made the choice to leave my community, to go to university, believing that I could at least personally outgrow the feelings of inferiority that colonialism breeds. I know this was not always a conscious thought. I thought: 'If I go to school; if I do well; if I win awards; if I graduate the top of my class, then people (White people) are going to believe that I am an equal.' Despite having accomplished a number of these things, I now understand that this was very naïve. Racism and colonialism are very much present in the everyday lives of First Nations no matter what we do or how much we succeed. It leaves people powerless. This is the essence of why race must matter.

Gratefully, in the last little while, it takes me less time to overcome the residual feelings of powerlessness that result from oppression. Usually it starts with getting mad. And on that day, rage started a flow of ideas.[25] The next day I was able to make a little plan. I remembered what an Elder had taught me about doing prison activism. He demonstrated, through his actions, that, often, things changed in the prison only when the wrongs (both individual and systemic) done to Aboriginal prisoners were exposed.[26] I decided that the university review process for tenure that I had been subject to (or the object of) needed to be made much more transparent. If the process was not transparent, then the fluid standards professors are judged against would remain subject to swings in interpretation, including manipulations that focus on getting rid of an undesirable colleague. Individual professors, whose scholarship challenges conventional norms, are left vulnerable and are protected only by appeal processes. But the process of appeal does not vindicate the professor when interpretation of standards borders on the manipulation of the system by those who know it better (that is, those who have institutional power). Given these concerns, I sent an email to a number of people I respected in the academy outlining briefly what had happened.[27]

As it turns out, this was a good strategy. It was a good strategy on both the personal and institutional levels. The dean of the College of Arts and Science received approximately fifty letters of support and concern from four different countries. On a personal level, whenever I read those letters it was impossible for me to feel like 'a stupid "Indian" woman.' I also believe that the fact that I had exposed the situation to a broader audience created a particular environment for the appeal. However, it was not a good strategy because it served to distance me further from my department colleagues, who were eventually provided with a copy of the widely circulated email requesting support.[28] I knew that this was likely to happen and was prepared to accept this as a possible consequence. The decision, here, was actually quite simple. I was already ostracized and constructed as a 'monster.' It could not get much worse.

Now I did have some people tell me, some combination of the following: 'Don't do that! Do not do that! Behave! Be a good girl! Just wait! Wait for the appeal!' No thanks! Some private matters should be made public, as this is the only way change can be secured. By this time the university had worn through my ability to trust their processes. I did send that email out very cautiously, though. I did not send it as broadly as I could have. You only received the email if you were an academic. If you were an Aboriginal person, you got the email because you were an academic, not because you were an Aboriginal person.

I did not send that email to my community, or communities, as I belong to more than one Aboriginal community. And the reason that I did not do that is because I am so tired of having to use that good brown community energy to straighten out a university in which my people do not really get to participate. I could have gone to the old folks (the Elders and ceremony people). I could have asked for ceremony, but I thought that was wrong. I thought that this is something that the university needs to fix, without our energy, without us pushing you so hard to do something (and something that equity principles would suggest you should have been doing all along). And I prepared to leave because after being challenged in that kind of way, I did not want to be at the university any more. Several years after the tenure challenge, I still found it a struggle to choose to remain at this university. It was the violation of the relationship with the institution that I have experienced as the harm (and this is why living in the way of peace is an important standard through which to refract the university). Receiving tenure did not 'fix' anything. In fact, it made things harder.[29]

Even before the controversy arose in either my tenure or promotion files, the processes were difficult for me. I was expected to do things and approach things in a way that my culture does not condone. I was expected to talk about myself overly proudly and to distinguish myself from the community in which I live. At the outset, this asks me to do something that is culturally forbidden. As an Aboriginal person living within the culture, you are expected not to attempt to distinguish yourself from the people, not to try and stand above them. The concept of 'leader' in my culture means 'the one who walks behind.' A leader is the one who looks after the needs of all of the other people and then worries about their own needs. I think this creates another layer of discomfort for Aboriginal people in these procedures, and the real crux of this problem is that it is invisible to others at the university who may be in a position and have the will to give us some guidance about tenure and promotion processes.

As I have already indicated, what the teachings of my culture focus on is creating and maintaining relationships (sometimes referred to as balance). For me, being granted tenure did not resolve the real issue because the brutality of the process was (and remains) the central issue.[30] The university did not fix what had happened. Although some months later, a senior university administrator did apologize to me, the university did not systematically deal with the chilly climate issues in the department that led to the tenure wars despite knowing in advance that these were vibrant issues in the department.

These issues that shaped the tenure wars were systemic, and I have only written about some of them; but because I was too often the only one who challenged these barriers, others had the opportunity to label me 'difficult' or 'the problem.' And the university was all too happy to accept such labelling, because it means they do not have to do anything proactive. I did the best that I could to ensure that the review of the College's negative decision by the University Review Committee encompassed more than just a review of the individualized merit standards and their application to my case. Over the December break from classes, I finally realized (in both my heart and mind) that what was going on was not about me at all. It was about the university. The fact that I was forced into an 'appeal'[31] was evidence of the inability of the university to actually implement equity standards in such a way that my 'difference' did not diminish my case but serve as the appropriate context to understand excellence in a new way. My opening words to the 'appeal' committee focused on the fact that I understood that this was not about me. The tenure challenge was about the university and their (in)ability to understand equity, do equity.

Equity is about the institution as a collective. It is not about 'us,' the equity candidates. It is not about the individuals who are perceived as 'different.' Equity is not as simple as the individualized task of allowing those historically excluded from the university to prove we are good enough. I think it is really important that this is understood. I do not want to see people of colour, Aboriginal people, Aboriginal women being battered by what the university does (or more correctly refuses to do) with standards and policies. As people the university chooses to cast as 'outsiders' or 'unequals' we have to be very careful to keep talking, writing, and exposing. Especially, we must keep praising each other, because, at least in my experience, when push comes to shove, the institutions in which we work do not support us in any kind of meaningful way. This is a significant violation if, as I believe, the contribution 'diversity' makes to the university is substantial. It means that the university is willing to take but gives little in return. This creates dysfunction in relations and not the harmony, to which we should aspire, that living in the way of peace suggests.

I have said this before and I firmly believe that the education system has to be sending the message and developing the understanding that our children, our people, and ways, are our solution. This has got to mean more than the empty rhetoric that we hear in Indian country such as the mantras of 'Indian control of Indian education,' 'We have our treaty rights,' or more recently, 'Education is our buffalo.' What our children need to know is what these slogans mean. This means that the knowledge (especially Euro-specific knowledge) is not so important. Such-and-such a content is not the essential ingredient of a good Aboriginal education, at least not in my mind. Building confidence and teaching to empowerment are more important ideals because they are the tools that allow us to confront Whiteness, oppression, and colonialism. That is why I am agitated, but it is also why I am still here. Teaching gives me the chance to build positive identities in First Nations students through access to Indigenous knowledges and ways in the classroom.

The paper that I gave at that Yale conference turned out to be an article called 'On Being Homeless: One Aboriginal Woman's "Conquest" of Canadian Universities, 1989–1998' (Monture-Angus 2002). I borrowed that idea of homelessness with great hesitation because I recognized the privilege I have. However, what I do experience in the university is an intellectual homelessness. About this I have no doubt. There are no indications in my experience that the Department of Native Studies is a location of decolonization. It is called a discipline. It has philosophies, supposedly, and theory and principles and methodology. Many claim it has those rigorous aspects. However, Native studies remains a part of a larger Euro-intellectual tradition within the university. Therefore, I also experience it as a compartment, a box – and as a contradictory one. The experience of containment is not how I think about the world. As I understand it, I have connections and responsibilities. My question now is: How do you move Native studies forward toward a tradition that includes Aboriginal ways and systems of knowing?

It is essential to see that the battles engaged in at the University of Saskatchewan were not battles of my choosing. They were battles that were forced onto me as applying for tenure and promotion are essential parts of university existence. I was not necessarily courageous, just determined to have a right to survive. And I was surviving in the way I know how, in the way I was taught – by writing, telling, and exposing. I recognized that I was writing what I am not supposed to be telling (Montoya 2005). Not only was I telling, I was writing this down and writing is a permanent form of telling. When I write things down I lose control of my story.

When I came to university teaching as a career choice, I had a lot of dreams. I had dreams about transcending isolation, oppression, and the ever-pervasive Whiteness. I now often admire how repeatedly naïve I was. But some dreams are not easily lost. Despite the fact that I know much of the 1990s for me were about mere survival, I still honour the tradition of peace and aspire to transcend to a place where survival is not the essence of my existence.

Conclusion

The 'tenure wars' are a decade behind me now. But, I just heard last week about another Aboriginal woman who is facing a tenure battle. The story continues. And the news that it is happening again only reinforces the fact that tenure denials must be understood as part of a systemic pattern of exclusion within both Canadian and American universities.

Over the years, I have noted several areas in which I continue to feel challenged and to struggle in my academic career. These areas are all structural issues which I would describe as university hiring, the creation of Aboriginal programs, research methodologies, research ethics, workloads, and curriculum structures. Each is about the illusiveness of being at peace in an academic setting and each requires constant reflection. Each of these topics could be a separate chapter.

In the employment standards at the University of Saskatchewan one of the seven categories of achievement considered is the 'research, scholarly and artistic work' of the professor. During my work with the college committee that reviews departmental tenure and promotion decisions, I have learned that 'meeting the standard' in this area means writing books and publishing in the journals, particularly publishing in *the* journal in the field. Sometimes it includes mention of research grants held or scholarly presentations made. But the focus is clearly on publications. As committee membership reflects those who are the 'stars' in the college – those who have shaped their careers on generating publications – the standards are safe and not questioned. Sometimes different career paths or choices are noted but, in my experience, these issues continue to sit on the periphery. Academic success is a one-dimensional standard. Only those who excel far beyond the standard will have their work in the classroom, administration, or the community acknowledged. Mixing up who sits on college committees, such as this one, might engender the kind of change that reflects the multiple of career choices that faculty make. The moments that I am most proud of in my career, such as when a First Nations student admitted I was the first teacher they had had who thought they were smart and capable, are not recorded anywhere.

My concerns about the process used to review faculty applications are not just about individual struggles of racialized persons, women, or anyone else who is othered. One situation develops when a White scholar's work is defined as the field of 'Indigenous knowledge.' To be knowledgeable about Indigenous people in my view requires that you have relationships with Indigenous people and relationships that follow Indigenous ways of being. Yet, this is not a recognized category in our standardized curriculum vitas. It is not required information shared in the documents that faculty share in their tenure and promotion files. The result is that someone who offends Aboriginal communities, a concern often shared with me and I assume other Indigenous faculty, proceeds through the process unchallenged. Yet someone, Indigenous or White, who works very hard at maintaining their relationships and understands those relationships as foundational for the accumulation of their knowledge and expertise in the 'field,' does work that earns them no university credit but is very time consuming. The result is to make invisible the work that is most important to Indigenous people and communities. And this will impact on the number of scholarly papers that an individual can produce. When the process of tenure and promotion relies on the counting of these papers, the process is ordered in favour of our not putting the effort into maintaining our relationships with Aboriginal peoples and Aboriginal communities. The consequence for an Indigenous scholar is that our communities will conclude that we are not behaving in a right way and we 'were not raised right.' It pressures us to stand outside of our communities. This could be called an academic process of assimilation, which also operates as a barrier. As such then the university reinforces colonial patterns of imposition, patterns that deny to Indigenous scholars the ability to maintain relationships, to be at peace, and living in peace.

The second situation involves peer review processes. A lot of energy is devoted by academics to ensure these processes are objective and without bias. However, accepted academic peer review processes can operate to deny the validity and scholarly rigour of 'new' methods of inquiry or interpretations of data that challenge the status quo in a discipline.[32] More important, academic review processes have not found ways to include Indigenous knowledge experts. Therefore, decisions about what is 'good for' any Aboriginal community are imposed from the outside. There are parallel situations; when a non-Indigenous academic's work is not valued in Aboriginal communities there is no mechanism in the review by other academics to discern if the work is highly criticized only within Aboriginal communities. Those who maintain relationships with communities often hear these complaints about other scholars. This causes complicated and contradictory situations for individual scholars that are not easily resolved because of the gaps in the peer review process.

There is an easy solution to both of these problems.[33] Scholars, both Indigenous and White, working in any field that has, central to it, Indigenous, Aboriginal, Indian, or Native should be required not only to provide the names of academic referees but three further referees from Indigenous communities. But the idea of Aboriginal community is not necessarily a simple thing to define. Scholars who work on women's issues may not be able to provide letters from Band or Tribal Councils. The letters from Indigenous referees should be from individuals who have earned the right to 'speak on behalf' (note not for) their communities. This means that university administrators must at least possess rudimentary knowledge about how Indigenous knowledge systems operate.

When I look back at these two examples, I can now see more ways that created disadvantage for me in the tenure and promotion process a decade ago. As the issues of securing tenure are seen as individual, there were no structural and systemic initiatives taken to ensure that the 'tenure wars' did not occur again. Approaching this from an Aboriginal standpoint, from the position of relationship and connection, and not individuality, the harm I experienced is not validated as it could happen again. The lessons were not learned, and if anything, a backlash occurred. Tenure and promotions rules were tightened leaving less room for diversity. A comparative review of all the tenure and promotion files of Aboriginal scholars at my institution would shed light on the size and the scope of the problem. Never has such a review been mentioned despite the fact that other cases for tenure or promotion of an Indigenous scholar have been problematic.

In the summer of 2004, my tenure was moved from Native Studies to the Department of Sociology. Along with me moved all of the Aboriginal justice classes offered by the Department of Native Studies. This made administrative sense to the university as the Aboriginal Justice and Criminology program had run in the Department of Sociology since about 1991. Moving to sociology means that I now have colleagues who understand my interest in the experiences of Aboriginal people in the Canadian criminal justice system. I now work with other criminologists and we share a theoretical framework of understanding. For me it is more than just sharing space with criminologists, because each of us is a critical criminologist so we do not end up in disciplinary tussles. I have been a sociologist now for nearly four years and have found an academic home after nearly twenty years of searching.

Part of the reason for my current contentedness in my job (and I do still worry about the roller coaster effect) are the structural differences between the two departments where I have held tenure at the University of Saskatchewan. Sociology is a respected 'old' department. Sociology classes were first offered at the University of Saskatchewan in the 1940s and the department was established in 1958. Native studies was a response (or reaction) to student demands and not established as a department until 1983. Since the mid-1970s the Sociology department has offered a variety of sociology courses that also have as their topic Aboriginal peoples. Presently, there are six courses offered by the department with Aboriginal peoples as their primary focus. In addition, there are two work-study experiences offered to students in the Aboriginal Justice and Criminology program. Hiring of Aboriginal people has mattered to the department when hiring both staff and faculty and I have not experienced sociology as the sole Aboriginal person around. I have been encouraged by colleagues to continue to research the relationship between sociology and Indigenous peoples.[34] This might be seen as surprising. But because sociology is an older, more established discipline in both the college and the larger academic world, it has a more powerful position in college 'politics' and power distributions across departments.[35] Unlike Native studies, no one challenges sociology's existence. There are those in the college who do still challenge the validity of Native studies as a discipline and department. One way to protect yourself and your discipline in the face of such hostility is to embrace the academic rules and rigour (that is Whiteness) with a passion.

As an academic, my experiences of the university are a little odd because I have been tenured in two different departments in the same institution and also spent five years teaching law at two other universities. The place I am able to reflect from allows me to comparatively consider the location of three different disciplines within the university. It allows for making comparisons that make clear the ways in which power is distributed in the university in ways which result in the creation of inequality and hierarchy. I am not saying this is how it should be. It is disturbing to me to see the way Native studies can be marginalized in the academy. However, it makes no sense to deny that these hierarchies do exist and that they do have an impact on individual professors. One conclusion I am able to draw is that the move from Native studies to sociology resulted in a shift in my position in the university, from outside power to inside it. As Aboriginal scholars continue to learn how to navigate the university, we need to remind ourselves that marginalization and isolation, as well as power, are individual, collective, and overlapping experiences. What we do with these experiences is an individual responsibility.

NOTES

I have borrowed the title 'Doing Academia Differently' from the women's conference hosted by the Canadian Association of University Teachers (CAUT) in February 2007. Portions of this chapter were presented at that conference. This chapter is also revised from a previously published paper (Monture 2003).

1 Although the use of only the masculine gender in this statement disturbs me, I do not believe the author's intent was to exclude women. In fact, at least historically, gender inclusion was a principle reflected in the Kaianer-ekowa ('Great Law of Peace').
2 Each of these examples was chosen because they reflect experiences I have had, some on a regular and ongoing basis. As my children know, being a well-dressed Aboriginal teenager on the streets of Saskatoon means you must be a drug dealer, gang member, or thief.
3 For further information see Reber and Renaud (2005).
4 Indeed, this means that my tenure application was not fully and well prepared. I had been instructed only to ensure that copies of my articles and book chapters were available to the committees. It is impossible to know what would have happened if my file were more complete. However, it would have clearly changed how I felt at the end of the process. Learning of the standard practices and expectations some time after tenure had been fought and won left me feeling as if I had not done everything in my power to ensure the success of the application.
5 Although lacking a mentor (perhaps better thought of as a cultural translator – and indeed the university is a culture) is a common experience for racialized scholars, I want to note that this is my experience *only* of my early years at the University of Saskatchewan.
6 This was one of the criticisms of my scholarship made by departmental members on my tenure committee. That committee was five persons, two from my small department and three who were seconded to help meet the number specified in the collective agreement.

7 At the time I applied for tenure, I had written one book (single authored), eight book chapters (four since coming to the University of Saskatchewan), seven refereed journal articles (one since arriving in Saskatchewan), three papers in journals that were not refereed, and two papers in conference proceedings and technical reports. Some of these references are reprints or revisions of early works. I was also the editor of another book, not included in my tenure application, on the chilly climate in the university published in 1995 by the 'Chilly Collective.' Our fears of retaliation kept me from mentioning my involvement in that project until very recently (I added it to my university curriculum vitae this past year).

8 Since 2004, I have been a member of the Department of Sociology at the University of Saskatchewan.

9 The most recent analysis of the state of affairs in Native studies is by Russell Thornton (Cherokee) (1989).

10 When considering an employment offer, a careful and critical review of a department's curriculum beyond the usual consideration of what you could teach might be a very good way of determining the kind of department you are considering joining. Include, in the review, the degree that an effort has been made to decolonize the space.

11 It is not only Native studies that are structured in problematic ways for Indigenous scholars and students. In my new department, we offer three third-year classes that look at sociological issues and Aboriginal peoples. These courses are titled 'Aboriginal People in Urban Areas,' 'Social Welfare and Aboriginal People,' and 'Institutional Racism and Aboriginal People.' The first two reinforce negative stereotypes about Aboriginal people. We have all heard the comments about Aboriginal people being 'welfare dependent' and too lazy to work (or worse). The other reinforces the myth that you are only a 'real Indian' if you were raised on and continue to live on the reserve. This makes invisible that the reserve is a colonial fact and imposition, never a good idea of Indians themselves. I celebrate that in my new department Aboriginal people are included in our curriculum in a significant way since the 1970s and to an extent not available in the majority of sociology departments in the country. I also know that if revisions are made to these classes I will have to lead the charge, even after there has been discussion in the department about the problematic nature of the titles of the courses. The need for change to these courses is, in fact, one of the reasons I was asked to chair the undergraduate studies committee of the department.

12 For a deconstruction of this idea see the work of Sylvia Van Kirk (1980) and Sarah Carter (1997, 2006).

13 Although this strategy worked very well for me, I am also aware that because I elected not to teach the class (and thereby not to address the issues
in the structure of the class), the department hired a sessional to teach the
class. At least one of the women who has taught this class in the last few
years is as aware as I am of the structural difficulties with the organization
and description of the course. But as a sessional, she has far fewer opportunities and options for addressing the issues with the structure of the
class.

14 This describes the state of the curriculum during the years surrounding
the 'tenure wars' (1988–9). In the 2004–5 academic year, all the Aboriginal
justice classes were transferred to the Department of Sociology.

15 As of July 1, 2007, with the restructuring of faculty positions, Native studies now has a full-time faculty of eight. This is the largest the department
has ever been.

16 Please note that this kind of dry humour is common as a coping mechanism among Indigenous peoples. It is not meant to be offensive to White
people, although on occasion one experiences backlash regarding this
tone. Nonetheless, it is an important way that First Nations people cope
with situations where we experience powerlessness.

17 This had been a conscious and deliberate interview strategy. I did not give
a standard academic paper at my faculty seminar. I breached academic
protocol and spoke from the heart, in the tradition of my people, about my
commitment to education. This was a strategy employed to ensure that
the department could deal with who I was, recognizing that others often
experience me and my ideas as radical and controversial.

18 For years, I have been thinking about writing a piece that considers the
trauma of having my work peer reviewed by people with little knowledge of the lived experiences of what I write about (including those who
still carry with them racist attitudes). Despite the belief in academia that
review processes contribute to excellence of scholarship through neutral
and objective acceptance processes, it can equally be a process of enforcement of the status quo in scholarship. For a fuller discussion see Johansen
(1998).

19 See the *Indian Act* (S.C. 1919–20, c. 50, s.3).

20 I am playing with power here. However, it should be noted that when you
turn the power relationships inside out there is a worry about offending
colleagues that I do not think exists when a White scholar takes an Indigenous person as their informant. It is a good example of why playing with
power is an important reflective strategy.

21 There are indeed some simple strategies to deal with this reality. I work at

home. There I am relatively safe from the place where I am called outsider. It is home where I can write. And writing, too, is a strategy that I have employed to ensure my survival. Seeing the pain ordered in neat lines, black on white, makes it bearable. It transforms pain into knowledge. But writing about my survival in the university means I am not producing the 'standard' research article or grant application. It repeatedly challenges the kind of scholar I think I am. Are my research interests 'employment equity' or criminal justice? I pursued my post-secondary interest because I had a passion for issues of criminal justice, yet I now find myself working in an area, equity and survival, to which I never had academic aspirations as a student. It means I am constantly returning to the question of who I am as a scholar and noting there are good reasons I feel turned inside out.

22 Indeed the irony does not escape me. One of the strategies, of those of us who gather at the kitchen table to discuss this, is to point fondly at Coyote (the people of this territory, the Cree, have many stories of this trickster) every time we note the contradictions. This is the strategy of culturalizing the madness (one emotive response to confronting the lack of respect for 'difference'). We draw out the things we cannot understand because of our lack of access to the parameters of university culture, then indigenize them privately.

23 My four children and I are now living in the city. They have been grounded in who they are as First Nations citizens because of the time spent on the reserve. My knowledge of Indigenous ways has been enriched by the time I spent at Thunderchild. However, now that we are back in the city we are dealing with the issue of racism within public institutions, from the education system to the criminal justice system, but especially the police.

24 The fact that few First Nations citizens hold positions as university professors seems most frequently forgotten in the equity discourses at the university, and there are very real issues of recruitment and retention at this level of participation as well.

25 For a discussion of the power of rage, see hooks (1998).

26 The Elder Art Solomon put it a little more bluntly. As he often told me, 'Shine a light on the rats and the rats will run.' I had the honour and privilege to receive teachings from Dr. Art Solomon in person, but he has also left behind two books. See Solomon, with Kneen and Posluns (1991); Solomon, with Posluns (1990).

27 In part the email that I forwarded to about forty people in November 1997 read: 'Yesterday, the College Review Committee (CRC) at the University of Saskatchewan failed to support the department's recommendation for my tenure. The CRC cited two reasons for their decision to deny me tenure.

First, I do not have a graduate degree [I had not yet finished my LL.M.] and second, that my scholarship is not up to standard because I have not published enough "refereed" pieces. I would appreciate very much that each of you direct a letter to the dean explaining your reaction to this decision. I would ask you to comment on my teaching, writing, contribution to the field of Native studies/law, support I have given you as a colleague, etc.' (at page 1, copy of file with the author).

28   The paragraph of the November 1997 email that, I believe, offended them, reads: 'e) My working at the university is a constant battle. I work in a very divided department. There are 5 tenure stream jobs – three of these positions are held by White men, one is a Métis man, and me. It is only the three White men who hold tenure, the Métis man has yet to apply. I feel marginalized on both gender and race/culture. I am the only tenure track person in the department willing to address issues of inclusion of Aboriginal knowledge and scholarship. It is absolutely a "chilly climate." The stories I can tell about the department are too many to go into detail about but I am sure that most of you can guess pretty well at the details. What is supposed to be a "safe place" for Aboriginal People at the university (i.e. a Native studies department) is not. It is not safe for me or the students, many of whom spend many hours in my office. This is not directly the issue; however, it does clearly overlap with the tenure decision. It negatively affects my ability to both write and teach. The process of being tenured is purely individualized and does not take into account any of these hostile work environment issues. This is one of the central problems in the private nature of the tenure process.'

29   Early in the tenure battle, I told two union representatives that receiving tenure would not feel like a victory but a life sentence. Over time, I have unpacked this sentiment and understood that what I lost was the opportunity to feel positive or even to celebrate the earning of tenure.

30   The sites of control within the university are multiple. In both the tenure and promotion battle, I received assistance from the faculty association. During the course of these struggles one union man told me, as unsolicited advice, that part of the problem was I had a chip on my shoulder. I still do not know what he meant. But how can I not have a 'chip,' when the university has not gone about fixing any of the harms done other than granting tenure and promotion? Yes I had (and perhaps still have) an attitude but calling this a chip makes it my responsibility, blames the victim. The problem for me has not been the possible denial of these applications, but the process I was put through to secure them.

31 This is not an appeal in the way that a lawyer would understand the term. The University Review Committee (URC) is the third committee to look at an application for tenure or promotion. Had the URC ruled against my application, then a further appeal is allowed.

32 For a detailed examination of these issues see Johansen (1998).

33 In my view, since the solutions and problem are both easily visible and solved, I am left wondering why it has to be me (a racialized person) who has to raise the issue. This reminds me of the fifty questions about privilege that Peggy McIntosh raises and should be read by all (1990, 31–6).

34 In 2007, I published in an introductory sociology text the chapter 'What Is Sovereignty for Indigenous Peoples?' (Monture 2007). In sociology, I have been encouraged to continue my work on Indigenous sovereignty, work that was challenged as not having academic merit when I was a member of Native studies.

35 For a longer consideration of Native studies as a discipline, see Duane Champagne (Chippewa, Turtle Mountain) (2007).

REFERENCES

Carter, S. 2006. *Categories and Terrains of Exclusion: Constructing the 'Indian Woman' in the Settlement Era.* Toronto: University of Toronto Press.

– 1997. *Capturing Women: The Manipulation of Cultural Imagery in Canada's Prairie West.* Montreal: McGill-Queen's University Press.

Champagne, D. 2007. 'In Search of Theory and Method in American Indian Studies.' *American Indian Quarterly* 31(3):353–72.

Cook-Lynn, E. 1997. 'Who Stole Native American Studies.' *Wiccazo Sa Review* 12:9–22.

Crichlow, W. 1999. 'Labelling Heroes: Role Models in Education.' In G. Hudek and P. Kihn, eds. (2001), *Labelling, Pedagogy, and Politics*, 147–60. London: Routledge.

hooks, bell. 1998. *Killing Rage: Ending Racism.* New York: H. Holt.

Johansen, B.E. 1998. *Debating Democracy: Native American Legacy of Freedom.* Sante Fe: Clear Light Publishing.

Luther, R., E. Whitmore, and B. Moreau. 2003. 'Making Visible the Invisible.' In R. Luther, E. Whitmore, and B. Moreau, eds., *Seen but Not Heard: Aboriginal Women and Women of Colour in the Academy*, 11–31. Ottawa: Canadian Research Institute for the Advancement of Women.

McCaslin, W.D. 2005. *Justice as Healing: Writings on Community Peacemaking and Restorative Justice from the Native Law Centre.* St. Paul, MN: Living Justice Press.

McIntosh, P. 1990. 'White Privilege: Unpacking the Invisible Knapsack.' *Independent Schools* 29(2):31–6.

Mohawk, J. 1989. 'Origins of Iroquois Political Thought.' In J. Bruchac, ed., *New Voices from the Longhouse: An Anthology of Contemporary Iroquois Writing.* New York: Greenfield Review Press.

Montoya, M.E. 2002. 'Celebrating Racialized Legal Narratives.' In F. Valdes, J. Culp, and A. Harris, eds., *Crossroads, Directions, and a New Critical Race Theory,* 243–50. Philadelphia: Temple University Press.

Monture, P. 2007. 'What Is Sovereignty for Indigenous Peoples?' In M. Hird and G. Pavlich, eds., *Sociology for the Asking,* ch. 15. Toronto: Oxford University Press.

Monture-Angus, P. 2003. 'In the Way of Peace: Confronting "Whiteness" in the University.' In R. Luther, E. Whitmore, and B. Moreau, eds., *Seen but Not Heard: Aboriginal Women and Women of Colour in the Academy.* Ottawa: Canadian Research Institute for the Advancement of Women.

– 2002. 'On Being Homeless: One Aboriginal Woman's "Conquest" of Canadian Universities, 1989–98.' In F. Valdes, J. Culp, and A. Harris, eds., *Crossroads, Directions, and a New Critical Race Theory,* 274–87. Philadelphia: Temple University Press.

– 1999a. *Journeying Forward: Dreaming First Nations Independence.* Halifax: Fernwood.

– 1999b. 'Selected University Experiences: A Preliminary Discussion of Equity Initiatives for Aboriginal Peoples.' In K. Armatage, ed., *Equity and How to Get It: Rescuing Graduate Studies,* 99–125. Toronto: Inanna Publications.

Reber, S., and R. Renaud. 2005. *Starlight Tour: The Last, Lonely Night of Neil Stonechild.* Toronto: Random House.

Solomon, A., with C. Kneen and M. Posluns. 1991. *Eating Bitterness: A Vision Beyond the Prison Walls.* Toronto: NC Press.

Solomon, A., with M. Posluns. 1990. *Songs for the People: Teachings of the Natural Way.* Toronto: NC Press.

Tator, C., and F. Henry. 2006. *Racial Profiling in Canada: Challenging the Myth of 'A Few Bad Apples.'* Toronto: University of Toronto Press.

Thornton, R. 1998. 'Institutional and Intellectual Histories of Native American Studies.' In R. Thornton, ed., *Studying Native America: Problems and Prospects,* 79–107. Madison: University of Wisconsin Press.

Valdes, F., J.M. Culp, and A.P. Harris, eds. 2002. *Crossroads, Directions, and a New Critical Race Theory.* Philadelphia: Temple University Press.

Van Kirk, S. 1980. *Many Tender Ties: Women in Fur Trade Society, 1670–1870.* Winnipeg: Watson & Dwyer.

Yazzie, R. 2005. 'Healing as Justice: The Navajo Response to Crime.' In W.D. McCaslin, ed., *Justice as Healing: Writings on Community Peacemaking and Restorative Justice from the Native Law Centre,* 121–33. St. Paul, MN: Living Justice Press.

4 Caribbean Students in the Canadian Academy: We've Come a Long Way?

CAMILLE HERNANDEZ-RAMDWAR

The face of Canadian universities has been transformed over the last twenty years. Campuses, particularly those in or near to large urban centres, reveal an increasing number of racialized minority students attending both full- and part-time studies. Do increasing numbers of students of colour, however, guarantee an end to racism? Furthermore, do the increasing numbers of racialized university students translate into an increased presence of faculty of colour in Canadian universities, as some of these graduates potentially move into the ranks of teaching assistants and professors? How are students of colour faring overall in the university setting? Numbers do not necessarily tell us the whole story, particularly the subtle nuances of everyday lived experience. Qualitative research, such as the use of interviews and the inclusion of personal narratives, is helpful in providing a more holistic picture of these experiences by using the words of students themselves.

One group of racialized students who are growing in numbers in university classrooms are Caribbean students, both those who migrate from the Caribbean, and the second generation born and/or raised in Canada. Caribbean students have been a part of the Canadian academic scene since the 1950s and 1960s when numbers of young migrants travelled from the British colonies or newly independent Caribbean nations to the great white north to seek a higher education, part of the 'brain drain' from the Caribbean (Trotman 2005; Bobb-Smith 2003; Henry 1994). Caribbean migration to Canada increased significantly after changes to Canada's immigration policies in 1967. Some of the Caribbean migrants are now sending their children, the second generation descendants, to university to claim their space on the academic scene.

Overall, one of the keys issues I am addressing in this research is the continued prevalence of racism in the academy, despite apparently increased levels of Caribbean students who are now attending university. Simmons and Plaza, in a 1998 study of African Caribbean migrants and their children in Toronto, stated that 'many Blacks are going to university, but fewer are going than will be necessary to achieve equality. It seems that those Caribbean-origin Blacks who are born in Canada are going on to university in higher proportions, hence as the second generation expands one can expect a decline in inequality.'

The concern here is that it will take more than simply numbers to challenge the inequalities, racist structures, lack of diversity in faculty and curriculum, and lack of support for racialized students in the academy. In Canadian universities, 17.1 per cent of full-time students and 15.3 per cent of part-time students are visible minorities, yet this is hardly reflected in the make-up of faculty at Canadian universities (Nakhaie 2004). Henry and Tator (2007) have pointed out that 'racism is deeply embedded in the culture of academia, as reflected in curriculum, pedagogy, hiring, selection and promotion practices, and in the lack of mentoring and support for faculty of colour' (24). All of these structural inequalities and omissions affect the quality of education received by Caribbean students in university, not to mention the retention and promotion of Caribbean faculty.

Methodology

I conducted a number of structured interviews[1] with Caribbean students, including graduate students who also teach part-time in the academy. One objective in the selection of participants was to aim for as great a diversity in Caribbean students as possible, in regard to racial / ethnic origin, gender, age, and generational status (first and second). Although the number of informants was small, the data reveal some of the experiences of Caribbean students in their own words, which is important in that many of the studies done on racialized students simply reduce them to numbers, disregarding the experiential component of their university experience. Of the fourteen students I interviewed, eight (Tricia, Pat, Mark, Angela, Cheryl, Sandra, Debby, and James) are undergraduate (or have recently completed undergraduate studies), four (Jean, Lawrence, Michelle, and Justin) are completing a PhD, one (Marie) is doing her Master's, and one (Rhea) has just entered graduate school. In terms of racial/ethnic origin, eight respondents are of Afro Caribbean origin (Tricia, Jean, Lawrence, Michelle, Rhea, Pat, Mark, and Debby), one is of mixed origin (Angela), one is Chinese Caribbean (Cheryl), and four are Indo Caribbean (Sandra, Justin, Marie, and James). Two of the respondents are recent Caribbean migrants (Angela and Cheryl), one (Marie) has moved back and forth between Canada and the Caribbean during her childhood and adolescence, while all other participants are second generation Caribbean Canadian. The varying ages of respondents will be included along with their narratives.

The University Experience

Especially for the younger informants, university was seen as a place in which important connections were made, socially and professionally. For example, Cheryl (24), who led one of the Caribbean student groups on campus, said that for her university was 'enjoyable – there was lots of interaction with people my own age, fun social activities ... it broadens your mind.' James (22) said, 'Socially it was good ... I was involved with the (West Indian) student group a lot,' while Mark (early 20s) said he 'enjoyed it, I learned a lot, made social and business connections.' Sandra (22) was involved with the West Indian student group, but also felt that socially everyone kept to their own ethno-racial clique: 'Everyone signs up and it segregates us from each other actually. In high school there was segregation, but not racially. Here, I will talk to everyone in a class, but out of class, I was always with my (West Indian student group) crew.' Sandra felt that in high school the cliques were based on style, clothing, and musical tastes, whereas in university social groups were based on ethno-racial origin.

In terms of broadening one's mind, most respondents, such as Michelle (30), commented that they had learned a lot in university: 'it was good intellectually, looking at the world in a different way.' Jean (38), now completing her PhD, reflected on how her early undergrad days were a critical turning point in identity formation:

> The shaping of my cultural and racial identity came when I went to undergrad at Guelph, and being sort of left away from home and really kind of having, getting into the U.S. civil rights movement, the issues around that, learning more about the issues surrounding Black beauty, coming into contact with visa students who are from various parts of the Caribbean, and having the reaffirming aspect of various aspects of Caribbean culture.

Pat (25) said the experience was 'good' in that she met 'both students and professionals,' and that she was also able to address issues of race and gender that they 'didn't talk about in public school.'

Overall, the students expressed meaningfulness in identity formation as it related to their own ethno-racial background, whether this was through student groups or by taking classes that had Caribbean/ Black content. This also seemed to be tied to the obvious lack of these kinds of academic offerings in their previous schooling, years K–12.

For some of the other participants such as Angela (25), the university experience has proven to be less than pleasant, especially in institutional terms. Angela described it as 'frustrating,' and explained how the university had 'shredded' her transcripts from Trinidad, claiming to have never received them; because of this she was never able to apply for transfer credits and ended up spending a longer time (and more money) to complete her degree, as she did not have the funds to request the transcripts a second time, nor did she wish to deal with the university administration ever again. As well, coming from a Caribbean educational background, Angela felt that her university courses were 'babyish' in comparison to what she had done in Trinidad, 'below par compared to UWI [University of the West Indies],' and that she spent a lot of her time 'teaching classmates in the library ... almost every night and weekends ... there was *so* much they did not understand.' The tutoring of her classmates, which she did voluntarily and without recognition or recompense, was a necessity in her eyes as the courses she was taking required group work which would result in a group mark. On a similar note, one of her professors did not recognize the mathematical methods Angela used, even though she would receive the same answer as he. She was marked wrong and even accused of cheating: 'This was stuff I had done from ten years old, Form One. I had to talk to him. I was bored out of my mind. But I got an A+.'

This differential treatment of students schooled in the Caribbean has been documented by researchers (Coelho 1988; Henry 1994; *Freshies* 2000), and usually revolves around the misperception by Canadian educators that Caribbean education is inferior by Canadian standards, and/or that Caribbean students are simply less intelligent. According to Henry, 'Systemic racism and the differential treatment of Caribbean students by teachers, administrators, and other students is a significant problem that directly contributes to the lack of achievement and high drop-out rates in some regions' (1994, 134). Marie (26), for example, was immediately put back a year in high school when she arrived in Canada from Guyana because 'Canada did not accept my credentials.'

Such experiences affected Marie's self-esteem, and led to feelings of frustration and of being undervalued by Canadian society; similar experiences and feelings continued to replay themselves in her life once she entered university years later.

Barriers to Completing Studies

Although for some of the students, such as Michelle, financial burdens were the greatest barriers (see Funding and Student Debt), there were other barriers which students had encountered that affected their academic performance. Mark and Angela both recounted instances in which they felt discriminated against by a particular professor, which was a definite barrier to their achieving good grades. Mark said, 'My second year was the most trying. There was one professor that I did not get along with. He was very instrumental in trying to hold me back.' Angela recounted an incident in which a lecturer 'was not realistic in teaching. He had a bias because of your name. He played favourites. The students proved this by submitting another student's A paper with a different name, and he marked it badly. It was brought to the department's attention.'

Sandra's barriers were the numerous deaths of both family and friends during her first two years of university, one of which was the highly publicized shooting death of a young female acquaintance of hers, the other, the murder of a family member. I spoke with Sandra at length about the impact of increasing violence in Caribbean communities on young people such as herself. She told me that she has tried her best to deal with the spectre of violence in her life, but has found she has become increasingly withdrawn. She also said that when she tried to appeal her grades due to all the death-related stress she was enduring, her department was not 'really understanding of my situation ... [even though] I submitted death certificates [and] newspaper clippings.' She eventually ended up on academic probation and had to repeat some of her classes (adding to her financial stress).

For Jean, Marie, and Lawrence, growing up in single mother households has meant added personal and financial responsibility. When Jean's mother died during the early part of Jean's graduate program, she had to take on the responsibilities of the funeral, sorting out her mother's finances, and taking on the role of the family member abroad who is responsible for sending remittances and barrels 'back home,' something her mother had been doing for years. Lawrence, as well, had family obligations he had to contend with when his mother was suddenly diagnosed with cancer: 'I have had financial and situational barriers. My mother got sick and I had to take on the responsibility of economic support during her illness.' Marie has been the primary breadwinner for many years in her household due to her mother's mental illness. She has also been a primary caregiver to her younger sister, circumstances that deeply affected her performance during her undergraduate years, and for which she received neither support nor advice from academic advisors.

Two important points came to mind when I heard the stories of these four students: 1) increasing levels of violence and violent crime in Caribbean communities and families are having and will continue to have an impact on the academic performance, health, and well-being of Caribbean people, and 2) two outstanding characteristics of Caribbean families – large numbers of single parent female-led households, and responsibilities and expectations placed on children by their parents regarding financial and other kinds of support – can directly affect the academic performance of Caribbean students (as well as contributing to stress and illness). I feel that these two points – increasing violence and specific family characteristics – need to be better understood by university faculty, administrators, and bureaucracies, but in a way that is sensitive and does not result in negative stereotyping. Caribbean students often face specific barriers that affect them differently from other students attending university. These need to be taken into consideration when decisions are being made regarding such things as academic penalties and leaves of absence. In Marie's case, she had to fight for many years with academic advisors and senior administrators to stay in university because her family obligations were adversely affecting her grades:

> In my first year of university I was put on academic probation. I was taking care of a child [her sibling], working two jobs. I was overwhelmed. I needed someone to help me manage my time, or tell me about petitioning options due to my circumstances … my main objective was to bring my younger sister out of foster care. My mom could not take care of her. I tried to explain this to the woman [academic advisor]. She told me 'university is not for everyone' … When I told her I would love to get into law school she told me I should lower my standards, that I should go to col-

lege. When I told her I worked in retail, she told me I didn't even need to go to college but that I can move up in the retail world.

Marie recounted many instances of discouragement and 'advice' from faculty and administrators to leave school altogether and to remain in the workforce full time; she strongly feels that this was due to her Caribbean ethnicity and racialized status.

Family Influences

The majority of students I interviewed were the first in their family to attend university, which could result in a mixture of expectations placed on them by parents, as well as a sense of responsibility on their part to succeed. Lawrence (38), who is about to complete his PhD, recounts how much he feels indebted to his mother, who raised him and his siblings single-handedly from adolescence: 'I dropped out of high school ... it was my mom who kept on insisting "when are you going back?" She motivated me to go back despite all the obstacles. It was the influence of my mom – that's why this degree is for me and my family.' None of Lawrence's siblings are even entertaining the idea of attending university, so he will be the first and only in his family to complete a university education. Tricia (20) is also the first and only in her family of thirteen siblings to attend university, even though she is the second youngest in the family. Being the first in a family to attend university can mean two things: a sense of obligation and responsibility toward the rest of the family (the 'shining example' syndrome), and a lack of practical support at home (for example, lack of books, knowledge and experience of university, a lack of practical support on how to negotiate the university system). Conversely, being the 'shining example' can also result in envy and resentment on the part of other family members who cannot or choose not to go to university.

For some students, part of the reason for their attending university is the parents' desire for status. Having a child in university is, for a Caribbean parent, grounds for bragging rights. Sandra explained how one of her friends had to change universities because it was not one that was well known 'back home': 'Her mom said "nobody in Trinidad know that university; you're going to find your way to ____ [the name of a more prestigious university]." It is more for show, to tell others "this is where my daughter goes." It can't be an unknown school. It has to be name brand, like clothes.' This too is part of Caribbean colonial history in which schools have been ranked according to the elite's preferences, enrolment, and patronage.

Funding and Student Debt

The link between racism and poverty in Canada has been well documented (Saloojee 2005; Hou and Balakrishnan 2004; Henry and Tator 2006; Galabuzi 2006). A Canadian Labour Congress study found that 'racial status is responsible for the growing gaps in income. Racialized workers earn substantially less than Whites' (Henry and Tator 2006, 97). A report entitled *Ethno-Racial Inequality in Toronto* also found that '"African, Black and Caribbean ethno-racial groups" experience much more poverty and family incomes significantly below the Toronto average' (Saloojee 2005, 189). Racism combined with poverty can be especially crippling for students of colour. Low income is one of the primary reasons many racialized students never make it through the doors of the university in the first place. For those who do, it also means they cannot count on their families for financial support during their studies. It also means that many Caribbean students who do graduate will carry a heavy debt load.

Two of the students I interviewed clearly demonstrated the impact of low-income families on their education. Tricia disclosed that she is currently the sole income earner in her family due to a car accident that has left both her parents disabled. She now partially supports her two parents and thirteen siblings through her job earnings while also attending full-time studies. Like Jean, Marie, and Lawrence, she feels obligated to support her family, despite how this may affect her education. Sandra has been working two jobs since she was seventeen years old, and also contributes to the household income in a family of four. She says, 'My hours are decreased during the school year, but in the summer I go crazy. I will work fourteen days in a row, double shifts. I work twenty hours a week during the school year. I also have a line of credit from the bank, which is why I work two jobs. I don't want to have thirty thousand dollars to pay back [at the end of my studies].'

Financial stress for students is a major source of concern. The pressure and debt load only increases the longer one stays in school. Michelle, now completing a PhD, considered dropping out of graduate school altogether due to the financial strain, and the fact that there was 'no help, not even from the places that are supposed to help.' She said that the base funding for graduate students in her department is below the poverty line. Lawrence, also completing his dissertation, had this to say:

> Funding, fees, increasing tuition have created an enormous debt load for me. As I went through the system from undergraduate to graduate school I became more aware of the different opportunities for the dominant group of students. We do not get the same opportunities as the dominant group of students in terms of funding, teaching opportunities, research opportunities, or support from family members.

The intersection of class and race as it pertains to Caribbean people in the academy definitely is a major concern that needs to be addressed. Further research on the number of Caribbean students who must access government or private loans in order to attend school is needed; as well, the debt load that graduate students and/or faculty of Caribbean origin carry needs to be assessed. Like class, the intersection of gender and race/class needs to be factored in. For example, although more African Caribbean women in Canada have a university education compared to their male counterparts, they are still on average earning less than Black men, and are also often heading single parent households (Plaza 2004).

Rhea (35) is a sole-support parent who is re-entering the academic field after a hiatus. She is only now able to return to studies as she has been working full time for a number of years and was lucky enough to receive a graduate scholarship. However, her scholarship is contingent on her fulfilling a graduate assistantship at her school; in addition, she needs to maintain her full-time job to support herself and her son. She suffers tremendous anxiety about how she will manage this work and study load, in addition to raising her son. She is determined that her son does not fall into the traps that many young Caribbean/Black males fall into in Toronto, that is, dropping out of school and falling into 'street life.'

Instances of Racism in the Academy

Existing research and evidence clearly speaks to ongoing levels of racism operating on Canadian campuses (Henry and Tator 2007, 2006; Nakhaie 2004; *Out of Sight* 2006). In my interviews, I wanted to provide room for participants to discuss both individualized accounts of racism and the larger problem of structural racism inherent in the institution of the university itself. When I asked the participants if they had ever experienced racism in the academy, I found a correlation between the number of years spent in the university and the greater the accounts of racism in the academy. Whether this was due to increments of racist instances as years go by, to higher levels of racism in graduate school, to a greater awareness of issues of racism as one progresses through university, or to an increasing political awareness due to maturing realizations about the society one lives in is uncertain. Responses to the question varied greatly, and I found myself at times probing the younger students who simply answered 'no' to the question 'Did you or are you experiencing racism in the academy?' by attempting to define racism broadly, not sure if they would consider certain forms of treatment or behaviour as 'racist.'

There were three participants who said they had never encountered racism in the academy; James, for example, said, 'I never received nothing to do with racism in all of university. I think it is based on the individual and that would determine how they were treated.' Cheryl said she had 'never noticed it,' while Sandra said she 'never felt any personal thing.' However, Sandra did admit to not knowing enough about the reality of structural racism to provide a more comprehensive answer: 'everything is designed to benefit the upper class. I don't know if there are different races in the upper class now. I don't know how to answer that question properly. Everything in society always has some racism behind it.' She admitted to having taken a Caribbean Studies course that dealt with racism, which had 'opened up my eyes a lot, that a lot more racism existed. I was so oblivious.'

As a professor of undergraduate students, and one who teaches on issues of racism, I have noticed that many of the students who come into my classroom are unaware of the entrenched levels of racism operating within society and the university, as well as the insidious ways in which racism operates. I was therefore not entirely surprised by the responses of these three students. Carl E. James, in his study of Black youth and career aspirations, commented on a similar attitude he encountered in his interviews:

The youth do not have any realistic notion of structural racism ... they see this racism as largely individual and to some extent institutional but not structural ... From their perspective racism cannot and must not be used as an excuse for not achieving ... Such belief in the individual's capacity to counter racism indicates that the youth are quite naive about the structural roots of racism. (1990, 110)

Both Sandra and James are Indo Caribbean, while Cheryl is Chinese Caribbean, and this may have something to do with their denial of racism. In several ways, racialized people who fall into categories between 'White' and 'Black' are viewed/used as 'model minorities' or buffer groups by the dominant group, and are therefore sometimes also positively stereotyped (as in, Chinese people are good at math and computer science, Indian people are good at business and know how to save money), whereas people of African descent are more likely to be stereotyped negatively (as, for example, criminals, violent, drug dealers). It certainly seems that the incidences of racism I recorded appeared to be highest for African Caribbean males in the academy, who, correlatively, have been one of the most negatively portrayed racial groups in the media and society at large (Roswell 2007; Benjamin 2003; James and Brathwaite 1996; Henry 1994). However, Sandra, James, and Cheryl are also all in undergraduate programs, and in their early twenties; this may also have to do with their limited perception of racism in university. By contrast, Marie, who is also Indo Caribbean, but in graduate school and in her mid-twenties, was much more aware of racism and able to discern and describe racist treatment in a number of ways.

Some participants recounted instances of racism they had either witnessed or experienced that came from other students. Debby said, 'I can't really say there is overt racism. There were little comments that I feel weren't necessary from other students. But I have the feeling that [the university] is racist – there was racist graffiti in the study carrel in the library, anti-Jewish, anti-Middle Eastern.' Sandra, who at first said she personally hadn't experienced racism, did recount an incident that happened to one of her classmates:

> He was a member of the ITM [Information Technology Management] Student Association, and last year they were having a boat cruise and gave him tickets to sell. Well he sold most to his West Indian crew, he sold a lot of tickets, the boat was full. He's also a DJ, so there was West Indian music and requests. This year he was told that there were too many complaints, that there were too many black and brown people on the cruise last time.

Apparently the complaints came from other students in the ITM department, who weren't happy about suddenly and involuntarily becoming minorities on 'their' boat cruise.

Sometimes the descriptions of racial discrimination were related to tensions between various groups of racialized students. As mentioned earlier, Sandra described an environment in which, even more than in high schools, students were encouraged to join and adhere to a specific ethno-racial student group, whose boundaries were often stringently monitored. Angela, who is Trinidadian of mixed racial background, provided a further example. She was really 'shocked' at the reception she got from her peers in regard to her racial identity, or more specifically, lack thereof. Coming from a country where multiracial identity is very common, she could not understand why she was being objectified in the way that she was:

> Students asked me 'What are you?' 'What's your background?' 'You're not black and you're not white – what are you?' My cousins who have lived here for some time told me I have to pick a side. I did not fit in with my classmates. I did not fit in with their model of blackness. I joined the Black and Caribbean students' group [but] I left because their version of Caribbean was Jamaica, playing pan, smoking weed, dub and hip hop. I fought to get soca played ... my culture is not that. I could sing old calypsos. I always felt uncomfortable there.

Divisions between racialized peoples operate to ensure a 'divide-and-rule' status quo which allows white supremacy to operate uncontested. One of the ways that racism is constructed in Canada is to maintain discrete boundaries between racialized groups (such as Aboriginal, Black/African, South Asian, Asian, European) when, in the case of the Caribbean, many of these racial groups share a similar cultural background. The ethno-racial divisions between students which operate through the propensity of student groups on campus can also work in a similar fashion. Instead of racialized students uniting to combat the larger structural oppressor, inner divisions and competition for resources keep students who are all affected by racism continually divided.

Cheryl, who is of Chinese Caribbean background, also experienced difficulties with other students who would be stunned when she would open her mouth and speak with a strong Trinidadian accent: 'People should not judge you on how you look or sound. My peers have done this. [When they react like that] I don't know what to say to comfort them.' Cheryl described instances of being shunned by other Caribbean students (who had difficulty in seeing her as 'Caribbean' since she is neither Black nor Indian) and also by Chinese international students, who shunned her upon realizing she was from the Caribbean, which somehow in their eyes then made her 'Black'! A recent graduate, Cheryl is now looking for work and finds that, once again, the inability for many people to synchronize Chinese and Caribbean together is creating problems for her. The stereotype of the hardworking diligent Chinese employee is destroyed once she opens her mouth: 'I had a [white Canadian] woman tell me she thought I was too laid back for the job, that people from the Caribbean are laid back. This was after she heard my accent.' Cheryl is now trying to speak 'like a Canadian' in order to secure employment.

On a structural level, the most predominant account by the students of racism in the university was in relation to the lack of diversity in the university, in terms of curriculum, faculty, student body, and administration. Pat was grateful that she had been able to take Caribbean Studies in university, but complained that 'any topic related to non-white people is "specialized" and not part of the core curriculum' and that this had been the way curricula were always structured since high school. Earlier research done in Toronto high schools correlates with this; for example, Frances Henry found that there was 'Eurocentrism ... a lack of Black teachers as role models [and a] persistent "invisibility" of Black studies and Black history within the curriculum' (1994, 124). Michelle echoed Pat when I asked her if she had taken any Caribbean Studies courses in university. She retorted, 'They won't allow me to. Why am I paying you all this money for you to tell me what to do?' Michelle is in a particular program that restricts her choice of elective courses; therefore, there are no 'ethnic' or 'area' studies available to her, a fact which she feels is grossly unfair. On the other hand, Mark had taken every Caribbean Studies course he possibly could and then he 'looked for more.' He enrolled in every elective course offered that might have some Black/African content, partly because 'I didn't get this in elementary or high school. I had to get it on my own. It was only in these types of classes that I could sit down with people like me and people not like me and talk about the state of the world.' Mark also had this to say about the racism within his program:

It came up the most in my last year. The programme [Radio and Television Arts] is a reflection of the industry in Canada, very white, old white men. The chair of the programme told me it was very important that I succeed to change that, the old white men thing. There was no reflection [of diversity] in faculty or students. In my programme there were seven Black males, a maximum of five at any one time in four years of the programme. That's one a year graduating. I didn't know anything about people out there [in the field]. There's no way you can tell me that there aren't nonwhite people in the industry who are very successful and can talk to a class or be hired. Every guest speaker that came – and there were more than five – all were white.

Although it seems that Mark's program chair was being supportive in telling him he had to succeed, this is also a burden placed on racialized students (and faculty) – that one must be superior, do better, strive higher, and, basically, be extraordinary and exceptional to change the status quo. The onus is somehow never on the people in positions of privilege and power to change the status quo, but rather on the racialized 'token' member. Too often we become 'representatives for the race,' overburdened with expectations and baggage that our white peers do not have to deal with (Henry and Tator 2007).

Students who are both racialized and recent immigrants face compounded problems compared to their Canadian-born counterparts. Angela felt that the administration of the university was not 'racist by choice,' but that it was lacking in its treatment of immigrant students. She said that within the departments there was nothing specific to deal with the needs of immigrant students, to explain the culture of Canada, 'no help with integration. Among the faculty and staff you have very few other than from the general Canadian culture.' She also felt this extended to the classroom in which professors would talk about the 'things in the general Canadian culture – I cannot relate at all.'

As aforementioned, it was the graduate students who had the most to say on the subject of racism in the academy. Marie, in the second year of a Master's program, described how throughout her undergraduate years she was repeatedly discouraged from remaining in university and was instead directed to pursue full-time employment; even when she studied diligently and worked under tremendous pressure to improve her GPA she was told that she 'still could fail'; 'I was left to feel that the university was doing me a favour by letting me in, that I was taking up space, that I shouldn't be wasting their time.' The treatment she received ('no encouragement, no advice, no bursaries, no support') affected her self-esteem so much that she became paranoid and felt that she was 'being watched' by university administrators in an effort to make her fail. In her fourth year she sought counselling because she felt that the academic advisor she had been assigned to throughout her undergraduate years, the same one who continually encouraged her to drop out and pursue a job in retail, 'was sitting on my shoulder. I am the first to go to university. I did not want to disappoint. I also felt guilt that I was choosing to stay in school rather than work [and support the family].' It was only in her final year when she began thinking about graduate school that a Caribbean professor advised her on how to apply. 'He gave me the courage. It was people of colour who helped me through – NOT the academic advisors who are paid thousands of dollars a year.' Marie eventually received acceptances from top graduate schools in both Canada and the United States, and chose to continue her studies in Toronto. The interlocking oppressions of race, class, and gender that Marie has experienced led her to comment that 'racism is not just this or that ... There are so many strands to consider.'

Michelle, nearly finished her doctorate, recalled how difficult graduate school was as a Black woman because 'the courses were biased and lop-sided ... only certain people and certain histories were presented. It was not very diverse. Graduate school is run by a dominant class of professors who do not teach from a minority perspective. The courses are taught from a privileged perspective, taught by those who are of this perspective.'

Michelle also told me one of her most upsetting experiences in graduate school has been attending academic conferences in Canada, in which she is the 'only Black person.' She recounted an incident which disturbed her in which, after her presentation, a white woman approached her to tell her that she was 'very articulate'; this upset Michelle as she felt she would not have received such a backhanded compliment had she been white. It is the same comment that has created a major controversy with African American politician and U.S. President Barack Obama, who was also repeatedly referred to by the media and some of his peers as 'very articulate.' Certainly, neither white academics nor white politicians are congratulated for being 'very articulate' by other whites; the assumption is that they would be nothing else, whereas an articulate Black person is somehow always seen as an anomaly.

Lawrence felt he has been particularly discriminated against in the academy in comparison to his peers. As a Black male who wears his hair in dreadlocks, he is often negatively stereotyped by students, faulty, and staff:

> I'm a Black man in the academy. Because I'm concerned with issues of social equality I'm seen as a threat and people respond to me in that way. Because I'm proud of my background and who I am I'm also a threat. I think all that is racialized. I have dreads and everybody assumes I'm Jamaican and not Canadian and that I sell marijuana, I'm a drug dealer. I see that stereotype rapping me more and more as I proceed through academia.

Indeed, during one of our meetings which occurred on the campus grounds, I was amazed to see a young white girl approach Lawrence, on the campus, outside the doors to the university, and ask him if he had 'any buds to cut' (marijuana for sale). He told me that this happens to him all the time, on and off campus. At the same time, Lawrence also feels the burden of racism that Mark had spoken about, that is, that he become the representative Black voice in the graduate studies setting: 'Because I'm usually the only minority in this field, as I go up the ranks I become the spokesperson, for example, "What do Black people think of this?"' However, he is also made invisible when he has to endure the racist comments of other members of the graduate department as if he were not in the same room: 'I have heard a lot of racialized comments by faculty members about minority students, other grad students, how Black males are lazy, how Black females are oversexed, and the rumours that they are sleeping with the professors.'

The Graduate Drain

All of the graduate students currently pursuing their doctorates (Jean, Michelle, Lawrence) expressed a sense of disillusionment after a long, hard struggle to acquire the PhD. For them, the sense of having sacrificed a lot, financially, personally, and emotionally over a number of years, and the toll that this sacrifice had taken on their lives, was deeply felt. Jean, who was very close to defending her dissertation at the time of our interview, was 'on the verge of a breakdown' as her committee kept changing the date of her defence. She despaired that she would ever finish, even though she was literally weeks away from completion. The whole experience had left her with a bitterness that made her want to leave academia altogether. Lawrence, as well, expressed that he is planning alternatives for his future that have nothing to do with academia, as, like Jean, he felt disrespected, disillusioned, and disheartened by the entire academic rat race. Michelle, who has been teaching undergraduate students for the last four years, is appalled by the level of racism and disrespect in undergraduate classrooms, an experience which she says is 'very emotional' and has 'taken a lot out of me. I teach in all white classrooms. The students are not seeing racism.' She also confessed that she would find it 'difficult to tell fourth year students to go to graduate school. I feel I need distance [after so many years in academia]. During my six years of graduate school there were only two Black students [in my department] the whole time.' All three of these graduate students, who also teach part-time in the academy, expressed feeling burnt out, disillusioned, frustrated, and undervalued.

Meanwhile, Rhea, who has just returned to academia, is feeling an increasing sense of anxiety and doom, and she stated, 'What have I gotten myself into?' She is worried she may not be up to the demands and pressures of graduate school, working full time, and raising her son single-handedly. She also worries about whether or not she is academically prepared for the intense demands of graduate school. Marie, as well, struggles with feelings of inadequacy due to the constant discouragement, lack of support, and prejudice she received from white academic advisors and professors during her undergraduate years. Although she is now in graduate school, she, too, worries if she has the academic ability to succeed.

The combination of studies and teaching which many graduate students undergo can be demanding, but more so for racialized students, who may be experiencing racism from within their graduate departments or their thesis committees, from undergraduate students in the classroom, and/or from other faculty. The three graduate students I spoke with who are in PhD programs and teaching in the university commented repeatedly on the heavy workload, long hours, lack of recognition, low pay, job insecurity, and general burn-out. They are also aware that they are being exploited by the academy, as Lawrence bluntly stated: 'Sometimes I feel like a slave because I work like a dog.' Some of the graduate students are seriously questioning whether or not it is worth it to continue teaching. The difficulty they have in finding full-time work (if they are graduates or close to graduating) and the way in which they are consistently passed over for promotion has resulted in a lot of bitterness. They do not feel that they are given the dignity or respect that is warranted them by the academy despite their high level of education, and often excellent credentials; they see no point in 'giving back' to an institution that does not 'give back' to them.

It is feedback such as this that raises the question of how many Caribbean graduates will actually remain in academia and how many will leave due to maltreatment and lack of viable opportunities, once again lessening the numbers of Caribbean people in positions of decision making.

'Was it worth it? Do you think it will pay off?'

On a positive note, all of those interviewed definitely felt that attending university was worth the experience, and that it would or already was paying off for them (for example, in terms of greater knowledge, job prospects, networking). However, most of the students were also quite cynical about the whole process of paying for the 'privilege' of an education when it is really the only means to an end in a society which especially discriminates against people of colour in the workforce. For Lawrence, one of the most important things about going to university was that 'now I am a role model to my nieces and nephews, now they see that it's possible for them to go to the same places.' However, he also added that 'at the same time I don't think I should have to pay thousands of dollars to learn these things.' Similarly, James stated: 'I don't think I need a university degree to justify intelligence. You can be a high school dropout and be a millionaire, but in terms of getting a well-paid job you need a university degree ... in terms of knowledge gained a lot of it is repetitive and common sense. You are basically paying for a piece of paper.' The feeling that one really has no other choice but to attend university, that to do otherwise would be to severely limit one's life chances in Canadian society, was also shared by Tricia:

> You pay twenty thousand dollars for a piece of paper. It's not important in life itself, but if you want a higher-paying job then society tells us we need this ... even so if you go to law school or medical school they still look down on you. Why is that? We are coming from the same background. It's not worth it! When you finish you're still not where you're supposed to be, where you want to be. I think it will pay off to the point where they allow me to let it pay off.

The 'they' in Tricia's last statement refers to the white Canadian power structure. At twenty years of age, Tricia is well aware that as a Black woman she will most likely experience inequality and discrimination in the workforce.

Increasingly, all young Canadians, regardless of race, are put into the bind of requiring a 'piece of paper' to qualify in the job market, but this is especially true for racialized Canadians. As aforementioned, racialized students have to work harder, continually prove themselves, be exceptional, contend with community and family pressures, economic challenges, structural and everyday racism, and, even if they manage to supersede these barriers and acquire the almighty 'piece of paper,' they are still seen as 'lesser than' in the Canadian workforce. As Tricia rightly points out, there are still racist barriers in place that penalize racialized university graduates, and the research is there to back up her sentiments; in *Canada's Economic Apartheid: The Social Exclusion of Racialized Groups in the New Century,* Galabuzi states, 'The racialized employment income gap is observable both among low-income earners and high-income earners. It persists among those with low and high educational attainment [among those with less than high school education and also among those with university degrees]' (2006, xix).

Angela was even more cynical than Tricia when she stated that her university education 'will not pay off.' When asked if it had been worth it, she had this to say:

> Yes, it will get you more money [but] it will not give you practical experience that you need in my field, a textbook does not tell you what to do. I do not feel my university education was worth it – too many courses were the same with the same professor, and he also gave lectures at another university, the same lectures with the same slideshows in three of my four courses ... I am a practical person. The theory they have thrown down my throat for four to five years has meant nothing to me.

Angela is one of the two Caribbean migrant students I interviewed, both of whom felt that the Canadian educational system overall was far inferior to what they had known in the Caribbean. For immigrant students, the challenges and barriers are even greater, the frustrations deeper. As well, job discrimination for racialized immigrants is even more severe than for their Canadian-born counterparts (Henry and Tator 2006; Galabuzi 2006; Saloojee 2005).

Conclusion

According to the evidence presented here, the increased presence of Caribbean students on the university campus has neither eradicated nor decreased racism. The pressures of structural racism take their toll on Caribbean students as they pursue a university education, particularly if they go on to pursue graduate studies. The structure of the university can actually work to create divisions and competitiveness between Caribbean students, for example, by funding student groups based on ethno-racial differences and refusing to fund 'politically based' student groups. Increased tuition fees, lack of proper funding, and heavy debt loads are all barriers to Caribbean students, many of whom are coming from families that face racism in the workplace and therefore fall within a lower-income bracket. At present, there is a lack of data that could reveal how many Caribbean students are graduating with heavy debt, which could also result in post-graduate poverty. As well, many of these students are coming from single parent families and/or from communities that experience higher levels of violence, factors that come out of historical legacies of colonialism and racism, legacies that contribute to the ongoing marginalization of Caribbean people. It remains to be seen how many of the Caribbean students currently enrolled in university will not only complete their education, but will also then be able to achieve employment equivalent to their educational qualifications, skills, and talents. It is not enough that Caribbean students complete university degrees, but it is crucial that we are able to move into positions of decision making and power within the university faculty and administration to ensure that structural change will be achieved. Still, Caribbean students, along with other racialized students, are enrolling in universities in unprecedented numbers, and are contributing to a groundswell of change, one that is challenging Canadian racism as it operates not only on a structural but also on an attitudinal level.

NOTES

1 I asked the participants a series of questions, which included the following:

a) Overall how has your university experience been?

b) Did you come from a family where education was highly valued? Were you expected to go to university? Are you the first and/or only one in your family to get a university education?
c) Have there been any barriers to your completing your studies (i.e., financial, family obligations, work, etc.)? Do you think that you will complete your degree?
d) Have you experienced racism in the academy? Do you think the university is a racist institution?
e) How did you/are you supporting yourself financially through school?
f) Do you think a university education is important? Do you think it is worth it? Do you think it will pay off?
g) Did you take any Caribbean Studies courses or courses that dealt with Caribbean content? If yes, was this experience important to you?

REFERENCES

Benjamin, A. 2003. 'The Black/Jamaican Criminal: The Making of Ideology.' PhD diss., University of Toronto.

Bobb-Smith, Y. 2003. *I Know Who I Am: A Caribbean Woman's Identity in Canada.* Toronto: Women's Press.

Coelho, E. 1988. *Caribbean Students in Canadian Schools: Book 1.* Toronto: Carib-Can.

Freshies (videocassette). 2000. Directed by Rudi 'Quammie' Williams. Toronto: Jamaican Canadian Association.

Galabuzi, G. 2006. *Canada's Economic Apartheid: The Social Exclusion of Racialized Groups in the New Century.* Toronto: Canadian Scholars' Press.

Henry, F. 1994. *The Caribbean Diaspora in Toronto: Learning to Live with Racism.* Toronto: University of Toronto Press.

Henry, F., and C. Tator. 2007. 'Through the Looking Glass: Enduring Racism on the University Campus.' *Academic Matters: The Journal of Higher Education* Feb.:24–5.

– 2006. *The Colour of Democracy: Racism in Canadian Society,* 3rd ed. Toronto: Thomson Nelson.

Hou, F., and T.R. Balakrishnan. 2004. 'The Economic Integration of Visible Minorities in Contemporary Canadian Society.' In J. Curtis, E. Grabb et al., eds., *Social Inequality in Canada: Patterns, Problems and Policies,* 4th ed., 273–84. Toronto: Prentice Hall.

James, C.E. 1990. *Making It: Black Youth, Racism and Career Aspirations in a Big City.* Oakville, ON: Mosaic Press.

James, C., and K. Brathwaite. 1996. 'The Education of African Canadians:

Issues, Contexts and Expectations.' In K. Brathwaite and C. James, eds., *Educating African Canadians*, 13–31. Toronto: James Lorimer.

Nakhaie, M.R. 2004. 'Who Controls Canadian Universities? Ethnoracial Origins of Canadian University Administrators and Faculty's Perception of Mistreatment.' *Canadian Ethnic Studies* 36(1):92–110.

Out of Sight (videocassette). 2006. Queen's Coalition for Racial and Ethnic Diversity. http://video.google.ca/videoplay?docid=-5037313042062349620&q=Queen%27s+University.

Plaza, D. 2004. 'Caribbean Migration to Canada: Mobility and Opportunity, 1900–2001.' In S. Courtman, ed., *Beyond the Blood, the Beach and the Banana: New Perspectives in Caribbean Studies*. Kingston, Jamaica: Ian Randle.

Roswell, T. 2007. *Constructing a Jamaican Crime Problem: Linking Race and Crime in Toronto*. Unpublished paper. Ryerson University.

Saloojee, A. 2005. 'Social Inclusion, Anti Racism and Democratic Citizenship.' In T. Richmond and A. Saloojee, eds., *Social Inclusion: Canadian Perspectives*, 180–202. Black Point, NS: Fernwood.

Simmons, A., and D. Plaza. 1998. 'Breaking through the Glass Ceiling: The Pursuit of University Training among African-Caribbean Migrants and Their Children in Toronto.' *Canadian Ethnic Studies* 30(3):99–119.

Trotman, D.V. 2005. 'Transforming Caribbean and Canadian Identity: Contesting Claims for Toronto's Caribana.' *Atlantic Studies* 2(2, Oct.):177–98.

5 'It Will Happen without Putting in Place Special Measures': Racially Diversifying Universities

CARL E. JAMES

> Working as an insider means that inquiry into 'how things work' into the actualities of socially organized practices, makes what we are part of visible. In exploring social organization, we explore our own lives and practices. Thus critique is investigation and investigation is a reflexive critique, disclosing practices we know and use.
>
> – Dorothy Smith, *The Conceptual Practices of Power: A Feminist Sociology of Knowledge*

In the process of working on this chapter, I attended the National Conference on Race and Ethnicity in American Higher Education (NCORE) (May 29–June 2, 2007) where a number of participants – in keynote addresses, panel presentations, and institutes – made presentations about the lack of racial diversity among the teaching faculty in many American universities, particularly in 'predominantly White institutions.' A common theme was that universities need to do more to recruit, appoint, retain, nurture, support, and promote faculty of colour if, as Robert Birgeneau, chancellor of the University of California, Berkeley, and former president of the University of Toronto, said, they are to 'claim excellence.' In his feature address, 'Creating an Inclusive Academy,' Birgeneau noted that being inclusive 'is a moral issue' and 'a key plank of our mission.' He went on to say that universities 'cannot claim to be excellent unless we try to capture the entire talent pool' that exists in the population (2007). Diversity among faculty, as Sidney McPhee, president of Middle Tennessee State University, contended, is not only about the attainment of excellence but an 'economic necessity.' Billed as a 'special feature,' McPhee was participating on 'a unique panel' of

'African Americans currently serving as president of a predominantly white public university.' Further, in her opening remarks on day two of the conference, Belinda Biscoe, an African American and assistant vice-president of Outreach, University of Oklahoma, made the point, 'Who teaches matters ... the student population is changing but the faculty remains the same.' Students, she said, need 'role models' (2007).

The argument for diversity among faculty has long been discussed by the presidents of American universities. In fact, in his 1996 report, 'Diversity and Learning,' Neil L. Rudenstine, president of Harvard University (1991–2001), wrote about the need to change the status quo in terms of faculty members. Drawing on the writings of John Stuart Mill, John Newman, and Charles Eliot (former president of Harvard University), Rudenstine argued that the diversity and related differences of individuals within university is 'integral to true learning at a profound level. They are not dispensable. They shape some of the fundamental ways in which knowledge itself is generated, tested and transformed into understanding' (4). Rudenstine maintains that 'it is not enough, moreover, for a person to read about or 'be taught' the opinions of others on a given subject,' for as Mill also asserts, 'to do justice to the opinions and arguments of others we must have contact with them, interact with them, hear from them, listen to them articulate and defend that which they believe in earnest' (4).

More recently (Autumn 2004), the president Don Randel, and provost Richard Saller, of the University of Chicago, wrote to their 'Colleagues and Friends' (2004) of the 'initiatives' at that university that were aimed at having 'a more diverse community.' In their letter, the president and provost 'reaffirmed' their university's 'goal' and 'commitment to diversity' asserting that this commitment 'has profoundly shaped the course of research and education at the University throughout its history.' They recalled that their university was always open to 'women as well as men,' was 'accessible to Jews in the mid-twentieth century when other elite institutions practiced discrimination,' was the first in the United States to award a Black woman a doctorate, and one of the first 'major non-historically black universities' to grant tenure to a Black faculty member. But despite this 'proud tradition of inclusion' and some 50 per cent increase in the 'faculty of color' over the past two decades, the administrators pointed out that their university's 'most difficult challenge ... is to attract and retain those faculty at the forefront of research, a growing number of whom are faculty of color.' Randel and Saller continued:

To increase the diversity of our faculty along the dimensions of race, gender, ethnicity and national origin is more than just a moral good, though it is certainly that. It has a clear impact on research across a broad spectrum of disciplines from art history, music, literature and religion, through the social sciences to the biological sciences. Of course, it is not essential for a researcher to be a member in order to study the culture of a particular group or its social experiences. But it is an undeniable empirical fact that what a researcher takes to be a significant problem for investigation is deeply influenced by her or his experiences. A more diverse faculty and graduate student body will certainly expand the range of research undertaken at this University, and we all will be correspondingly intellectually enriched. (2004)

Moreover, as Randel and Saller recognized, 'Recruitment of underrepresented minority faculty will succeed in the competitive environment only if the President, Provost, Deans and Department Chairs together with their faculty display a serious commitment' to recruit and retain minority faculty members (University of Chicago 2004).

I have not experienced such discussions taking place among administrators at Canadian universities. Nevertheless, it is the case that, as in the United States and Britain,[1] our student population is quite diverse (particularly in urban universities), but we do not see that diversity reflected in the faculty. This point was made by Peter Cole, keynote speaker at a Canadian Association of University Teachers (CAUT) conference in Ottawa in 2003 that was aimed at engaging university association members in dialogue on issues of equity related to bargaining. Professor Cole, an Aboriginal scholar at the University of Victoria, British Columbia, emphasized that diversity is not merely about having different ethno-racial bodies of students and faculty members on campuses, but also about recognizing what they add to institutions. At the same conference, a panel presenter talked of the 'chilly climate' that exists on university campuses for 'equity seeking group' members making it difficult for them to fully participate in the institutions. Specifically, the perception of minority faculty members as 'token hires' and the related lack of respect and recognition of their knowledge and experiences in institutions continue to undermine the contributions that they are able to make toward truly 'diversifying' the institutions. And in a small group session in which the recruitment of minority faculty members was discussed, some participants agreed that there is a need for clear measures in collective agreements that address the barriers which 'equity seeking group' members face in their bid to access and retain positions at universities. But other participants suggested that 'things will correct themselves' because, as they have observed, there have been changes in the ethnic and racial composition of faculty members on today's university campuses. In challenging this claim, participants questioned whether these observed changes were indeed 'corrections' – in other words, 'the system correcting itself' – or a situation in which racialized faculty members are trying desperately to meet expectations by operating as best they can within the existing Eurocentric structure of institutions. Certainly, the present situation was not created by chance (see James 2003a; Mukherjee 2001); hence there is a need for purposeful measures to ensure systemic changes that will facilitate equitable access, inclusion, and treatment of minority scholars, and accept the knowledge, ways of knowing, voices, and epistemologies that everyone brings to the teaching, learning, and research that take place in universities.

In this chapter, I reference the literature pertaining to the situation of minority scholars, as well as my shared acquaintance of the issues and problems evidenced, in part, through my experience working in the area of affirmative action, participating in a number of local and national university committees and fora, and communicating with colleagues at other universities on issues pertaining to affirmative action/employment equity.[2] I discuss how the culture of the Ivory Tower, the recruitment and appointment processes, and the treatment of racial minority faculty members are impediments to the racial diversification of Canadian universities. The structures and practices of universities, informed by Western European middle-class, patriarchal ethics and traditions in combination with the state's discourse of multiculturalism – with its notions of cultural democracy, freedom, racelessness, and colourblindness – contribute to a false sense of neutrality, fairness, objectivity, and 'public good'[3] (Brayboy 2003; Henry and Tator 1994, 2007; James 2003b; Morrison 2000; Mukherjee 2001; Spafford et al. 2006). As such, the values, norms, and principles by which universities operate help to maintain a homogeneity which, as Randel and Saller (2004) rightly observe, 'perpetuates unchallenged assumptions – the very antithesis of what the University stands for.' In such a context, identifications such as race and ethnicity operate in systemic ways to enable or limit access to university faculty positions, the determination of 'qualification,' and the retention and promotion of faculty members. Indeed, as Henry and Tator (1994, 86) write, 'the university has generally used the same approach as the other liberal institutions by initiating conservative actions which do little to change the status quo.'

But while a number of Canadian universities have affirmative action or employment equity programs (no doubt influenced by the Federal Contractors Program), and in their job advertisement explicitly encourage 'designated group' members – women, Aboriginal peoples, visible/racial and sexual minorities, people with disabilities – to apply for positions asking that they self-identity, it is still the case that the representation of racial minority faculty members remains quite low on university campuses (see Alfred 2007; Henry and Tator 2007; Luther, Whitmore, and Moreau 2003a; Nakhaie 2004; Spafford et al. 2006). Reversing this situation requires addressing the interrelated structural and individual factors such as the seeming ambivalence (sometimes reluctance) of candidates to self-identify, the ways in which the cultural norms and values of the institution and disciplines influence the expectations and treatment of candidates in the interview process, the tendency to make appointments based on the perceived capacity of the candidate to 'fit' into the existing culture of the faculty, and the assumed relationship that is made between particular scholarship and minority status of candidates.[4]

If these structural and individual issues are to be addressed, then race and racial differences need to be acknowledged as salient to individuals' experiences and knowledge. Doing so means disrupting the existing claims and related practices of colour-blindness, individualism, neutrality, social justice, objectivity, meritocracy, and academic freedom that contribute to an 'institutional culture of denial' that fosters 'apathy and resistance' to equity programs and practices (Law, Phillips, and Turney 2004a, 96; see also Spafford et al. 2006). The challenge, therefore, for universities is to come to terms with the disruptions that 'special measures' – in terms of recruiting, retention, and promotion – signal. The challenge also is to ensure equitable and respectful treatment of racial minority faculty members, whereby they are not mere bodies 'representing' the various racial groups that exist in our society, but recognized as offering colleagues and students new, additional, enriched, and alternative insights, knowledge, and pedagogical approaches based on their scholarship and experiences.

I understand diversity to be differences among people, based on such things as race, ethnicity, skin colour, gender, social class, sexuality, and religion, and that these interrelated characteristics inform the experiences and perspectives that individuals bring to their lives, their scholarship, and interactions. Recognition of difference is necessary if institutions are to operate on principles of equity. By equity, I mean ensuring that minorities' access to and presence in university are not merely based on increasing their numbers but on the fact that their scholarship and contributions are recognized as a legitimate part of the university. This understanding of equity also takes into account the historical and contemporary conditions that have operated to affect their participation in the institution. Contrary to the argument put forth by Michaels (2006) that our concern should be about class and economic inequality and not race, I take the position that class and race are not inseparable – racism, classism, sexism, and the other 'isms' and phobias operate to maintain the inequities in society. Indeed, enough evidence exists to show that race and ethnicity, as well as gender and other factors, combine to determine the earnings and economic situation of racial minorities in Western societies. For instance, Pendakur and Pendakur (*Toronto Star* 2007) found that despite being born and educated in Canada, racial minorities still earn less than White Canadians.[5]

To fully understand the economic disparities between minority groups and Whites, one has to take into account historical context. While history can and does function as a 'distraction from the present injustices' and serve to perpetuate them (Michaels 2006, 18), it is able to do so because the structural factors that have maintained the inequities have been misrepresented, unaddressed, and/or denied. A case in point is one in which employers, as Michaels references within the context of the liberal multicultural discourse, seem more willing to recognize or 'celebrate' cultural events in terms of ethnic, religious, and/or national origin rather than providing the merited earnings or economic benefits. This pretence at being inclusive of difference is unlikely to produce equitable social and economic outcomes in the context of unchanged and unaffected racist, classist, and sexist structures; hence the status quo remains. Even so, it is incongruous to conclude, as Michaels does, that identity is 'the least important thing about us' (19). For while there is no scientific basis to race, people still do relate to racial categories as 'if they were fixed and natural. [And while] social scientists now tend to talk more about ethnicity and culture than race, assumptions that once related to concepts of race often continue to proliferate and structure understandings of self and other' (Law, Phillips, and Turney 2004a, 95). Furthermore, as Halperin (1995, 98) declares, identity constructions 'are very real. People live by them, after all – and nowadays, increasingly, they die from them. You can't get more real than that.'

Following Stanley (2006), I reference critical race theory (CRT) as a means by which to critically examine how the liberal ideology that underpins the taken-for-granted notions of colour-blindness, equality of opportunity, merit, and accommodation of minority members in fact 'reflect[s], create[s] and perpetuate[s] institutional racial power' (Roithmayr 1999, 2). CRT also exposes how the myths of meritocracy, in advocating race-neutrality and colour-blindness, continue to justify the exclusion of racial minorities from full participation in society and their access to its institutions. Indeed, colour-blindness does not make sense in a society where race operates historically to affect the different ways in which people get treated (Aylward 1999; Henry and Tator 2007; Stovall 2006; Yosso 2005). Taylor (1998, 123) points out that 'the danger of color blindness is that it allows us to ignore the racial construction of whiteness and reinforces its privileged and oppressive position.'

In positioning the experiences of racial minorities at its centre, CRT names and discusses 'the pervasive, daily reality of racism in society which serves to disadvantage people of color' (Stovall 2006, 244):

> Racism, like capitalism, is an accepted structural phenomenon centered in maintaining the status quo. It is not, and never has been, the result of individual bigotry it is often reduced to. Instead of race as a category, racism (i.e., White supremacy) should be understood as a set of systemic structures that maintain a racial ruling elite as demonstrated through enforcement of policies and laws that govern the land. (250)

Furthermore, as Taylor (1998, 122) points out, White superiority is 'so ingrained in the political and legal structures that they are often unrecognizable.' So too are racist acts which often are wrongly interpreted as isolated instances of bigotry, rather than reflections of larger structural and institutional patterns of White hegemony. As such, the normalization of race-based practices in employment and education 'makes the racism that fuels it look ordinary and natural, to such a degree that oppression no longer seems like oppression to the perpetrators' (123). The point here is how institutional racism operates. It is embedded in the policies and discourses, the stereotypes and biases, the assumptions and practices that are rooted in the collective psyche of members of the institution. Rangasamy (2004) writes that 'institutional racism is not the proverbial grit in the machine that conventional programmes of race awareness training can remove. Rather, it is organic in nature and functions and grows in cunning and resilience with each challenge it successfully overcomes' (28).

CRT provides a useful and important lens through which to examine how race and racism operate individually, institutionally, and structurally to affect the varied experiences (which, of course, are not uniform) and treatment of racial minority faculty members in Canadian universities. It questions the belief in the meritocratic and culturally neutral claims of universities, indicating that these socially constructed concepts that have operated to benefit the majority White members of society must be challenged in an effort to bring about institutional changes (Stanley 2006). These changes will, in part, come about through race consciousness (as opposed to race-neutrality or colour-blindness) and genuine commitment to the recruitment, appointment, and retention of racial minority faculty. In this regard knowing about the power-laden cultural construction of universities is necessary.

The 'Ivory Tower' Culture

In his essay, 'Ivory Towers? The Academy and Racism,' Les Back (2004) observes that 'there is a deep resistance in the academy to reckon with – what might be called the sheer weight of whiteness. These are the value-ridden maxims that govern seemingly neutral ideas like academic freedom, objectivity and fairness' (1). Therefore, to insist that through these value-ridden maxims, universities remain neutral, non-judgmental, accessible, and tolerant of differences[6] requires, as Morrison (2000) contends, 'a sensitivity and alertness so intense it can descend to the absurd when not merely distracting' (2). The fact is, universities function on the basis of White-norm culture which sustains a discourse characterized by subtle ambiguities and murkiness that is most powerful in its 'embodiment of the normal' (hooks 1992, 169). This discourse is evident in the claims by institutions that the predominance of White faculty is unintentional – it is just that universities, as the rationalization goes, are not able to recruit qualified minority members, for it goes without saying that all 'qualified' individuals can apply and will be appointed. It is farcical that this constructed notion of 'racial *unintentionality*' (emphasis in original, Bérubé 2001) remains and will persist as long as individuals continue to believe that minority members 'are always welcome even though they are not there' (252). In such a context then, the 'Whiteness' of the institution does not have to be examined because it is unintentional.

Whiteness is not simply an individual's identity that is lived, learned, relearned, contested, and struggled-over, but it is embedded in the institutional structure, thereby benefiting those with related social and cultural capital (Henry and Tator 2007; James 2007; Leonardo 2004; Levine-Rasky 2000; Spafford et al. 2006; Steinberg 2005). The story of a student as told by Audrey Thompson (2003) serves as a good reference here. Not only does it indicate how White students are socialized into the 'White' values and ways of the institution but also how it can operate in their favour. Thompson writes that the student 'who displayed a sophisticated intellectual understanding of whiteness theory ... prided herself on her intellectual antiracism and counted herself as a friend of people of color.' But as the student admitted, if her anti-racism activities translated into her being 'a race traitor' and would 'jeopardize her chances of being a professor, she could not do it ... she planned to play the academic game the white way' (16).

Evidently, the constructed culture of Whiteness is mediated by factors related to ethnicity, religion, gender, class, sexuality, and others. Rangasamy (2004) spells this out:

> Universities have evolved over several centuries on the basis of assumptions that heterosexual, white men from the economically and socially privileged classes were naturally endowed for university education. Consequently, the socio-economic and cultural values that govern the operational mode and management of universities, particularly the older ones, are derived from those social groupings. (32)

Moreover, the constructed Whiteness of universities is not merely about race but also about a constructed Europeanness and related Christian religious beliefs and practices, which are particularly evident at convocations. Indeed, as Toni Morrison points out, 'higher education is unabashedly theological and conscientiously value-ridden and value-seeking' (2000, 1). And in so far as particular individuals are perceived to represent the values and practices consistent with the culture of the university, those who do not are thought of as not belonging or 'out of place' and marked as trespassers whose presence will lead to a disruption of the historically and politically circumscribed understanding of the space as open and neutral (Purwar 2004, 51). That is why a big deal was made of the appointment of Mamdouh Shoukri as the new president of York University. The media made a point of telling us of his Egyptian background and that 'he will be the first Muslim appointed as head of a Canadian university' (*Toronto Star* 2007). Years earlier, in 2005, similar references were made to Indira Samarasekera's immigrant background when she was appointed president of the University of Alberta. One report notes: 'She is the first president of visible minority, growing up in Colombo, Sri Lanka (then Ceylon), as part of a large Tamil family' (Sinnema 2005).[7]

It is significant that in 2005 and 2007, both Samarasekera and Shoukri were reported to be 'firsts.' So during the closing years of the twentieth century when minorities were calling for diversification of university faculty, and while some universities (including York University) had supposedly put in place affirmative/employment equity action policies, these policies seem not to have applied to the upper level positions of Canadian universities. In fact, as Nakhaie (2004) demonstrates, while the student population at Canadian universities is becoming more diverse (mirroring the increasing diversity of the Canadian population), racial minorities are still vastly under-represented among university administrators. Analysing the ethno-racial distribution of university administrators between 1951 and 2001, Nakhaie noted that administrators (presidents, vice-presidents, and deans) are still predominantly of British origin. 'The decline in their share as university administrators was lower than their decline in the general population' (98). While there was a significant increase in the representation of administrators of non-British origins, French and especially non-European administrators remain significantly under-represented. In 2001, university presidents of British origin were 76.8 per cent, vice-presidents 69.9 per cent, and deans 61.5 per cent, compared to 4.5, 4.6, and 7.6 per cent for those of non-European descent. Nakhaie concludes that his findings point to evidence of 'blocked ethnic mobility' suggesting that 'ethnicity is a significant impediment to achieving top positions at institutions of higher education' (102). It seems, then, that university administrators of British origin have enjoyed the ride provided by 'glass escalators' while individuals of other origins often come upon 'glass ceilings' in their rise within the university structure.[8]

Individuals' access to and experiences in faculty positions is connected to Whiteness as a racialized identity/identification and its function in relation to ethnocentrism as part of racism (Law, Phillips, and Turney 2004a; Henry and Tator 2007). It is racism that accounts for the glass ceiling and the 'glass cliff' – the 'risky or precarious' positions (Ryan and Haslam 2005) – in which minorities find themselves in universities. Indeed, as Back (2004) acknowledges, 'racism has damaged reason, damaged academic and civic freedoms and damaged the project of education itself' (5). And as Rangasamy (2004) writes with reference to his experiences in universities in Britain, in addition to helping to create 'a comfort zone' for institution members, racism 'helps to preserve and safeguard the emotional, [intellectual], moral, political and other investments of the dominant sector for the dominant sector' (33). Further, according to Lensmire (2007), referring to his U.S. context, 'As white people, we need stereotypes of people of color to give us some relief from the guilt of participating in and benefiting from a society that at every moment betrays a founding principle – that all people are created equal' (15). This wilful ignorance of the institutional and structural character of racism, Lensmire says, functions to preserve White privilege, colour-blindness, and ambivalence about race in the face of the 'massive inequality that exists all around us' (20), contributing to 'dilemmas and conflict' that remain at the core of White racial identities, thus protecting the 'white self from any chance of being implicated in racism' (21).

Writing about this desire not to be implicated in racism, Back (2004) contends:

> The temptation to present the persona of an exceptional 'alright white person' ... is another version of a political masquerade where bad white academics can be denounced roundly by those adopting the comfortable position of exception-to-the-rule. There is something deeply disingenuous about this move because it forecloses critical reflection rather than opening it up ... 'Alright Whites' can castigate new white colleagues for their complicity in benefiting from exclusionary employment practices without ever questioning the status of their own tenure. The logic is that 'racism couldn't have been applicable to me and my employment fortunes because I am an exception – I am an alright white person!' Delusions of this kind give false comfort and they are vulnerable to attack from anyone who pays close attention. (5)

Indeed, as Back concludes, 'education and sophistication produce no immunity from racism and white supremacy' (6). Nevertheless, many in the university community continue to operate as if they can avoid being implicated in racism.

This avoidance is reflected in the tendency of researchers to conflate race and ethnicity and/or not name race as a demographic variable about which to collect data. Even in the twenty-first century, Canadian sociologists and other social scientists will gather data by gender, age, ethnicity, language, place of birth, and citizenship/immigrant status but not race. If these demographic factors inform the experiences and lives of Canadians, is it not the same for race? The recent issue (Feb. 2007) of the *Journal of Higher Education: Academic Matters* is illustrative. The lead article of the journal reports on how women are doing in university after forty years of feminism. But the authors, Drakich and Stewart, were unable to provide information of minority women.[9] Conscious of this limitation, the authors write: 'We are acutely aware of the absence of race, class, disability and ethnicity in this article. To speak of gender in the 21st century is an anachronism perpetuated by the failure of universities and Statistics Canada to collect these data for faculty and students. The only window available on diversity in universities is the limited data in the Canadian census' (2007, 9). The other authors in the journal whose analyses were based on their own research data make no mention of the diverse experiences of women in today's universities. The various research respondents were presented homogeneously, simply as women, leaving one to assume that in the 'gendered' and 'feminized' experiences and expectations that the researchers talk about, the situation of Black, South Asian, or Asian women are represented (see Acker 2007; Dillabough 2007; Webber 2007). Similarly in their article on masculinity, Kaufman and Laker (2007) speak to and about men as if they are homogeneous. They write that there is a need to 'support and encourage the creation of spaces for young men to gain awareness and to learn to challenge both their unacknowledged fears and the extant privileges of males … [and] become active in issues promoting gender equity, challenging homophobia, and … men's violence against women' (17).

Of the eight journal articles, race was only taken up in the reflections of the minority contributors, Clarke (2007) and Alfred (2007), as well as in that of anti-racism scholars Henry and Tator (2007). In their discussion of 'enduring racism in the university campus,' Henry and Tator assert that 'academics of colour as well as Aboriginal faculty believe that institutions of higher learning remain a zone of whiteness – which reflect the dominance of white Eurocentric values and exclusions' (24). This idea of a 'white zone' and its endurance was demonstrated to me recently (December 2006) when I was invited to comment on a document that was developed by a group of female colleagues to investigate the situation of women in universities. In the colour-blind tradition, there was no mention of minority women or any attempts through the questionnaire to solicit information that would tell about the particular situation of minority women. Quite revealing was the fact that in an organization that claimed to recognize diversity among faculty members and to be operating on principles of equity, the document got passed by two committees (both of which were populated by all White members). It seems, then, that it is only with minority academics and conscious White researchers that race as a demographic variable will get incorporated into 'mainstream' research or investigations. Its absence from these investigations sends a signal and reinforces the myth that race has no bearing on the experiences of individuals – especially those working in 'race neutral' university environments. And this idea of being race neutral or colour-blind makes it difficult for all concerned to work toward recruitment and appointment processes that would produce the sought-after diversity.

Who Gets Hired? The Recruitment, Application, Interview, and Appointment Processes

In most instances, job advertisements for universities will say something like the following, taken from two universities websites:

> The [University] is strongly committed to diversity within its community and especially welcomes applications from visible minority group members, women, Aboriginal persons, persons with disabilities, members of sexual minority groups, and others who may contribute to the further diversification of ideas.

> [The University] is committed to equity in its academic policies, practices, and programs; supports diversity in its teaching, learning, and work environments; and ensures that applications from members of traditionally marginalized groups are seriously considered under its employment equity policy. Those who would contribute to the further diversification of our faculty and its scholarship include, but are not limited to, women, Aboriginal peoples, persons with disabilities, members of visible minorities, and members of sexual minority groups. The [University] invites you to apply to our welcoming community and to self-identify as a member of one of these groups ... To ensure that you are considered within the priorities of the Employment Equity Program, you may *self-identity* in your letter of application or in a separate letter to the [Employment Equity Office]. (emphasis added)

On the basis of advertisements such as these, one would assume that universities would be advertising in places where 'visible minority group members, women, Aboriginal persons, and members of traditionally marginalized' groups would easily gain access to the career opportunities presented. This would mean placing advertisements in a diversity of sources as well as traditional sources. And, in addition to conducting interviews at conferences – knowing that not all potential candidates might have the funding or resources to attend the conferences – universities should have alternative means of reaching 'members of traditionally marginalized groups.' If indeed universities are committed to equity and diversity, then attempts should be made to ensure a diversity of recruitment measures – something that appointment committees and/or equity officers and committees should ensure happens. In this regard, individuals involved in the recruitment process cannot afford to be colour-blind, and must be committed to ensuring that advertisements reach individuals of a range of communities – particularly members of communities who are absent from the faculty. This would mean disaggregating the 'visible minority' group/category, thus taking into account the particularities of the respective racial minority groups. It also means explicitly acknowledging and talking about the identities of faculty members, noting who should be recruited in order to have a diverse faculty – one that not merely reflects the student population but also, and importantly, represents different perspectives.

However, my experience has been that faculty and appointment committee members tend not to talk about the racial composition of their faculty and whom they might try to recruit in order to have a more diverse faculty. This failure to explicitly talk about race or the identities of faculty members is related to the notion that to raise questions of race or identity is to be prejudiced or backward. But isn't prejudice one factor that accounts for the homogeneity in faculty membership (Henry and Tator 2007; Spafford et al. 2006)? How else do we explain the fact that racial minority members today hold expertise in most disciplinary university programs, yet in many cases university faculties remain largely White and male? And how else can we explain cases in which members of 'traditionally marginalized groups' are perceived to be likely candidates only when faculty positions 'apply to them' – say, for example, positions in race and ethnicity in the social sciences (see Henry and Tator 2007)? Indeed, as Clarke (2007) maintains, there need to be better strategies when it comes to 'diversifying the pools and short-lists of candidates. Visible minorities must be considered *seriously* for teaching "mainstream" Canadian literature as well as British canon, from Beowulf to Pinter. White privilege, in these areas and others, must end. The ivory tower must become a prism' (emphasis in original, 19).

It seems appropriate and inoffensive to expect that members of 'traditionally marginalized groups' would self-identify in order to participate in the employment equity/affirmative action programs of universities. In fact, one might think that such applicants would willingly or enthusiastically self-identify in order to at least get the chance of an interview. But in many cases minority applicants are refusing to self-identify. The implication is that appointment committees and 'equity' officers claim that they have no way of ensuring diversity among the shortlisted candidates. Hence, the question: Why are minority candidates not self-identifying? One likely reason is distrust and uncertainty about how the self-identity information will be used.[10] The perception is that, while universities suggest they have a 'strong commitment to diversity' and 'equity' and would 'seriously' consider 'applications from members of traditionally marginalized groups,' marginalized group members do not have confidence that this will happen; and why should they when the culture of the institution remains White, Euro-centric, and male (Henry and Tator 2007; Law, Phillips, and Turney 2004b; Luther, Whitmore, and Moreau 2003a).

It is not only the culture of the university or faculty that influences the decision not to self-identify; it is also the culture of the discipline. That is, in some disciplines, members argue that identity is irrelevant; rather it is the scholarship and productivity of an individual (a rejection of the link between these factors). The idea is that it is on the basis of merit and not 'who they are' that applicants will attain the job. In such a context, applicants who call attention to their identity (in terms of race, ethnicity, gender, sexuality, etc.) would be perceived to be contravening the code of ethics in the discipline, even though the university has a policy that requires applicants to self-identify.

What about when candidates do not self-identify – what should be done? What if his/her name signals a particular ethno-racial identity? And what if you know the candidate to be a member of a 'designated group' – like someone who currently teaches in the faculty or is known to faculty members – do you treat the candidate as if she/he did self-identify? What if the candidate objects to being identified as a member of a 'designated group' because he/she expects to attain the position on the basis of merit? A noteworthy scenario is one in which the faculty, where there is very little diversity, sees the opportunity to hire a member of a 'designated group' who has similar credentials – a PhD, same years of teaching experience, and refereed journal publications – to the White candidate. If in such a case both are considered 'equally qualified,' how, in the absence of self-identification, should the committee decide on whom to recommend for appointment? Do you try to persuade the minority candidate to self-identify thus making it easy for the appointment committee? What if the candidate self-identified after she/he attended the interview, feeling convinced that identifying would not be a liability – that is, satisfied that there is a genuine commitment to diversity and equity – will the appointment committee or the faculty accept that? When in the appointment process is it inappropriate to accept self-identification – after the interview is completed, before the candidate arrives on campus? And is the candidate not a minority group member unless he/she identifies as such?[11] My experience has been that in situations in which these questions arise and in which faculty members are uncertain of what to do, there is a tendency to resort to a rigid interpretation of the employment equity/affirmative action policy.

While it is true that candidates are assessed on their scholarship, given human relations, it is fair to suggest that they are also observed, viewed, or judged during the interviews, colloquium, luncheon, dinner and/ or reception[12] in terms of their cultural capital and capacity to 'fit' into the existing culture of the faculty. As Luther, Whitmore, and Moreau (2003a) stated, universities perform a 'gate-keeping' role permitting 'entry only to those who are most likely to fit within and help reproduce its established culture and traditions' (29). An example of how this cultural reproduction takes place is illustrated in Razack's (2003) essay on 'racialized immigrant women as Native Informants in the academy.' She recalls a colleague's support for the appointment of a particular minority candidate on the basis of the candidate's bravery. 'She was brave,' Razack writes, 'because, as part of her work on the Middle East, she had written against Islam' (62). One interpretation of the appeal of this candidate is that, not only did she fit into the culture of the faculty, she also represented the views of the collegium, hence would become an effective 'Native Informant' – a role (as anthropologists) that minorities are expected to play in representing the academy to, and working with, those considered different. In this regard, as Razack's experience on hiring committees has shown, 'you can't be a proper Native Informant if you embody a stereotype that is threatening' (61).

In addition to the deliberations of appointment committees, in some universities, there are employment equity/affirmative action program personnel and committees that are responsible for monitoring and/or reviewing the appointment process to ensure fairness and equity. But after years of having such programs in place, there is no evidence that minorities are gaining positions in universities in larger numbers. In part, this is because of the seeming apathy or ambivalence in institutional commitment (from presidents to deans to faculty members) to the recruitment of minority faculty members, and concomitantly, that of minority graduate students who are important to the process of diversification (see Mahtani 2006). It is important, therefore, to examine the structures and mechanisms that are in place to facilitate faculty diversification. As such, we need to examine the role of the employment equity/affirmative action personnel such as the director and equity committee members, noting the extent to which their authority enables them to influence the appointment process. Evidently, where they are positioned within the organizational hierarchy informs their authority and power to influence things.[13] Due to the lack of (or limited) education about and ambivalence toward faculty diversification, it is not surprising that those involved in diversity and equity activities tend to be marginalized.

A further issue pertaining to the hiring process is the failure (as I have already mentioned) to explicitly discuss the demographic make-up of the faculty. While the gender breakdown of faculty members in most institutions is reported and discussed, there is silence on matters of race. How then will universities know that they are making progress with the composition of the faculty unless they take a count?[14] The reason often given for not disclosing racial composition has to do with confidentiality and the fact that some minority group members do not wish to publicly identify themselves but will do so if the information remains confidential. Indeed, in some faculties the small number of minority members makes it easy to identify them in any publication. But, regardless of the theory or politics of it, aren't some individuals 'obvious' by their skin colour or raced on the basis of skin colour (see Hunter 2005)? Granted, skin colour does not necessarily signify race or racial identification, but despite the liberal notion and pretence of colour-blindness, skin colour continues to operate in institutions and society to inform our perceptions, attitudes, and behaviours toward each other. And when we consider that in many cases the individuals involved in diversity and equity activities tend to be members of 'designated groups,' their marginalization, junior positions (such as assistant and associate professors), small numbers, and recent membership, coupled with the perception of them as having a biased agenda (see Razack 2003; Spafford et al. 2006), mean that they are unlikely to be able to influence the hiring process that will produce the changes needed to increase diversity among faculty members. One tenured racial minority faculty member who was nearing retirement once commented that even if s/he knew that racism or sexism played a part in the hiring process, s/he would 'never say it openly' because s/he did not 'want to alienate the people [with] whom I have to work ... The silent majority exercises its power very effectively. They have to work so little to keep things going the way they are. Those of us who want to change it, have to work so much harder' (cited in Spafford et al. 2006, 16).

Despite the issues, problems, and ambivalences, the fact remains that minority members do want to be part of the academy, not only because it is their right to be there, but because they also recognize that through their research, teaching, and service to the university, they will be able to address issues related to their communities (Luther, Whitmore, and Moreau 2003; Stanley 2006). Stanley reveals that faculty of colour endeavoured to use their service activities – including '(a) mentoring students of color, (b) serving on university and national recruitment and retention committees focusing on diversity, (c) helping local communities in their educational efforts, (d) mentoring faculty of color, and (e) educating majority White faculty, administrators, students, and staff about diversity' – to contribute to the development of their communities (including their campus community) and create avenues from which to build their research agenda (719). But the experiences of minority members in universities often make it difficult for them to pursue or realize their ambitions.

Experiences of Minority Faculty

In writing about the treatment and experiences of 'faculty of color' in predominantly White colleges and universities in the United States, Stanley (2006) sought to break the 'silence' and give voice to these members for whom the 'silenced state is a burdensome cycle that is rarely broken' (710).[15] In examining issues related to tenure and promotion, teaching, access to mentors, collegial relationships, and the service expected of them, Stanley tells of how racism operated in their experiences, particularly in ways that position the experiences of Whites as normative, and the standard by which faculty of colour were evaluated. It was found that many faculty of colour perceived that higher expectations were held of them, they were not acknowledged when they made efforts to respond to what was required of them, and as such they had 'to prove and "overprove" their presence and worth in the academy' to their White colleagues (715).

The most dominant theme in the minority faculty members' narratives was the challenges they experienced in their teaching. This was particularly evident in the questions students raised in their course evaluations pertaining to the 'authority and credibility' of minority faculty (Stanley, 709; see also Mukherjee 2001; Scott 2003). Stanley also writes: 'Excerpts from these narratives illustrate that race matters in the classroom. Many faculty of color perceive that students treat them differently than they treat their White colleagues' (711). In terms of the service activities, Stanley mentions that faculty of colour

> are often at a crossroads: On the one hand, they are recruited to diversify the faculty and further the university's diversity agenda (because of perceived or real expertise), and, on the other hand, they often engage in these activities only to be told that they are of little value in merit and personnel decisions. Participation in service activities remains a critical area to which many faculty of color fall prey, and it is often a component that costs them greatly when they are being evaluated for promotion or tenure. (Stanley 2006, 721; see also Essed 2000)

One of the most notable and reported cases pertaining to the experiences of a minority faculty member is that of Cornel West at Harvard University. The president, Lawrence Summers, who succeeded Rudenstine (who wrote about the need for diversity initiatives – see Rudenstine 1996), questioned West's 'scholarly' work and his political activities (at the time West was an advisor to Bill Bradley who was running for president). At issue was the fact that West's newly published hip-hop CD, *Sketches of My Culture,* was thought to be 'an embarrassment' and not commensurate with his position at the university (Cowan 2004). So despite an exemplary scholarly record – having authored or edited over twenty books in his career and having had published over forty-nine articles in academic journals in the previous five years[16] – West's attempt to make his work accessible to a large community of people brought him disrespect and criticism, which reflects the fact that, as Cowan concludes, universities are

> locked in the elitist premise that 'legitimate' scholarship is that read by those within one's respective field rather than by the masses. This is the crux of what Summers was getting at when he urged West to write a book more likely to be reviewed in scholarly journals than in newspapers. However, West's critics tend to overlook the fact that he pursues non-traditional scholarship, such as the CD, *alongside* acclaimed traditional scholarship. (emphasis in the original, 77–8)

Similar to the experiences of minorities in the United States (see Essed 2000; Stanley 2006), minority and Aboriginal faculty members in Canadian universities reported feeling 'tokenized,' ghettoized, watched, judged, and 'forced to meet and exceed expectations and standards that had been set by others.' As well, they are perceived to have expertise primarily in areas related to racial, cultural, and Aboriginal issues, and as such are limited in their 'intellectual interests, capabilities and energies'[17] (Luther, Whitmore, and Moreau 2003a, 24; see also Graveline 1994; Henry 2006; Mahtani 2006; Spafford et al. 2006). Henry and Tator (2007) report that there are inordinate demands placed on faculty of colour, for instance, minority students wishing to have them as mentors and role models, the broader student population seeking their expertise, their colleagues asking them to speak on issues of diversity and racism, and administrators needing their 'physical presence on committees to prove that the committee is representative' (25). Mahtani (2006) found that minority female faculty members were expected 'to take on gargantuan tasks simply because they were seen as being a '"two-fer" – both a woman and a woman of colour' and this contributed to their isolation, exhaustion, and the decision by some to leave the institution (23). Minority members who stay, as Henry (2006) found at one Ontario university, are faced with an 'inhospitable' climate and resentment from other faculty members that contribute to feelings of self-doubt as to whether their appointments were based on their qualification or identity, as in 'equity hires' or 'token hires.'

In response to perceptions of them as 'equity' or 'token hires,' some minority faculty members worked hard to prove that they belong in the institution, and in doing so avert possible marginalization and isolation. Therefore, aware of the potential backlash against actual or perceived affirmative action or employment equity hires, one racial minority participant in a study conducted by Spafford and colleagues (2006) commented:

> I feel I should do well – extremely well, so that nobody will say ... 'It's because of her colour she is sitting there.' I really don't want that to happen, so I work very hard. I always have that drive to feel that I have to do much better, or as good or much better than others, to be seen as worthy of the position that I am in and to be seen as contributing equally as the others. (cited in Spafford et al. 2006, 8)

Some minority members manage such racialization by denying that race has something to do with their employment; others claimed that it was a matter of 'personal choice' (Spafford et al. 2006).

The experiences and narratives of minority scholars can be characterized by ambivalence, conflicts, contradictions, and denial (Dlamini 2002; James 2001; Mahtani 2006; Spafford et al. 2006), as well as 'self-doubt, apprehension, frustration, and disappointment' (Henry and Tator 2007, 25). Some of these issues are evident in the essays by Clarke and Alfred. In his essay, 'Professing Blackness,' Clarke (2007) explains that 'academic critics fretted that my focus on black literature underlined my wasteful attention to woeful inferior works ... White authors were posited as the unimpeachable and objective interpreters of black history and culture' (19). Likewise, Alfred (2007) maintains that being an Aboriginal in the academy and

> accepting one's indigeneity means a constant fight to remain connected to our communities, to live our culture, and to defend our homelands all the while fulfilling our professional duties inside what is, essentially, a central institution of colonial domination ... Our experiences in universities reflect the tensions and dynamics of our relationships as Indigenous peoples interacting with people and institutions in society as a whole: an existence of constant and pervasive struggle to resist assimilation to the values and culture of the larger society ... Indigenous people in universities have for the most part proven unprepared mentally, emotionally, and physically to carry on the struggle of their nations inside academia. (22–3)

In their study of the 'experiences of inclusion and isolation among racially minoritized faculty in Canada,' Spafford and her colleagues (2006) found that most had 'experiences of *being a mentor* but not in *being mentored*' (emphasis in the original, 13).[18] And as a consequence of their scarce representation in their institutions, they felt an obligation 'to mentor and act as a role model to racially minoritized students' (13). One Aboriginal respondent stated: 'I think that there [were] ... four or five [Aboriginal academics] in Canada so I felt ... an interest and also a certain degree of responsibility to role model' (13). Their role modelling and mentorship activities combined with onerous committee work and teaching loads were at the expense of their research productivity. Yet, even as they experienced blatant discrimination, minority faculty members were careful about raising such issues. For instance, when 'a less qualified, White external candidate' was hired in a tenure-track position over a minority candidate who held a 'contingent position' in the department, nothing was said, because as the minority candidate reasoned, 'In these issues, discretion may be the better part of valour ... because I was still looking forward to future competition. I did not think it was tactically wise to come up strong about my observations of the recruitment process' (cited in Spafford et al. 2006, 17).

The experience of Dr. Kip-Yin Chun, a professor in the physics department at the University of Toronto, is particularly instructive. Hired as a research associate in 1985, his contract was terminated in December of 1994. However, in the intervening years, Dr. Chun applied to four tenure stream positions in that department but was unsuccessful even though he was widely published, internationally recognized for his scholarship, and had positive student evaluations and letters of recommendation. In three of the competitions, Dr. Chun was the only shortlisted racial minority candidate. In 1992, he was informed that the university would not approve any new contract applications, effectively setting in motion his termination. Dr. Chun's complaints to the university about unfair treatment, and later racism, resulted in an even more inhospitable environment in which he was excluded from faculty meetings and not given opportunities to teach as was expected. After an earlier agreement with the university had failed, a commission comprising Backhouse, Anderson, and Black was appointed by the Canadian Association of University Teachers (CAUT) in 2004 to investigate Chun's allegations of discrimination. In their report on the case, Backhouse and her colleagues concluded that the treatment of Dr. Chun was unfair and, in some aspects, racist. They claimed that it was likely that he could have won the job competitions but because of the 'set up ... he could not win' (2006, 31). Dr. Chun eventually left the university.

In concluding their study on the experiences of minority faculty

members, Stafford et al. (2006) noted that they coped in academic institutions by

> over-performing in order to compete with their White colleagues, mini-
> mizing racially-based aspects of their negative experiences, and less often
> because of the risks involved, confronting their colleagues and superiors
> about racially intolerant or insensitive behaviours ... By necessity, [they]
> often chose a 'don't rock the boat' approach, even when seeking to act as
> social change agents ... They struggled with their visibility in that they
> were frequently invited to participate on committees as a 'representative'
> of a marginalized group but the time commitment and lack of recognition
> often became problematic.' (18)

In some instances, minority faculty members experience colleagues
who, as Minami (1995) found, 'are at least as biased, envious, petty
and pusillanimous as your everyday Six-Pack Joe.' In a tenure situation they are influenced by a combination of intelligence and arrogance
that allows them to 'murder tenure candidates with daggers instead of
machetes' (360). He continues to say:

> Although we tend to idealize universities as centers of enlightenment, the
> level of racism and fierce politicking is numbing. Thus, candidates who
> do not socialize with other professors, who have many interests outside
> the university, who study subjects not considered significant or not well
> understood by their colleagues, and who do not play the game of courting
> favor with those in power in their department may find themselves out
> of a job at tenure time. Moreover, departments dominated by white males
> usually select for tenure those like themselves, i.e., other white males.
> There is good reason why universities are called 'Ivory Towers.' (361)

Conclusion

In so far as the culture of the Ivory Tower, structured on White Eurocentric values and mores, remains 'invisible' to those within it, and while
individuals – especially those with the power central to its construction
– remain convinced of its neutrality, universalism, openness, fairness,
objectivity, racelessness, colour-blindness, and public good, then it is
unlikely that racial diversity will result. In such a context, the claims
that the under-representation of racial minorities on university campuses is a product of institutional racism and discrimination, and the

resulting 'inhospitable' or 'chilly' climate that exists there, will continue to be contested (Graveline 1994; Henry and Tator 2007; Law, Phillips, and Turney 2004b; Luther, Whitmore, and Moreau 2003; Mahtani 2006; Nakhaie 2004; Spafford et al. 2006; Stanley 2006; Thompson and Louque 2005). Instead, the under-representation of minority faculty will be rationalized in terms of them 'not having "acceptable" credentials, "not making an effort," being a "poor fit," or being "unable to adapt" to the institution' (Nakhaie 2004, 104). Paradoxically, under these conditions, the presence of the few minorities in the academy will indirectly function to reify the status quo and maintain the marginalization of minority faculty and diversity issues (Brayboy 2003, 73).

The fact is, implemented within the existing institutional structure, diversity and equity programs seem to be a useful public relations exercise (especially when we consider that institutions are largely publicly funded). For not only are the few bodies of minority faculty seen as representing the 'implementation' of diversity, they are expected to offer new courses related to 'diversity' in terms of race, indigeneity, ethnicity, multiculturalism, religion/faith, and globalization; help to recruit other minority faculty; participate in committees to show diverse representation; work with and/or supervise minority students or students interested in Aboriginal or race-related issues; serve as mentors and role models; 'offer helpful suggestions on how institutions can be more user-friendly to minority students' and communities; and help 'to assuage white guilt' (Brayboy 2003, 73). Furthermore, in the White-normed context, White professors can continue to be 'good' teachers, researchers, and scholars and avoid the extra and contentious demanding work with minority students and communities (Brayboy 2003). Unfortunately, minority students tend to be oblivious to the expectations and extra work of minority faculty members, who as a consequence are likely to be perceived as unsupportive of the intellectual and political needs and aspirations of minority students – a situation which is not helpful for minority faculty members and students in generally (see James 2001).

Brayboy (2003) refers to the situation as 'unnatural' in which minority faculty members find themselves, because working with students, teaching large classes, serving on committees, and publishing 'at the rate expected to be retained, promoted, and tenured[19] ... raise questions about the abilities of faculty of color to participate in the culture of [universities]; a somewhat favorable situation can quickly become a closed situation if faculty of color are unable to do all that is being asked of them and not achieve tenure' (77). Hence, if universities are to become congenial spaces for minority faculty, then it requires the commitment of all faculty colleagues and staff, and importantly, the 'active, enlightened, and compassionate leadership' of administrators and union/association leaders, to promote, encourage, manage, and monitor the changes that are 'so urgently needed in the institutional culture and language' (Rangasamy 2004, 33).

The evidence, therefore, points to the fact that diversifying universities requires more than having 'free-standing' policies but also fundamental changes to the academic structure with its cultural assumptions, norms, values, and ethics that 'operate almost invisibly but leave their imprint' (Henry and Tator 2007, 24). As part of that structure, scholarly associations and academic journals (their editors, editorial boards, and reviewers) must also attend to how mechanisms such as racism, classism, sexism, xenophobia, and Islamophobia, which are encoded in their activities and decisions, operate to affect the intellectual life and academic careers of minority scholars. So, too, it is necessary for university support staff, with whom faculty members have much interaction (in many cases they are the ones with whom individuals first make contact with the university), to understand their need to be fair and respectful in their treatment of minority faculty. Ultimately, racially diversifying universities requires 'pursuing the kind of resolute and ongoing reckoning with whiteness. This is not a matter of an end point, or an achievement; rather it is an ongoing questioning that strives to step out of whiteness' brilliant shadow' (Back 2004, 5).

NOTES

For this chapter's epigraph, see D. Smith (1990, 204).

1 See, for example, Thompson and Louque (2005); and Law, Phillips, and Turney (2004b).
2 Critical race theorists maintain that the stories of racialized people can be used to challenge the existing normative discourse based on whiteness (Stanley 2006; Taylor 1998). As Taylor states: 'Stories can not only challenge the status quo, but they can help build consensus and create a shared, communal understanding. They can, at once, describe what is and what ought to be' (122).
3 Toni Morrison (2000) writes that 'the real or imagined search for "good-

ness" in some figuration is still part of the justifying, legitimizing language of the academy' (2).

4 For example, the assumption that a minority person is suited for a race and ethnic relations position in social science as opposed to a position in European history or philosophy.

5 According to Pendakur and Pendakur, as reported in the *Toronto Star* (2007), Black women earn 12 per cent less than their White counterparts, while Black men earn 16 per cent less. Chinese women earn substantially more than White women while Chinese men earn the same as White women. While the earnings gap for South Asian women was not as glaring as those for women from the Caribbean and/or Blacks, South Asians experienced earnings similar to those of Caribbean and Black men (*Toronto Star*, Saturday, June 2, 2007, p. ID7).

6 I think here of comments by the incoming president and the outgoing president of York University published in the summer (2007) issue of the university magazine, *Yorku*. The incoming president, Mamdouh Shoukri, was quoted by Burton Woodward as saying, 'York stands for accessibility, fairness and social justice, York stands for being part of the community' (4), and the outgoing president, Lorna Marsden, writes, 'York is modern, secular, engaged and concerned with social justice' (6).

7 As if to remind us of her 'unusual' name, the media also provided readers with a pronunciation guide (Sinnema 2005).

8 The terms are borrowed from Ryan and Haslam's (2005) discussion of the over-representation of women in 'precarious leadership positions' in corporations. They also make the point that in 'achieving more high-profile positions' women face 'additional, largely invisible, hurdles' in their workplaces (81). The same could be said of minorities in universities.

9 See Mahtani (2006), Mukherjee (2001), Luther, Whitmore, and Moreau (2003), and Spafford et al. (2006) for a discussion of minority women experiences.

10 Reporting on their research pertaining to the experiences of minority faculty members in Canadian universities, Luther, Whitmore, and Moreau (2003) noted that many of their respondents talked about their 'need to be vigilant of others, to be continually cautious about developing trust in either individuals or structures, to question the motives behind initiatives, and to look for possible hidden agendas' (28).

11 What about the case of a woman, would she be considered a member of a 'designated group' even though she did not self-identify? What is done with the gender information signalled by her name and the gender pronouns in her letters of recommendation? Are they to be ignored, or

can they be ignored even as we engage in discussions in which the same gender pronouns are employed in discussions of candidates? Resorting to a rigid interpretation of the policy, one person once said to me that 'a woman is not a woman unless she identifies as such.'

12 I have heard some faculty members object to these social events during the hiring process because of how they are used to evaluate candidates.

13 Some American universities have a vice-president who is responsible for diversity and outreach with the necessary staff and budget.

14 In an article that examines the representation of 'equity-seeking groups' in Canada, the United Kingdom, and the United States, the Canadian Association of University Teachers (CAUT) (2007) noted that 12.4 per cent of all university teachers 'self-identified as visible minorities in the 2001 Census, up slightly from 11.7 per cent in 1996' (1). It was pointed out that this figure was merely 0.3 per cent less than the percentage of 'visible minorities' 25 years and older in the 2001 workforce. The article concludes that the data on equity seeking groups in Canada has 'serious limitations.' It is unreliable and as such 'poses significant problems. It makes it difficult for policymakers, administrators and academic staff associations to grasp the full extent of the problem and, consequently, to develop the most effective tools to promote equity' (4). 'In contrast, the United Kingdom and the United States gather data at the institutional level, which allows for important equity performance comparisons between institutions' (4).

15 Such stories in powerful ways not only serve 'to challenge the dominant mindset of society – the shared stereotypes, beliefs, and understandings … [and] the status quo, [but] they can help build consensus and create a shared, communal understanding. They can, at once, describe what is and what ought to be' (Taylor 1998, 123).

16 Cowan (2004) raises the question: How then did the debate come to involve affirmative action and the perception that West was a 'second-rate' scholar and beneficiary of affirmative action?

17 For example, Henry (2006) mentions that a newly hired faculty member was 'cautioned by a colleague about not publishing too much in the areas of racism and anti-racism.' The message, as Henry points out, 'was that this is not a legitimate field of research and that it would not be taken seriously in terms of future promotion and tenure decision' (144).

18 One person stated that a mentor was not necessarily 'someone with whom he could racially identify but as someone who could facilitate his connection to the people with power in his profession.' The reality was that such persons were mostly White men who associated more with others similar to themselves (Spafford et al. 2006, 13).

19 Todd (2007), a journalist who recently spent six months in an internship at the University of British Columbia, reminds us that 'faculty tenure committees (which are made up of peers, not administrators) are not supposed to judge' faculty members 'only on their publications, but also on their teaching and public service.' The expectations and process make it difficult for faculty members to make needed contributions to the community/society as 'public intellectuals.' Todd continues to write, 'But I've been constantly told the unfortunate academic reality (for academics, students and the public) is that virtually all of one's academic worth is based on one's research and publications, often in obscure journals. Publish or perish is not an empty cliché. It's virtually the law in academia. And it's crushing many hard-working, devoted, up-and-coming scholars.'

REFERENCES

Acker, S. 2007. 'Breaking through the Ivy Ceiling.' *Journal of Higher Education: Academic Matters* Feb.:10–11.

Alfred, T. 2007. 'Indiginizing the Academy.' *Journal of Higher Education: Academic Matters* Feb.:22–3.

Aylward, C.A. 1999. *Canadian Critical Race Theory: Racism and the Law.* Halifax, NS: Fernwood.

Back, L. 2004. 'Ivory Towers? The Academy and Racism.' In I. Law, D. Phillips, and L. Turney, eds., *Institutional Racism in Higher Education,* 1–6. Trent, UK: Trentham Books.

Backhouse, C., P.W. Anderson, and W. Black. 2006. 'Report of the Independent Inquiry Commissioned by the Canadian Association of University Teachers into Alleged Discrimination against Dr. Kin-Yip Chun at the University of Toronto.' Toronto: Canadian Association of University Teachers.

Bérubé, A. 2001. 'How Gay Stays White and What Kind of White It Stays.' In B.B. Rasmussen, E. Klinenberg, I.J. Nixica, and M. Wray, eds., *The Making and Unmaking of Whiteness,* 234–65. Durham: Duke University Press.

Birgeneau, R.J. 2007. 'Creating an Inclusive Academy.' Keynote presentation at the 20th Annual Conference on Race and Ethnicity in American Higher Education (NCORE). San Francisco, April.

Biscoe, B.P. 2007. Opening remarks at the 20th Annual Conference on Race and Ethnicity in American Higher Education (NCORE). San Francisco, April.

Brayboy, B.M.J. 2003. 'The Implementation of Diversity in Predominantly White Colleges and Universities.' *Journal of Black Studies* 34(1):72–86.

CAUT Equity Review. 2007. 'A Partial Picture: The Representation of Equity-Seeking Groups in Canada's Universities and Colleges.' Ottawa.

Clarke, G.E. 2007. 'On Being an African-Canadian Professor.' *Journal of Higher Education: Academic Matters* Feb.:18–19.

Cole, P. 2003. 'Diversity among University Faculty Members.' Canadian Association of University Teachers (CAUT) Equity Bargaining Conference, Ottawa.

Cowan, R. 2004. 'Cornel West and the Tempest in the Ivory Tower.' *Politics* 24(1):72–8.

Dillabough, J. 2007. 'Parenting and Working: A Model Change Needed.' *Journal of Higher Education: Academic Matters* Feb.:14–15.

Dlamini, N.S. 2002. 'From the Other Side of the Desk: Notes on Teaching about Race When Racialised.' *Race, Ethnicity and Education* 5(1):51–6.

Drakich, J., and P. Stewart. 2007. 'After 40 Years of Feminism, How Are University Women Doing?' *Journal of Higher Education: Academic Matters* Feb.:6–9.

Essed, P. 2000. 'Dilemmas in Leadership: Women of Colour in the Academy.' *Ethnic and Racial Studies* 23(5):888–904.

Graveline, F.J. 1994. 'Lived Experiences of an Aboriginal Feminist Transforming the Curriculum.' *Canadian Woman Studies* 14(2):52.

Halperin, D.M. 1995. *Saint Foucault: Toward a Gay Hagiography.* New York: Oxford University Press.

Henry, F. 2006. 'Systemic Racism towards Faculty of Colour and Aboriginal Faculty at Queen's University,' Report on the 2003 Study: 'Understanding the Experiences of Visible Minority and Aboriginal Faculty Members at Queen's University.' Kingston, ON: Queen's Senate Educational Equity Committee.

Henry, F., and C. Tator. 2007. 'Through a Looking Glass: Enduring Racism on the University Campus.' *Journal of Higher Education: Academic Matters* Feb.:24–5.

– 1994. 'Racism and the University.' *Canadian Ethnic Studies* 26(3):74–90.

hooks, b. 1992. *Black Looks: Race and Representation.* Toronto: Between the Lines.

Hunter, M.L. 2005. *Race, Gender, and the Politics of Skin Tone.* New York: Routledge.

James, C.E. 2007. 'Who Can/Should Do This Work? The Colour of Critique.' In P. Carr and D. Lund, eds., *The Great White North? Exploring Whiteness, Privilege and Identity in Education,* 119–31. Rotterdam: Sense Publishers.

– 2003a. 'Collective Bargaining and Economic Benefits Conference: Bargaining for Equity.' Canadian Association of University Teachers. Retrieved May 26, 2007, from http://www.yufa.org/news/jamesreport.html.

– 2003b. *Seeing Ourselves: Exploring Race, Ethnicity and Culture.* Toronto: Thompson Educational.

– 2001. '"I've Never Had a Black Teacher Before."' In C.E. James and A. Shadd, eds., *Talking about Identity: Encounters in Race, Ethnicity and Language*, 150–67. Toronto: Between the Lines.

Kaufman, M., and J. Laker. 2007. 'Masculinity in the Quad.' *Journal of Higher Education: Academic Matters* Feb.:16–17.

Law, I., D. Phillips, and L. Turney. 2004a. 'Tackling Institutional Racism in Higher Education: An Antiracist Toolkit.' In I. Law, D. Phillips, and L. Turney, eds., *Institutional Racism in Higher Education*, 93–103. Trent, UK: Trentham Books.

– 2004b. *Institutional Racism in Higher Education*. Trent, UK: Trentham Books.

Lensmire, T.J. 2007. *Ambivalent White Racial Identities: Fear, Religion, and an Elusive Innocence*. Paper presented at the 2007 Annual Meeting of the American Educational Research Association, Chicago, April.

Leonardo, Z. 2004. 'The Color of Supremacy: Beyond the Discourse of "White Privilege."' *Educational Philosophy and Theory* 36(2):137–52.

Levine-Rasky, C. 2000. 'Framing Whiteness: Working through the Tensions in Introducing Whiteness to Educators.' *Race, Ethnicity and Education* 3(3):57–71.

Luther, R., E. Whitmore, and B. Moreau. 2003. *Seen but Not Heard: Aboriginal Women and Women of Colour in the Academy*. Ottawa: Canadian Research Institute for the Advancement of Women (CRIAW).

Luther, R., E. Whitmore, and B. Moreau. 2003a. 'Making Visible the Invisible: The Experience of Faculty of Colour and Aboriginal Faculty in Canadian Universities.' In R. Luther, E. Whitmore, and B. Moreau, eds., *Seen but Not Heard: Aboriginal Women and Women of Colour in the Academy*, 11–32. Ottawa: Canadian Research Institute for the Advancement of Women (CRIAW).

Mahtani, M. 2006. 'Challenging the Ivory Tower: Proposing Anti-racist Geographies within the Academy.' *Gender, Place and Culture* 13(1):21–5.

Marsden, L. 2007. 'Remembering the Future.' *Yorku – The Magazine of York University* 4(5):6–7.

Matsuda, M. 1996. *Where Is Your Body? And Other Essays on Race, Gender and the Law*. Boston, MA: Beacon.

McPhee, S. 2007. 'Embracing Diversity in a Flat World: A Mandate for Presidents and Board of Trustees.' A Special Feature Panel, National Association of Race and Ethnicity (NCORE). San Francisco, May.

Michaels, W.B. 2006. *The Trouble with Diversity: How We Learned to Love Identity and Ignore Inequality*. New York: Henry Holt.

Minami, D. 1995. 'Guerilla War at UCLA: Political and Legal Dimensions of the Tenure Battle.' In D.T. Nakanishi and T.Y. Nishida, eds., *The Asian Educational Experience: A Source Book for Teachers and Students*, 358–73. New York: Routledge.

Morrison, T. 2000, April 27. 'How Can Values Be Taught in the University.' Paper presented at the Center for Human Values, Princeton University, Princeton.

Mukherjee, A. 2001. 'The "Race Consciousness" of a South Asian (Canadian, of course) Female Academic.' In C.E. James and A. Shadd, eds., *Talking about Identity: Encounters in Race, Ethnicity and Language*, 212–18. Toronto: Between the Lines.

Nakhaie, M.R. 2004. 'Who Controls Canadian Universities? Ethnoracial Origins of Canadian University Administrators and Faculty's Perception of Mistreatment.' *Canadian Ethnic Studies* 36(1):92–110.

Purwar, N. 2004. 'Fish In or Out of Water: A Theoretical Framework for Race and the Space of Academia.' In I. Law, D. Phillips, and L. Turney, eds., *Institutional Racism in Higher Education*, 49–58. Trent, UK: Trentham Books.

Randel, D.M., and R.P. Saller. 2004. Dear Colleagues and Friends. Chicago: University of Chicago. Retrieved September 28, 2006, http://www.uchicago.edu/docs/education/pimi.pdf.

Rangasamy, J. 2004. 'Understanding Institutional Racism.' In I. Law, D. Phillips, and L. Turney eds., *Institutional Racism in Higher Education*, 27–34. Trent, UK: Trentham Books.

Razack, S. 2003. 'Racialized Immigrant Women as Native Informants in the Academy.' In R. Luther, E. Whitmore, and B. Moreau, eds., *Seen but Not Heard: Aboriginal Women and Women of Colour in the Academy*, 57–68. Ottawa: Canadian Research Institute for the Advancement of Women (CRIAW).

Roithmayr, D. 1999. 'Introduction to Critical Race Theory in Educational Research and Praxis.' In L. Parker, D. Deyhle, and S. Villenas, eds., *Race Is ... Race Isn't: Critical Race Theory and Qualitative Studies in Education*, 1–6. Boulder, CO: Westview Press.

Rudenstine, N.L. 1996. 'Diversity and Learning.' Harvard University, January. Retrieved May 1, 2006, http://www.hno.harvard.edu/gazette/1996/02.08/ExcerptsfromDiv.html.

Ryan, M.K., and S.A. Haslam. 2005. 'The Glass Cliff: Evidence that Women are Over-Represented in Precarious Leadership Positions.' *British Journal of Management* 16:81–90.

Scott, K.A. 2003. 'My Students Think I'm Indian: The Presentation of an African-American Self to Pre-service Teachers.' *Race, Ethnicity and Education* 6(3):211–26.

Sinnema, J. 2005. 'New Spirit on Campus.' June 26. Retrieved June 5, 2007, http://www.engineering.ualberta.ca/news.cfm?story=36461.

Smith, D. 1990. *The Conceptual Practices of Power: A Feminist Sociology of Knowledge*. Boston: Northeastern University Press.

Spafford, M.M., V.L. Nygaard, F. Gregor, and M.A. Boyd. 2006. '"Navigating the Different Spaces": Experiences of Inclusion and Isolation among Racially Minoritized Faculty in Canada.' *Canadian Journal of Higher Education* 36(1):1–27.

Stanley, C.A. 2006. 'Coloring the Academic Landscape: Faculty of Color Breaking the Silence in Predominantly White Colleges and Universities.' *American Educational Research Journal* 43(4):701–36.

Steinberg, S. 2005. 'The Dialects of Power: Understanding the Functionality of White Supremacy.' In L. Karumanchery, ed., *Engaging Equity: New Perspectives on Anti-racism Education,* 13–26. Calgary: Detselig Enterprises.

Stovall, D. 2006. 'Forging Community in Race and Class: Critical Race Theory and the Quest for Social Justice in Education.' *Race, Ethnicity and Education* 9(3):243–59.

Taylor, E. 1998. 'A Primer on Critical Race Theory: Who are the Critical Race Theorists and What are They Saying.' *The Journal of Blacks in Higher Education* 19(Spring):122–4.

Thompson, A. 2003. 'Tiffany, Friend of People of Color: White Investments in Antiracism.' *Qualitative Studies in Education* 16(1):7–29.

Thompson, G.L., and A.C. Louque. 2005. *Exposing the 'Culture of Arrogance in the Academy.'* Sterling, VA: Stylus.

Todd, D. 2007. 'Free Expression Often Stifled: Scholars Seem Reluctant to Discuss Certain Subjects for Fear of Being Labeled "Culturally Insensitive."' *Vancouver Sun,* Jan. 9.

Toronto Star. 2007. 'Education Has Little Impact on Minority Earning Power: Even Non-white Men and Women Born Here are Paid Less Than White Canadians, Study Finds.' (Petti Fong) June 2: ID7.

University of Chicago. 2004. Annual Report: Provost's Initiative on Minority Issues, AY 2003–04, October 25. Retrieved Sept. 28, 2006, http://www.uchicago.edu/docs/education/pimi.pdf.

Webber, M. 2007. 'Cultivating Miss Congeniality.' *Journal of Higher Education: Academic Matters* Feb.:12–13.

Woodward, B. 2007. 'Top People: An Era Spanning Two Presidents.' *Yorku – The Magazine of York University* 4(5):4, 6–7.

Yosso, T.J. 2005. 'Whose Culture Has Capital? A Critical Race Theory Discussion of Community Wealth.' *Race, Ethnicity and Education* 8(1):69–91.

6 On the Effectiveness of Anti-Racist Policies in Canadian Universities: Issues of Implementation of Policies by Senior Administration

ENAKSHI DUA

Introduction

A survey undertaken in 1989 by the Association of Universities and Colleges of Canada of thirty-seven Canadian universities on the extent to which these institutions had developed policies and practices for addressing race relations found that only a few had developed formal or comprehensive policy statements that addressed racism (cited in Henry and Tator 1994, 201). In the past two decades, however, a series of reports and articles have documented the overwhelming patterns of racism and whiteness in Canadian academia (for example, see the Henry Report), and there is now a sustained interest in and focus on bringing anti-racist policies to the academy. As a result of patterns of discrimination, anti-racist activists on Canadian campuses have been advocating that universities adopt a range of anti-racist policies and mechanisms to deal with racism.[1] These mechanisms range from anti-discriminatory statements that propose to prevent discrimination from occurring in the first place, to audits to identify systemic discrimination, to anti-discrimination policies and clauses that address racism, to employment equity policies that address the systemic under-representation of Indigenous scholars and faculty of colour. In this chapter I describe a preliminary investigation on the extent to which universities in Canada have developed anti-racist policies and practices. I also ask the complicated and challenging question of whether these policies and practices are effective in addressing the many forms of individual and systemic racism.

In contrast to the situation in 1989, today many, if not most, Canadian universities have developed a number of different kinds of mechanisms that are directed toward the elimination or redress of racism. The wide emergence of policies to address racism in the past fifteen years throughout Canadian universities is not only surprising but raises a number of important questions. First, what kinds of policies and procedures exist? Which policies have been adopted? How extensively have they been adopted? Second, what is the history behind these practices? How did these practices emerge? What forces shaped their emergence? Third, how effective are these policies and mechanisms in dealing with the patterns of racism? Indeed, in the same time period as Canadian universities were adopting such policies, there were a series of reports and articles about the continued patterns of racism and whiteness in Canadian academia. And, finally, if these policies are not effective, what limits their effectiveness?

Notably, with the exception of Henry and Tator (1994), there has not been such an evaluation of the effectiveness of anti-racist policies in Canadian universities. There is, however, a small body of work that examines the effectiveness of employment equity and anti-harassment policies in addressing gender inequities.[2] These investigations suggest that equity policies have had a moderate effect in addressing gender-based discrimination. For example, in a review of gender-based employment equity programs within Canadian universities, Drakich and Stewart (2007) conclude that the past three decades have witnessed moderate changes in the proportion of white women in the academy. In addition, research by Thomas (2004) has found that anti-discrimination clauses have also been effective in addressing and providing a remedy for sexual harassment. Importantly, much of this research suggests that the effectiveness of gender-based policies is tied to whether such policies include strong mechanisms for implementation. As a result, much attention has been focused on formulating gender-based policies in ways that will allow for effective implementation.

In addition, researchers have noted two interrelated factors that significantly affect the success of gender equity policies; one is the degree to which there is feminist activism on campuses, and the second is the willingness of university administrations to respond to feminist demands for equity. As Drakich and Stewart (2007) note, 'Universities, not always willingly, responded to employment equity demands with changes to university policies and practices to improve the climate and academic career prospects for women' (6).

Anti-Racist Measures

In this chapter, I offer a preliminary exploration of current anti-racist measures that are in place in Canadian universities. In order to address these questions, I have employed a range of material. First, I reviewed available anti-racist policies in thirty-seven Canadian universities. This includes a review of policy statements and mandates of equity and human rights offices and collective agreements. Second, in order to evaluate the effectiveness of these policies and practices, I have interviewed anti-racist practitioners in ten universities in Canada. The anti-racist practitioners were employed as directors of human rights and equity, counsellors, and policy analysts. In those universities where faculty associations have taken leadership in equity initiatives, I supplemented these interviews with interviews with officials within faculty associations. Thus, in three universities I carried out interviews with either equity or grievance officers.

In addition, I interviewed the equity officer for the Canadian Association of University Teachers (CAUT). A total of fourteen interviews were conducted. The ten universities were chosen in ways to reflect regional, large/small urban centres, and rural/urban distribution of Canadian universities. Finally, I have supplemented these interviews with internal reviews of these policies. These internal reports have been useful in evaluating the effectiveness of current practices in universities other than the ten chosen for interviews.

The interviewees were chosen in a number of ways. I approached those practitioners that I had come into contact with in past anti-racist initiatives. In addition, I asked individual interviewees if they could refer me to others. Finally, I asked colleagues engaged in anti-racist work if they could refer me to anti-racist practitioners. In the process, I was sensitive to include those who were in a variety of positions – directors of equity and human rights offices, grievance officers, and equity/anti-racist officers. Through this process, of those interviewed, eight were employed as directors of human rights and equity offices, one as CAUT's legal counsel and as the professional officer on the CAUT Equity Committee, one as a policy analyst, one as an equity counsellor, two as anti-racist/equity officers, and one as a grievance officer.[3] Of note, I found that the kind of position that anti-racist practitioners were located in did not affect their responses. As there has been little research on anti-racist policies in the academy, open-ended questions were deployed so to allow interviewees to identify the history and effectiveness of policies. In the interviews, anti-racist practitioners were asked the following questions:

- What policies and practices exist in your institutions to address racism?
- How did these policies emerge?
- To what extent are current anti-racist policies and mechanisms effective?
- Are there policies that are particularly effective? Are there policies that are particularly ineffective? What are the limitations in current policies?
- What do we need to do to address these limitations?
- What meaning do these policies have for the institution?

Because of the lack of funding and the spatial distance, many of these interviews took place as phone interviews.

My review of policies within Canadian universities found that most Canadian universities had developed a number of policies designed to address racism within the academy. Three kinds of policies were particularly prevalent: employment equity policies, anti-harassment policies and clauses, and anti-racist workshops. In addition, most universities had structures within the university mandated to address racism, such as anti-racist, human rights, and equity offices.[4] Despite the proliferation of employment equity and anti-harassment policies, my preliminary investigation also suggests that these policies have had a limited effect in addressing racism. In fact, what emerges is, at times, an overwhelming picture of limitations in addressing racism within the academy. My investigation suggests three important limitations.

First, in many universities, policies that address racism did not emerge as a response to anti-racist initiatives, but rather through a response to feminist activism and legal changes. As a result, it is not clear that the introduction of these policies was tied to a commitment to address racism. The forces that have led to the emergence of anti-racist policies raise concern over the degree to which the underlying spirit of these policies has taken hold institutionally.

Second, in examining these policies, it becomes clear that these policies are constructed in ways that do not allow for effective implementation. This is particularly true in the case of employment equity policies. As we shall see, employment equity policies most often exist at the level of general statements, and thus lack the procedural requirements that would allow them to be effectively implemented. There is greater variation in anti-harassment policies. A number of anti-racist practitioners noted that in their universities these policies were effectively formulated. In particular, anti-harassment policies seem be to more effective if these policies include mechanisms to deal with systemic racism. However, others pointed to a number of important procedural limitations that limited their effectiveness at their universities.

Third, and most importantly, all but one of those interviewed for this study reported that the most significant limitation in implementing current policies and practices was located in the forms of resistance that these policies invoked among members of senior administration. As a director of human rights and equity succinctly stated: 'Nothing is effective in dealing with racism. You can have all of the policies in the world, but none of these policies will be effective if you do not have the will to implement these policies. There is no intention of implementing policies when it comes to racism.'

What was remarkable was that all but one of the anti-racist practitioners reported similar attitudes among members of senior administration – that they experienced a lack of support from senior members of the administration when they attempted to address incidents of racism. Some reported hostility from senior administration, including intimidation and condescension. Some spoke of the pressure they felt to be silent about the racism within the university. Some of those interviewed were ostracized as a result of their efforts to implement anti-racist policies. Importantly, some of the interviewees tied the resistance of senior administration to the way in which whiteness dominated their worldviews. Simply put, members of senior administration denied that racism existed in their institutions, and would respond defensively to cases of racism. As these twelve practitioners reflected on the meaning of such policies within their universities, they noted that the policies worked as 'window dressing,' as they allowed university administrators to appear to meet their legal obligations to address racialized inequities. As a result, my preliminary study suggests that despite having a number of anti-racist policies and procedures in place, these policies have failed to take hold institutionally.

The Emergence of Institutional Responses to Racism in Canadian Universities

My review of anti-racist mechanisms found that in all of the thirty-seven universities surveyed, these mechanisms did not emerge as a result of anti-racist initiatives, or from an acknowledgment of racism. Rather, in all the universities, these mechanisms are embedded in two interrelated factors; first, pressure in the late 1970s and early 1980s from feminist activists to address sex-based discrimination on campuses, and second, decisions by human rights tribunals that accorded employers with the responsibility of addressing discrimination. As a result of these forces, between the late 1970s to the early 1990s, most universities began to develop sexual harassment policies. In response to pressure by feminist activists, a few universities also introduced gender-based employment equity policies. In many universities, sexual harassment and employment equity policies emerged through the process of collective bargaining. Accompanying these policies has been the emergence of human rights and equity offices. Initially these policies focused on gender-based discrimination. It was not until the 1990s that other forms of discrimination were included.

As many feminist scholars have documented, the late 1970s and early 1980s witnessed a surge of feminist activism on many university campuses. In order to address gender-based discrimination, feminist groups asked for mechanisms that prevented and addressed sexual harassment, centres that promoted initiatives in gender equity in employment to address the under-representation of female faculty, and mentoring programs that would assist new female faculty with career development (for a more thorough review of this history, see Drakich and Stewart 1995; Stalker and Prentice 1998). Perhaps the most important starting point for the development of equity measures within the academy was the introduction of sexual harassment policies and clauses. CAUT's legal counsel and professional officer for the CAUT Equity Committee reports that interest in sexual harassment language began in the late 1980s and early 1990s when university administrators were facing a number of sexual harassment cases. As the mechanisms to deal with sexual harassment within the universities were weak, many of these cases were referred to human rights offices or commissions. In making decisions in these cases, arbitrators noted that the employer lacked internal mechanisms to prevent sexual harassment, and as a result were failing to fulfil their obligation to protect their employees from sexual harassment. These cases provided a strong incentive for universities to initiate sexual harassment statements and clauses.

Related to the development of sexual harassment clauses has been the emergence of offices of equity and human rights. In most universities, it was not until human rights practitioners pointed out that the cases dealing with sexual harassment, which set out that employers had a 'positive' obligation to ensure employees did not face harassment, also extended to other forms of discrimination. As a result, sexual harassment policies became extended to include fifteen other prohibited grounds, including racism, ableism and Indigenous peoples. More recently, these policies have been extended to include gender and sexual orientation. In this period, centres for sexual harassment and gender equity began to be broadened into centres for human rights and equity.

As noted earlier, in addition to demanding policies that addressed sexual harassment, feminist activists were also advocating for gender-based employment equity initiatives. Notably, while this was taking place, in 1986, the federal government introduced an employment equity program, called the Federal Contractors Program. This program requires that employers that receive public funds implement employment equity plans to increase the representation of four designated groups: women, Aboriginal peoples, visible minorities, and those with disabilities. By the 1990s, a number of Canadian universities had implemented gender-based employment equity programs (Drakich and Stewart 1995). Even though the Federal Contractors Program also identified visible minorities, Aboriginal people, and those with disabilities as designated groups, when employment equity policies began to be implemented, very few universities integrated these groups in their policies. For example, in 1990, only three universities had equity policies that included people of colour and Aboriginal peoples (Dua 2000).

Thus, a brief review of such policies indicates that equity-based policies emerged to address gender-based inequities within the academy. As a result, it is not surprising that they have been somewhat effective in achieving these goals. However, there still remains the question of how effective these policies and procedures are for dealing with racism. In the following sections, I evaluate the effectiveness of three policies: employment equity policies, anti-racist workshops, and anti-harassment policies. As will be seen, in each of these kinds of policies, the efforts universities are making to effect change vary significantly. Some universities rely on general anti-discrimination and employment equity statements, which have tended to achieve little. Other universities have more specific mechanisms and procedures for implementing these objectives. As this is a preliminary investigation, my focus will be to identify patterns in these policies.

Employment Equity

In the 1990s, most universities had failed to include 'visible' minorities in their employment equity policies, but in the last two decades the extension of employment equity has been one of the most important sites for anti-racist activism on campuses. A number of internal reports and scholarly articles on racism within academia have identified the under-representation of faculty of colour and Indigenous faculty as a site in which racism begins. For example, from Kobayashi and Peake: 'Without the presence of academics of colour in the academy, the risk and harm that racism creates will remain uncontested ... the inclusion of geographers of colour is the most important "racial project" in which the discipline can engage' (2002, 50–1). Increasing the representation of faculty of colour and Indigenous faculty relates to the larger issue of challenging the ways in which academic institutions and the academic curriculum are embedded in a culture of whiteness. Several writers have argued that such hirings would facilitate the transformation of the university curriculum. For example, Mahtani (2006) has suggested that 'our differences as women of colour generate a potential diverse range of effective ways of teaching, leading, and learning' (24; see also Dua and Lawrence 2000).

My survey of employment equity policies in thirty-seven Canadian universities in 2007 suggests a number of universities have added the other designated groups to their employment equity policies. Indeed, all but one university had some form of statement that specified a commitment to hiring faculty of colour and Indigenous faculty. Employment equity initiatives ranged from those universities that have general statements on employment equity to those that have developed specific goals and mechanisms to achieve them, have integrated equal employment opportunities into strategic planning exercises, and communicate the employment equity policy and activity to the university community regularly and through several avenues. As much research on gender-based employment equity has demonstrated, there exists a positive relationship between employment equity programs that have goals and mechanisms to achieve them and women's employment profiles (see, for example, Drakich and Stewart 1995; Burton 1997). The crucial question is whether employment equity policies include similar goals and mechanisms to increase the representation of visible minorities and Indigenous peoples. However, a closer examination of the ways in which the categories of visible minorities and Aboriginal peoples have been integrated into employment equity policies suggests that the addition of these groups remains at the 'non-performative' level. Only one university had developed a meaningful employment equity policy for Indigenous peoples, and only two had a meaningful policy for visible minorities.

Notably, in seven universities, employment equity was constituted through a statement of a commitment to 'equity and diversity.' A typical example is that of Ryerson University:

> Ryerson University is committed to principles of equity and diversity in the workplace. Employment equity is a principle at the core of Ryerson's overall mandate as a community leader and an institution of higher learning. The University is committed to promoting employment equity within the University community, and to ensuring there is equal opportunity and equitable representation in employment for all current and potential faculty and staff. Employment equity involves hiring the best-qualified candidate while ensuring a fair and equitable hiring process for all persons. The University shall hire and make employment and promotion decisions on the basis of qualifications and merit. Within this context, the University shall make proactive efforts to increase the participation from the four groups designated for employment equity, namely women, visible minorities, persons with disabilities and aboriginal persons. (htp://www.ryerson.ca/hr/working/docs/1-employment-equity.pdf)

While these statements are accompanied by employment equity 'plans,' these plans did not have targets, nor were there mechanisms for the implementation of these plans. Moreover, as in the case of three of these universities, formulating employment equity plans is voluntary. Thus, as one anti-racist practitioner noted:

> We have an employment equity policy that is designed to attract more faculty of colour and indigenous faculty. Under our policy each unit had to formulate an employment equity plan with goals to increase the representation of these two groups. However, there was no mechanism to monitor this. The policy worked on a volunteer basis. Many units and departments did not even respond to our request for a plan.

Eighteen of the universities surveyed had employment equity policies that specified that if two candidates were equal in qualifications, then the candidate who is a member of a designated group will be appointed. A typical example is Carleton University:

The parties agree that the best available candidate should be hired, regardless of membership or non-membership in a designated group. However, where the qualifications of two candidates for appointment are demonstrably equal, and one of these candidates is a member of a designated group that is under-represented in the unit(s) or sub-unit(s) then, all else being equal, the candidate of the under-represented group should be offered the position. (http://www.now.carleton.ca/2007–11/1816.htm)

While these policies do identify a process by which employment equity candidates are to be hired, as many of those interviewed noted, such clauses are difficult to implement since the clause 'demonstrably equal' is difficult to prove. Moreover, as faculty of colour and Indigenous faculty often carry out research in areas that are under-represented in the academy, their research profiles are at times undervalued. Another important limitation of policies is that they fail to identify procedures to choose candidates especially when more than one designated group is represented among the shortlist. An anti-racist practitioner noted that such policies often have the result of increasing the proportion of one of the designated groups – white women. As a result, such policies give the illusion that 'all women' are being hired, but, in fact, candidates of colour and Indigenous candidates continue to be marginalized:

> One of the difficulties with the employment equity policy is the way in which data was put out. It was very problematic because it did not report on intersections. So while the data said that by the late 1990s women were doing well, that they were close to 40% of faculty, the data did not tell us who these women were. We could not tell where women of colour or aboriginal women placed on that grid. The difficulty is that the term women is used to refer to all women when it in practice is limited to one group of women – those who are white. When we asked for such data, the University was reluctant to provide it. We finally were able to obtain data – and found that indeed it was mainly white women who were being hired and promoted and that the reasons for such hirings and promotion were that these women were seen as a better 'fit.'

Thus, one of the limitations of such policies is that they do not put forward procedures that ensure that members of one of the designated groups are not favoured over members from the other designated groups.

Indeed, such patterns of favouritism can be seen in the case of six universities that place goals for increasing the representation of women before that of visible minorities or Indigenous peoples. Six universities have employment equity policies that place the hiring of women over other designated groups. These universities were also those universities that had incorporated specified mechanisms, such as targets to increase the representation of women, into their employment equity policies. Significantly, these mechanisms prohibited the hiring of racialized faculty and Indigenous faculty until these targets were met. A typical case is that at Brock University:

> For the purposes of this Article, the Parties recognize women, Aboriginal peoples, persons with disabilities and members of visible minorities as designated groups. Any department/centre with more than 40% representation of women (i.e. women hold more than 40% of the probationary and tenured positions in the department/centre) will be deemed to have achieved a gender balance and, in this instance, the employment equity procedures in this Article will apply to men and *women* from the other designated groups (i.e. Aboriginal peoples, persons with disabilities, and members of visible minorities). (emphasis added) (http://www.brocku. ca/hr/labour/BUFA_Collective_Agreement_2006.pdf)

In these cases, the employment equity policy placed the hiring of visible minorities and Indigenous peoples after the composition of female faculty reached 40 per cent. As one of the anti-racist practitioners reported, in her/his university such a policy can perpetuate systematic discrimination against candidates who are Indigenous or visible minorities:

> We have an employment equity policy that specifies that in units where women are under 40% of the faculty complement, women need to be hired over other groups. The policy comes out of the 1980s when women were very underrepresented in the academy. The difficulty with our policy is that because we do not have publicly available data on the proportion of faculty of colour and Indigenous faculty – though by walking through the halls anyone should be able to see there are not many – people assume that faculty of colour are not underrepresented. We had a situation in a hiring where there were two candidates, one who was a white woman and a candidate who was a man of colour, who were short listed for the position. The white women was offered the position. In this unit, the percentage of women was 35% but the percentage of people of colour

was less than 5%. When racialised faculty on campus raised questions about this hiring, the Chair of the Hiring Committee claimed that s/he had no choice but to offer the position to the white woman. S/he pointed out that to not do so would violate the university's employment equity policy. So here is a case where our policy worked to discriminate against a candidate of colour.

As some of those interviewed noted, the emphasis on gender equity over other forms of equity in such policies has resulted in tension and conflict as anti-racist faculty struggle to get other designated groups included in employment equity policies:

> There is a lot of tension around employment equity. Employment eq-
> uity is not working in my institution. We have a policy to increase the
> representation of women. It has worked as it has goals and targets that
> are enforced. But for racialised minorities, the policy has no goals and
> targets. We know that [having goals and targets is] the most effective
> way of increasing representation because what gets measured is what
> gets done. Both I and racialised faculty have been working to get the em-
> ployment equity policy extended to include racialised faculty – but have
> been unable to do so because of the reluctance to have such a policy at
> both the level of the leadership in the Faculty Association, as well as the
> administration.

Some of the anti-racist practitioners noted that, despite the need for equity policies that include racialized groups and Indigenous peoples, there is no will to have such policies. The experience of anti-racist practitioners was that there was a very different attitude in the university when dealing with issues of racism compared to other equity issues. I will return to this issue in the last section of this chapter.

Discouragingly, my survey found only one university had an equity policy that focused on increasing the representation of Indigenous scholars, and there was only one university that had policies that specifically focused on increasing the representation of faculty of colour. While it is important to note such limited improvements, my preliminary survey results illustrate that most universities have failed to develop equity policies that are effective in addressing the systemic barriers to hiring Aboriginal people and people of colour. None of the universities reviewed coupled measures to increase the representation of visible minorities or Indigenous faculty to broader planning frameworks. As a result, it would not be surprising if these groups continue to be under-represented in faculty ranks.[5]

Anti-racist Education

As a one of the anti-racist practitioners noted, while employment equity policies are the starting point for anti-racist policies within the academy, other kinds of policies are also required to address racism within the academy. In particular, institutions require policies that address 'climate issues,' as in the social and working atmosphere or culture. 'We can struggle for employment equity, but it is not the whole piece. If we only do the front end, we don't do the whole job. We have to deal with what happens to people once they get here. The climate issue is not well addressed. This means addressing how we deal with racism in our organization.'

One of the strategies to address racism within the organization is to offer anti-racist workshops. Anti-racist workshops are seen as the central way through which racism on campuses can be challenged. As a result, all of the universities surveyed have invested resources in offering such workshops. In most cases, these workshops are offered through the human rights and equity offices. For example, the mandate of the Human Rights and Equity Office at the University of Alberta is to offer workshops to help create inclusive work environments. The expectation is that such workshops will allow for social transformation through active dialogue and learning.

In my review of these workshops, I found that anti-racist workshops took a number of different forms. First, most universities offered workshops that introduced issues of discrimination and racism. An example of such a workshop is at the University of Alberta. The description of this workshop states:

> We can each prevent harassment and discrimination by being aware of the impact of our behavior on others. Think about things from another person's perspective. Would a reasonable person find the behavior offensive? When it comes to harassment, it is the impact that matters, not the intent. Be aware of how you treat people. Does everyone have the same opportunity, regardless of race, gender, ethnic origin, religion, colour, sexual orientation, disability, marital status, etc.? (http://www.uofaweb.ualberta.ca/humanrights/)

In addition, these workshops provide education and information on the discrimination and harassment policies. Second, a number of universities offered anti-racist workshops that highlighted the intersection between the academic work in the areas of ethno-cultural diversity, critical race-related issues, and issues of relevance to the larger community on campus. Such workshops included events for Black History Month, International Day for the Elimination of Discrimination, and International Women's Day. Other examples included workshops that addressed issues such as pluralism, multiculturalism, debates over faith-based schools, racial profiling, and Islamophobia. Third, a number of universities also offered workshops that focused on providing a forum for individuals and student groups to meet and discuss racialized tensions and think about how to form coalitions and programs for change. Examples of such workshops are workshops that bring together Muslim and Jewish students to think through racialized tensions.

Those interviewed for this study were asked how effective such workshops have been in addressing racism. All but one of those interviewed noted that the main limitation in these workshops is that attendance is voluntary. As a result, those who attend are those who are sympathetic to addressing racism. Thus, those interviewed questioned whether these workshops impacted the broader university community. As one director of a human rights office stated, 'We have fantastic educational programmes. They are beautifully designed, well executed … but rarely achieve the goals we want to achieve; because they are voluntary [they] do not get at the people who are the problems. Those who volunteer tend to be committed to such policies.'

Many of those interviewed noted that two groups within the university constituency were particularly difficult to reach, and these are faculty and administrators. As a director of a human rights and equity office noted:

Education is a powerful way of talking and crafting a space to look at how we include people, to look at climate, to talk about equality. The difficulty is that faculty are quite resistant to educational efforts. We have a chairs school for new chairs and Deans where we spend a half a day on equality. Problem is getting people to come. Last session had only five or six people there. Of those who come, they are the ones who know that equality can be a problem.

Since one of the major limitations in the effectiveness of anti-racist workshops was in reaching all of the constituencies of the academy, many of those interviewed raised the question of whether such workshops would be more effective if they were mandatory, 'but even then there is a drawback. Mandatory workshops create backlash, fear mongering.'

Two of those interviewed worked in universities where anti-racist workshops were mandatory. Indeed, one of the two interviewed did report that such workshops resulted in a backlash. In part this was because of the way in which university faculty dismiss those who do not have academic credentials:

> The principal vehicle for addressing racism was obligatory training for employment equity. There was considerable backlash that took place in these workshops. We had to spend inordinate amount of our time making sure that faculty took these courses. It took the energies of two full time staff people. And we experienced a high degree of resistance and hostility by those who took these workshops. Where they were effective is in illustrating the degree to which racism operated. Some of the faculty took great pride in exposing violations to the labour code – in how they interviewed candidates to 'look for the fit in the department.' The workshops generated wonderful material on the worse case scenarios that take place. But the workshops were totally ineffective. There was not enough thinking about the academic investment required to change faculty behavior. Faculty members do not entertain interventions from people who are not faculty. The mandate was folly to begin with.

However, one of those interviewed noted that in her/his institution these workshops have had the positive impact of educating members of the university around what is discrimination and harassment. 'Our human rights policy has been successful because people know it is there because we offer workshops in relation to discrimination. It is mandatory that every staff member of the university take a four hour workshop. We have had this for university staff and for VPs. They just do it.' This interviewee did note that there has been more difficulty implementing these workshops for faculty. While such workshops have been initiated, they have been less successful because 'you cannot make faculty do anything.'

A number of those interviewed noted that such workshops may be limited to having temporary effects. As one director of a human rights office noted, 'A problem is that there is no follow up. How do we know what is effective?'

Finally, some of those interviewed noted that it was not clear that workshops were effective in addressing situations of harassment, particularly when the perpetuator was someone in a faculty position. As a director of human rights noted, 'The difficulty with educational initiatives is the lack, for lack of a better word, of a hammer. I have had a number of faculty say to me, I have tenure, what can you do to me?'

In order to be able to address racist behaviour, including that which arises from systemic structures, anti-racist practitioners often turn to anti-harassment policies.

Anti-Harassment Clauses

Today all universities have some form of anti-harassment policy that includes racism. These policies range from general statements to policies that specify investigation and remedy mechanisms. An example of a typical clause under the human rights framework is that which is employed by Carleton University:

> The University prohibits discrimination and harassment, including conduct on the basis of race, ancestry, place of origin, colour, ethnic origin and citizenship that: Is abusive, demeaning or threatening, including behavior such as name calling; derogatory remarks, gestures and physical attacks; or display of derogatory or belittling pictures and graffiti; or Biases administrative and appointment decisions, employment and workplace practices, tenure, promotion, appointment, leave, and salary determinations; or Biases academic decisions such as admission, grading, the application of regulations and requirements and scheduling of academic activities; or Misuses power, authority or influence; or Discriminates in the provision of goods and services or access to premises, accommodation and other facilities. (Carleton University, Diversity Office, 2007)

In all universities, anti-harassment policies are administrated through offices of human rights and equity. In addition, in some universities, collective agreements also include an anti-harassment clause. As a result, a faculty person who is a member of a designated group and who experiences discrimination has the possibility of pursuing a complaint through either the grievance process through their faculty associations, or through the human rights office in their institution. The two different routes entail slightly different processes. In order to be able to evaluate the effectiveness of anti-harassment clauses in both cases, I also interviewed officers within faculty associations in those universities where collective agreements were employed to address harassment.[6]

In all of the thirty-seven universities surveyed, complaints are processed by human rights offices. These offices have websites that state the process for filing a complaint. There are two processes in dealing with anti-harassment complaints: either informal or formal mechanisms to resolve the complaint. The first step in this process is for the complainant to meet with an officer of the human rights office, where complainants are informed of two different avenues with which they may proceed, and the advantages and disadvantages of each process. For example, the University of Alberta Human Rights and Equity Office website noted:

> The advantage of the informal resolution process is that it gets people talking in a confidential setting, and there is little record of the complaint or the outcome. It is often the most effective and fastest way to resolve a conflict, and often the people involved are able to maintain some kind of relationship afterwards, be it a civil work relationship, or a close friendship. This may be important to people who will still need to work together after the dispute is over. Parties are often encouraged to try an informal process prior to proceeding with a formal complaint. (University of Alberta, Human Rights Office, 2007)

There is great variation in who decides what mechanism will be employed. In some universities, such as McMaster University, the complainant is able to choose, though with counselling from staff in the human rights office. In other universities, the director of human rights has some authority to determine how to proceed with a case. And finally, some universities, such as the University of Western Ontario, only offer an informal resolution process. If the complainant decides to employ the informal resolution process, an officer in the human rights office attempts to negotiate an informal resolution. This involves getting the parties to reach a resolution. The vast majority of complaints are processed through the informal methods. As we shall see, many of those interviewed for this study noted that informal processes had a number of advantages.

In contrast, the formal resolution process involves taking written complaints and an investigation by the human rights office in which both parties have the right to see and respond to the complaint. It can also involve other university personnel, such as administrators, union representatives, and witnesses. Many directors of the human rights office see this process as legalistic, costly, time consuming, and very adversarial, and opening up a greater possibility of criminal action. As the website at the Human Rights and Equity Office at the University of Alberta noted, 'It is difficult to share a work/study or living environment with someone throughout or following this process. However, there are times when the formal resolution process is more appropriate than an informal process' (University of Alberta, Human Rights Office, 2007).

In either formal or informal complaints cases, officers of the human rights offices are mandated to mediate resolutions, carry out investigations, and, in some cases, make final decisions. As a result, these officers are expected to be impartial, as they represent both the complainant as well as the person against whom the complaint is being made. In some universities, such as the University of Western Ontario, the final decision is made by a tribunal or hearing panel. The tribunal conducts a single formal hearing. Such tribunals are often composed of the various constituencies of the university: faculty, staff, undergraduate and graduate students, and those appointed by the Senate.

If the complainant approaches the faculty association, complaints are processed differently.[7] The complainant approaches the grievance officer, who, after consulting with the executive or the grievance committee, decides if the case warrants further attention. Thus, complainants do not have an automatic right to have their grievance heard. If the faculty association agrees to pursue the complaint, the complaint is directed towards the university administration as the employer rather than a specific individual, chair, or unit. The administration is asked to provide remedy for the situation of harassment. Often grievance officers begin the process by employing informal resolution mechanisms. If informal mechanisms fail, the faculty association again determines whether the case warrants going to grievance. After a grievance is filed, informal resolutions are still pursued. Failing such a resolution, the case goes to an outside arbitrator. In making a case, the faculty association represents the complainant only. In many universities, administrators ask the human rights office to carry out an investigation. Of note, if the complainant files a complaint through the human rights office against another faculty member, the faculty association is responsible for representing the faculty against whom the complaint has been filed.[8]

In examining the effectiveness of anti-harassment policies designed to address racism, a number of limitations emerge. On the one hand, many of those interviewed reported that these policies, especially when informal resolution mechanisms were employed, are somewhat effective and allowed human rights and grievance officers to raise incidents of racism with members of administrations and with department chairs, and to negotiate limited redress. On the other hand, some of those interviewed (five of fourteen) noted that there are important limitations in how anti-harassment policies are formulated. In particular, concerns were raised about the autonomy of the complaints process since complaints are processed and investigated by the same office. Indeed, a number of those who were interviewed reported that members of senior administration often impeded the impartial resolution of such cases.

The first concern about anti-harassment policies is that the limited data available suggest that people experiencing racism underuse such policies when compared to people experiencing other forms of discrimination. For example, data from annual reports of human rights and equity offices from six universities in large urban centres, where we would expect significant proportions of people of colour, illustrate that the proportion of race-based complaints in all complaints ranged from 9 to 20 per cent. In the cases of York and Ryerson universities, data on the university websites reported that students of colour represented more than 50 per cent of the student population. Thus, the data suggest that racialized members of the university communities do not see anti-harassment policies as a method to address incidents of racism.

A number of factors can inhibit members of the university from pursuing race-based complaints. The first is the difficulties involved in proving a complaint. As one director of human rights and equity noted:

Race-base complaints take longer to process than other kinds of complaints. Why? Because of the way in which they transpire. Race-based discrimination is much more sneaky ... it takes place over time ... It involves poisoned work environments, isolation ... incidents where someone has been shortchanged in terms of salary increments. It results in tense relationships within the department, that extends between a lot of people. As a result, the investigation takes more time.

Table 6.1
Complaints about racism, as a percentage of all
complaints, for selected Canadian universities,
2004

University of British Columbia	17
McMaster University	9
Ryerson University	14
Simon Fraser University	7
University of Windsor	15
York University	20*

*Data for York University were available only for
2005/6.

Notably, a number of those interviewed said that complainants, especially when employed as untenured faculty, are hesitant to employ anti-harassment policies as they fear retaliation from colleagues and members of the administration. For example, one director of a human rights office noted, 'There is enormous backlash against complainants. They are made the villain, and ostracized because they made a complaint … As a result, coming to the Office can do more harm than good.' Indeed, as the equity officer at CAUT notes, anti-discrimination policies have very weak language in protecting complainants from retaliation. In particular, proving retaliation becomes difficult as it is often subtle. A number of those interviewed noted that the fear of retaliation often makes complainants walk away from filing legitimate harassment claims.

Those interviewed reported a number of factors that made the informal resolution process more effective. One director of human rights and equity noted that she/he found it more productive to employ informal resolution processes than formal ones, because those involved in making the final decisions often did not understand the complexities of racism: 'I found the most effective way of assuring a resolution of the issue was to keep the issue out of the official process and deal with it through mediation. The difficulty with the process at my university is that once it gets to the level of a hearing it gets bogged down. The people who are responsible for the hearing are not sophisticated enough to deal with the complexities of racism.'

Another noted that because, often, the person against whom the complaint is being made holds more power and prestige than the complainant, informal mechanisms allow him/her to negotiate partial resolutions. 'The University will protect who they see as their own. So if this is a white faculty versus racialised faculty, the University will protect the white faculty. These kinds of differences in power mean that formal mechanisms often do not work. In these situations, I found that mediation is the only mechanism that allows for a partial solution.'

When implementing anti-racist workshops, a number of those interviewed noted that one of the difficulties in employing anti-harassment policies is that faculty feel that such policies encroach on their autonomy. As one director of a human rights and equity office reported:

> I come up against having to define what is discrimination, and who has authority to tell faculty what they can do. Faculty often use academic freedom to make arguments against claims of racism ... Academic freedom is to provide safe space for research. But when it is used to allow a faculty member to make statements that use the racial characteristics of who is asking questions to undermine that person's research, then this is discrimination. One of the questions to tease out is the relationship between academic freedom and inclusion. This is important for these policies to work better.

The reliance on informal mechanisms to address racism raised concerns about how effective anti-harassment policies are in dealing with systemic issues. As I noted earlier, four of those interviewed for this study raised concerns that anti-harassment policies did not effectively address the way in which specific incidents of racism are imbedded in systemic issues. As one director of human rights and equity noted, despite the inclusion of an equity framework, the office tended to work under a human rights framework, which focused on resolving individual cases of discrimination rather than systemic forms of racism and whiteness. Another director of human rights and equity reported:

> I can deal with individual complaints ... but it is more difficult to deal with systemic issues. Let me give you an example. I had a case where a half a dozen untenured racialised faculty of colour from several different faculties came to me about racism. They all reported similar experiences. But they did not want it to go on file as it was too dangerous for them as untenured faculty. After an investigation I found there was no way of pursuing the complaint. I put together a proposal for the President to look

at this as a systemic issue. The President had the power to say yes or no. The President said no. It was seen as too dangerous for the university.

Others noted that in their institutions anti-harassment policies were unable to address systemic issues, such as climate and curriculum. 'Students could not go to the Equity Office because it was complaints driven. If the issue was a systemic issue such as curriculum issues then the Equity Office was unable to address these issues.' As the equity officer at CAUT notes, there is often a lack of awareness in the broader university community around how harassment is located in systemic issues. She points out that many cases of harassment arise from systemic structures, thus requiring contextualization and often broader kinds of interventions. This, in turn, requires that anti-harassment policies need to include the ability to carry out broader workplace audits. Notably, in some universities, the director of the human rights office is empowered to request such audits. For example, at the University of Alberta, if the director of the human rights office, in dealing with a specific case, feels that it warrants an investigation of systemic issues, she/he can request an audit of that workplace:

> This Policy recognizes that a Vice-President may initiate a review of the work, study and living environment in a department or unit which may be affected by accusations of discrimination or harassment. The purpose of such a review is to assist in the creation and maintenance of a healthy work, study and living environment, to enhance and improve the environment through education and awareness of issues of harassment and discrimination, and to facilitate ongoing productivity and creativity in the workplace. (University of Alberta, http://www.uofaweb.ualberta.ca/humanrights//pdfs/D&HPolicy,GFCsection44.pdf)

Another concern with anti-harassment policies is that, in most cases, these policies empower the same officer to 'wear multiple hats'; therefore, the same person is often responsible for counselling, mediation, and investigation. In particular, the lack of an independent investigatory body means that, in most cases, investigations are carried out by equity offices. The equity officer at CAUT notes that given that most equity officers are hired by the president, and report to him/her, complainants are often concerned about whether an investigation carried out by an equity office is truly independent of the president of the same university.

While the vast majority of those interviewed for this study (10 out of 14) did not see the range of functions as problematic, thirteen of these fourteen anti-racist practitioners did report that interference from members of senior administration did restrain their ability to implement anti-harassment policies. As one director of human rights and equity noted, 'Unless your HRO is independent and reporting to the Board of Governors it is fundamentally flawed. My University is the prime example of this. I report to the President ... while the President never discussed cases with me, another President might ... You cannot have someone in the system policing the system.'

These anti-racist practitioners reported that when implementing these policies in cases of racism they experienced resistance from members of the senior administration. Even in cases where universities employed tribunals to make decisions, those appointed to tribunals often were also tied to the administration. As one anti-racist practitioner reported:

> People involved on the hearing panels are generally well placed people in the academic community. They got into these positions because they have been supporters of the institutions. They are on the inside of the university. So there is a self selection process that takes place in constituting hearing boards. They see their jobs to protect what makes them powerful rather than to be open to grievances. They are often closed to cases of racism.

In the opinion of all of these thirteen interviewees, such interference worked to legitimate and perpetuate racism. For example, one director stated unequivocally that in his institution 'it is the behavior from people in authority that contradicts what we are trying to do. Complaints are not dealt with. In one case a person who made a complaint against another faculty had that faculty made their supervisor.' Another anti-racist practitioner stated, 'Racism happens because it is permitted. When complaints are not dealt with, what message does it send? The message is clear – racism is not taken seriously, not dealt with, so people can do this.'

Policies or Implementation: Leadership and Resistance at the Level of Senior Administration

In the last three sections, we have seen that as anti-racist practitioners evaluated the effectiveness of anti-racist policies, according to thirteen of the fourteen who have been interviewed, the most serious limitation was not in the policies themselves, but in their implementation. As one director of a human rights and equity office stated, focusing on constructing 'correct wording' for policies, while important, shifts the attention from the most serious handicap in addressing racism – the lack of leadership from members of senior administration and executive members of faculty associations:

> The problem is not in the policy, or in the words of the policy, or what the policy says. These are not problems. The problem is that when we apply the policy in this particular culture it can be met with a lot of resistance … Thus the issue is not so much around the language of the policy. Rather the issue that needs to be looked at is the environment in which the policy will be applied. Are the people who need to step forward to make sure policy is applied, are they doing that or are there other factors getting in the way? … I am frustrated that the leadership in my University fails to step up and say that this kind of work is important.

Another anti-racist practitioner stated: 'I have become very disillusioned. I don't know what it will take to change my university. It is clearly not coming from the leadership.'

Most of those interviewed (13 out of 14) reported that members of senior administration not only failed to implement policies that addressed racism but, moreover, blocked these policies. One effective method of blocking anti-racist policies was to refuse to act in instances of racism. Interviewees reported numerous examples of such refusals to act in incidents of racism:

> Let me give you an example – one of the more progressive deans who was very sensitive to equity policies ended up with a situation where a racialised faculty member who was applying for tenure had a peer reviewed letter in his file which denigrated his research interest on … with a backhanded reference to the candidate's 'race.' The letter was included in the package that went forward for tenure evaluation. The candidate heard of this letter and approached the HRO to have the letter removed. The Dean who had been very open to equity issues refused to have the letter removed. The Dean claimed that the letter was part of the process – that peers have the right to criticize however they want … This situation illustrates that rules can be there, there was nothing wrong with what the

policy says, nothing wrong with the remedy ... the letter should have been removed, but the academy in the person of the Dean would not do it. S/he just said no.

Another reported a similar incident:

Let's take the case of a half a dozen untenured racialised faculty from several different faculties who came to me to talk about their experiences with racism in their units. They were continually asked to volunteer for committees; their research was dismissed. After gathering the data, I realized there was no way of pursuing the complaint. So I put together a proposal for the President for an audit of systemic discrimination ... The President had the power to say yes or no. The President said no. How do you look at a complaint like that when you report to the President? And that particular experience is common place ... there are many more like it ... what does that mean for anti-racist work? It means that it is nothing more than window dressing.

Another anti-racist practitioner reported about an incident when s/he raised student concerns about racist course material: 'When I went to the director with students' concerns regarding Eurocentric course material or racism in the classroom, nothing was ever done. No conversation took place with faculty members about the students' concerns.' Another anti-racist practitioner reported that one practice administrators employed to avoid dealing with incidents of racism was to exclude him/her from decision making: 'I raise issues that create discomfort – that people would rather not talk or hear about ... What I struggle against is when it is amorphous. When decisions are made in places that I am not invited. Decisions made where I am not. In these situations there is a failure of the leadership to invite me into these discussions.'

Most of those interviewed reported that, in their opinion, the reason for the lack of support by members of senior administration is that those in these positions do not have an understanding of racism, to the extent that they do not believe that racism exists on campuses. One director of human rights and equity noted, 'One of the issues is that people do not get racism. There is a notion that people of colour are looking for favors rather than being treated equally.' Another stated, 'Decision makers do not have the understanding of what racism is, they resist even acknowledging that racism exists. Two of the most influential people in senior admin in my university love the University. They do not believe that my University could do anything wrong.'

Similarly, another anti-racist practitioner reported how the president of her/his university denied racism in a public forum:

> The President of my University was invited to a forum on racism. At this forum s/he stated that 'I don't know that racism exists. I have not heard of racism in my University.' How is that possible that the President of the University does not know about systemic racism, and how is it that the President does not get to hear about racism? What is preventing this? Is it that information does not move up to the top? I would speculate that rather it is located in the denial that racism exists. People in power deny it. So people of colour and Indigenous people are othered in that. They are constructed as angry, emotional and dangerous and denied validation. So attention is not paid to the painful lived experience of marginalization and exclusion.

Most of the anti-racist practitioners (12 out of 14) reported that not only did they face an unwillingness among senior administrators to acknowledge that racism takes place on university campuses, but in addition, in addressing either individual complaints against racism or issues of systemic discrimination, they faced a defensiveness response. The result was that it was very difficult to implement these policies effectively. As one director of a human rights and equity office stated, 'To suggest that there is systemic racism, to raise racism as a problem within the university, is to get an angry and defensive response. Those are the people who get into administrative positions. Their job is to protect those in power.'

Another stated, 'The big big issue with racism is the word. As soon as you use the word racism there is a problem … it leads to the response that we don't have a problem with racism, there is not racism at our university. We don't have to deal with racism because none of us are racist. In this context, the word racism creates a problem. It causes an immediate rift in being able to deal with the issue.' And yet another stated, 'When I raise issues of racism, I am perceived as an alien, as problematic, as angry.'

Many of those interviewed noted that members of senior administration often 'attack the messenger' as an attempt to make concerns illegitimate. As a result, most of those interviewed reported that senior administration personalized the concerns: 'The more I raise the issue of racism in the university, the more I get marginalized and dismissed. I get identified as the problem, not the issue.' Similarly, another stated: 'The resistance got to the point where I felt like I was betrayed, questioned, and had to defend myself. It got to the point where the President of my Faculty Association wrote a public letter calling into question the things that I was asking for, made a personal attack of me.'

A number of those interviewed (10 out of 14) reported such attacks escalated from personal attacks to incidents of intimidation and retaliation. For example, one director of a human rights and equity office reported: 'Even though I report to the President, I find members of senior administration are constantly trying to silence me, to the point of intimidation. For example, when I raised a specific issue around racism, a VP who was uncomfortable with my actions suggested that my ability to keep my position is precarious.' Another reported: 'People like myself who have spoken openly about racism are squeezed out – the administration finds a way to get rid of us. I was squeezed out of my position at the University ... I was never considered for administrative positions ... and I gave up on my dreams of working in this field after seven years of applying for positions.'

The inability and unwillingness of members of senior administration to address issues of racism raised questions of who gets promoted to such positions. Notably many of those interviewed registered concerns about how such appointments are being made. As a number of interviewees pointed out, the process of making such appointments does not include assessing candidates' understanding about racism, or, as important, candidates' commitment to addressing it. As a director of a human rights and equity office stated, 'This gets into the problem of how leaders are chosen in academia. Do we choose them for their research portfolios or because they have the skills to understand how University environments work? ... The flip side of this is that these people ... do the most harm by not being skilled at coping with people issues ... this affects everyone in the University, faculty and students.'

Another director of a human rights and equity office reported that at his institution, rather than promoting senior administrators who were sympathetic to issues of racism, the opposite was taking place: 'I work in an institution that does not have a history of promoting senior administrators who may support such work. In fact, it is the opposite. Two of the senior administrators who were sympathetic to such issues have not been renewed.' Another director of human rights and equity reported, 'The limitation in an office like mine, where we have people who understand and care about racism, is that we report to someone in administration who does not understand nor is committed to the issues. These people are often VPs who get hired for skills other than their understanding of human rights.'

Many of those interviewed (10 out of 14) saw the failure to deal effectively with racism as tied to the way in which whiteness structures the academy. In part, this points to the under-representation of faculty of colour and virtual exclusion of Indigenous faculty in administration. All of those interviewed reported that in their universities the vast majority of the administrators were 'white': 'Problem is the administration. The upper levels are lily white.'

This issue was not simply one of the predominance of those racialized as white in these positions, but more importantly, the ways in which a discourse of whiteness shaped the way in which senior administrators viewed the academy. As one anti-racist practitioner reported, 'I sat on a Senate Committee. The discourse of the committee was one that did not allow me to raise equity issues. I would have to do an enormous amount of education before people would begin to understand what I am taking about.'

Some of those interviewed (6 out of 14) connected the unwillingness of senior administrators to implement anti-racist policies to their difficulty in facing the resistance such policies evoke among members of the academy. For example, a director of human rights and equity noted that

> there is a tension concerning the rate of movement or the amount of advocacy that is appropriate for the Equity Office. The majority of the senior administrators are pleased with the current rate of progress and feel it is appropriate. They express concern that too much advocacy could destroy the current effectiveness of the office due to a possible backlash. They feel there is a need to be cautious.

Notably part of the hegemony of whiteness was that those sympathetic to addressing racism felt compelled to be silent: 'I have had a new dean say to me that she/he would not come to me with issues of racism in her/his profile because she/he saw what happened to her/his pre-decessor.' As another reported in such a context, doing such work was extremely difficult: 'I felt like I was trying to push a big rock up the hill. A few white people had sympathy, but the resistance was so intense that they were silent. This really tells us about the hegemony of whiteness. There was a personal cost to doing this work. I was the one taking the first blows.'

All of those interviewed reported that in their experience members of senior administration addressed racism very differently than other forms of discrimination. All of those interviewed reported that when they raised other forms of discrimination and harassment, they rarely received the same resistance. Such resistance made dealing with racism very different from dealing with other forms of discrimination. As one anti-racist practitioner reported:

> Race is completely different than gender. There is a willingness to deal with sexism, to set targets for women. When it comes to people of colour – it is a very different agenda. I don't know why. I wonder what the resistance is? Is it the feeling that people of colour will take our jobs? Is it that these people will come in and change our institution? Our departments? Or is it excellence? That people of colour will erode our departments? Maybe it is the fear of having your own world view challenged, the very work you do.'

Similarly, another stated:

> Racism is definitely dealt with differently than other forms of discrimination. Why is it that gender, homophobia and disability are issues that are more easily taken up? Why is racism so difficult to deal with? ... Why is the resistance so intense ... there is a language missing around race. People do not 'talk about it' allowing racist assumptions to go unnamed. It becomes emotional, explosive. It becomes the elephant in the room.

A director of human rights and equity noted that the difficulty in addressing racism is tied to the way in which whiteness works:

> I always wonder why racism is not the same as other forms of discrimination. Maybe it is because white folks have one of the other categories of marginalized people at home, but they don't have one of me. It is the same

for employment equity. Men have women at home who need to have jobs, so it is easier for them to accept employment equity for women, or other marginalized groups.

All of those interviewed (including those located within faculty associations) reported that faculty associations in their institutions also did not take leadership in addressing racism. The equity officer at CAUT notes that based on the anecdotal information that she receives, there is a lack of capacity among faculty associations to deal with racism. While one might expect that faculty associations would be at the forefront of asking for equity initiatives, those interviewed reported the opposite. Often executives of faculty associations and membership expressed the same form of resistance to employment equity and anti-harassment policies as did members of senior administration. Of those who worked through their faculty association (3 out of 14), all reported that the executives of their faculty association often prevented and undermined anti-racist policies. This was the case for anti-harassment clauses, employment equity policies, as well as anti-racist workshops. For example, someone who worked as a grievance officer in his/her faculty association stated, 'I don't think Faculty Associations are innocent in putting forward equity. When I put forward language on anti-harassment clauses I faced intense resistance from the President and Executive of the Faculty Association.'

A director of a human rights and equity office reported similar resistance in his/her university:

Recently the Faculty Association has replaced the clauses that deal with harassment and human rights with clauses on academic freedom. Why is this an either/or? Moreover, this was put forward in a manner that lacked transparency. The Equity Committee was not aware of it. The Executive put this through. Where is the enemy here? What makes an environment that allows this to happen? Don't we need a transparent process for minority faculty members who don't know how decisions are being made? When executive members make such changes, there is no voice, it is lost. This is an abuse of power that is very hard for a policy to deal with. It is about culture, it needs leadership of organization to question processes that don't work for everyone. What gives them the permission to take out clauses that pertain to Human Rights? Why was there no conversation about this?

Another anti-racist practitioner who worked within the faculty association reported:

> I experienced so much resistance when I was the Equity Officer. As the Chair of the Equity Committee in my faculty association, we came up with a number of policies and programs through which we could enhance anti-racism. Two of the policies we proposed were to negotiate for a full time Equity position within the University. The other was for an equity audit. I was then tasked with taking these proposals to the Executive. Most of the time, I experienced resistance. I was quite shocked at the resistance I faced.

Many of those interviewed noted that, as with the membership of senior administration, those elected or appointed into leadership positions within the faculty association tend to be predominantly 'white.' As one of those interviewed stated, 'My Faculty Association is so predominantly white. Where you see it most clearly is in the Executive and in the Stewards Councils. Also there are no people of colour on the staff of my Faculty Association.' In addition, as one of those who was interviewed pointed out, there is also an issue with the lack of autonomy of the staff of these associations: 'There are issues with the hired staff in the Faculty Association. Because the executives of Faculty Associations have particular world views, the staff tend to support this world view. The person assigned to work with me resisted much of what I tried to do. I always felt that she/he was trying to contain me.'

As a result, it is not surprising that faculty associations do not provide an inclusive atmosphere for racialized faculty. Those who worked as either equity officers or grievance officers within their faculty association (three of those interviewed) noted that racialized faculty felt uncomfortable with approaching their faculty association. For example, someone who served as a grievance officer noted, 'I had the sense that people of colour do not feel comfortable with the Faculty Association – and coming to them with issues. This is not surprising as there is a lack of recognition of racism.' As a result of this discomfort, all of the anti-racist practitioners who worked within their faculty associations noted that the grievance process was not always effective in dealing with incidents of racism. As one grievance officer stated, 'Grievance officers have an idea of what is worthy of taking forward, and there are even policies that specify what is harassment. Even if you have policies, there is a reluctance at the level of the executive to take some of these grievances forward.'

Someone who worked as an equity officer noted that in her/his university, there was a limited understanding of how incidents of racism constitute harassment: 'One of the difficulties is that when a complainant comes forward with a complaint of racism, the language that they use to describe their experience is not recognized by the Faculty Association.' Another person who served as an equity officer within the faculty association noted, 'It is surprising how little faculty of colour use the grievance process or the Faculty Association.' As all three of these practitioners noted, one of the challenges for faculty associations is to take up ways of becoming more inclusive. As one anti-racist practitioner stated, 'How is the Faculty Association going to take up the issues? They need to become more inclusive. They need to insure that they are representative. Faculty Associations have acknowledged that they need to have women on executives and on committees – but I do not know of one that acknowledges the importance of being representative of race.'

The professional officer for the CAUT Equity Committee notes that as the officers of staff associations rotate regularly, they lack training in anti-racism. As a result, these officers often approach these issues in ways that are similar to other members of the academy.

Conclusion: The Anomaly

My review of anti-racist policies within Canadian universities found that most Canadian universities have implemented some form of employment equity policies, anti-harassment policies and clauses, and anti-racist workshops to address racism. For many decades, the attention of anti-racist activists on university campuses has been focused on advocating for anti-racist policies; the deployment of such policies across so many Canadian universities is encouraging. However, as my closer analysis of these policies suggests, this achievement may be incomplete. While a number of policies have come into being, rarely are these policies effectively implemented. And, as we have seen, the most serious impediment to the successful implementation of such policies is the unwillingness of senior administration to address racism.

This finding is significant for those of us who have been actively engaged in bringing anti-racist policies to the academy. Much, if not all, of our attention has been focused on thinking through ways of constructing effective policies. As a result, we most often focus on finding wordings that would allow policies to be implemented. We have also focused on insuring that policies include mechanisms and procedures that insure their implementation. As my study suggests, there is still much work to be done in this regard. However, anti-racist activists have less often focused on the question of institutional support for anti-racist policies (for exceptions, see Henry and Tator 1994; James, chapter in this volume). My study suggests that support from senior administrators may be the most important factor determining effectiveness.

Throughout this chapter I have eluded to one of the interviewees who reported that s/he did not experience resistance from members of senior administration. It is useful to take a closer examination of this case – as it further illustrates the importance of administrative support for effective implementation of anti-racist policies in the academy. Notably, the director of human rights and equity at this university began our interview by raising the importance of administrative support: 'My university is a testament of what can take place if you have strong support at the top. Then things can happen.'

This practitioner described the president of her/his university as 'someone who was cut from the same cloth as equity.' As a result of such a commitment to equity the president has made equity a standing item on the agenda on the president's executive council. Not only does this place the responsibility for equity at the highest level of the university, but equally important, 'the President has set high water marks that people have to follow … Deans and Chairs increasingly know that this is something that can and should be done.'

In the case of this university, the president's commitment to anti-racism is further demonstrated by putting into place measures that allow anti-racist policies to be effective. Three kinds of measures have further reinforced the successful implementation of anti-racist policies. First, when an incident of hate takes place on campus, the president is required to communicate with the entire university about the incident. This clearly establishes that creating an inclusive university is an administrative responsibility. Second, staff and their supervisors are required to undertake equity training, insuring that there is an understanding of how to address race-related concerns. Finally, employment equity has been made a performance measure for all vice-presidents. Thus, vice-presidents are made accountable for implementing anti-racism. The director of human rights and equity reports that while there is resistance, especially at the middle administrative levels, the commitment of the senior administration has had significant impact. In particular, it has resulted in a significant increase in racialized faculty within the university.

This case reinforces the most important finding of this preliminary study – the importance of support from senior administrators for the effective implementation of anti-racist policies. It suggests that the most crucial, though overlooked, challenge that we face is the question of how we are to facilitate such support. The challenge is to think through how to insure that anti-racist policies take hold institutionally.

NOTES

1 In the past two decades there has been a resurgence of anti-racist activism on Canadian campuses, as racialized students and faculty have formed ad hoc committees and caucuses to document the forms of racism and ongoing colonialism, as well as to put forth agendas for change. For example, at the University of Toronto, faculty formed the Advisory Committee on Race Relations and Anti-Racist Initiatives; at York University, faculty have formed the Race Equity Caucus; at Queen's University, students and faculty formed the Principal's Advisory Committee on Race Relations; at the University of Calgary, students and faculty formed the Anti-Racism and Decolonization Network (ARDN); at the University of Guelph, students and faculty organized the Task Force on Anti-Racism and Race Relations.

2 Notably, in Britain and Australia researchers have begun to evaluate the effectiveness of anti-racist mechanisms. See, for example, Ahmad 2004, 2006.

3 Those interviewed included those who were racialized as white, as well as those racialized as people of colour. The people of colour include Canadian-born people of East Asian, South Asian, and African descent. Notably missing in these positions were Indigenous peoples.

4 As the focus of this chapter is on the kinds of mechanisms that impact faculty, I will concentrate on policies that impact the working conditions of faculty. For a review of anti-racist policies directed at students, see Henry (2006).

5 Notably, there is very little data on the representation of faculty of colour in Canadian universities. This is, in part, because of reasons of confidentiality; most university administrations do not report data on the number of visible minorities or Indigenous faculty that have been hired in ways through which meaningful trends can be observed. In the absence of such data, it is

often assumed that the proportion of Indigenous faculty and people of colour has increased. However, one recent systematic study of hiring in a particular university noted the exact opposite. Recently, Smith and Dhamoon (2006) have found that at the University of Alberta, while the percentage of visible minority faculty was increasing in faculties such as Engineering and Business, there has been a *steady decline* in visible minorities in the faculties of Arts and Education. In addition, there has been *no significant change* in the representation of Aboriginal people in any faculty at the university over the past twelve years. Similarly, Chandrakant and Svoboda (2007) calculated that if the University of Toronto continues to hire people of colour at its current rate, 'the results suggest that there is less than a 2.5 per cent chance of achieving our desired goal of 15 per cent visible minority faculty within the next 25 years ... There is also a greater than 50 per cent chance that it will take more than 54 years to achieve this goal.'

6 It is important to note that, in contrast, one of the grievance officers who was interviewed noted that a large number of grievances in his university were brought forward by faculty of colour. However, there are no data on grievances. As a result, it is difficult to assess whether the same pattern occurs in other universities.

7 Some universities have developed mechanisms to harmonize these two parallel procedures. In some of these cases, such as the University of Western Ontario, collective agreements override the procedures of the human rights office. In other universities, such as the University of Alberta, specific templates have been developed to harmonize the two procedures.

8 One of those interviewed noted that in her/his university, the faculty association was more likely to represent the person against whom a complaint is being made if it is a race-based complaint.

REFERENCES

Ahmed, S. 2004. 'Declarations of Whiteness: The Non-Performativity of Anti-Racism.' *borderlands e-journal* 3(2):421–43.
– 2006. 'Doing Diversity Work in Higher Education in Australia.' *Educational Philosophy and Theory* 38(6):745–68.
Burton, C. 1997. 'Report on Gender Equity in Australian University Staffing.' Evaluations and Investigations Program, Higher Education Division. Department of Employment, Education, Training and Youth Affairs. Government of Australia, Dec.
Canadian Federation for the Humanities and Social Sciences. 'The Academy as Community.' http://www.fedcan.ca/.

Carleton University, Diversity Office. 2007. Website 2007.

Drakich, J., and P. Stewart. 1995. 'Factors Related to Organizational Change and Equity for Women Faculty in Ontario Universities.' *Canadian Public Policy/Analyse de Politiques* 21(4):429–48.

– 2007. 'After 40 Years of Feminism, How Are University Women Doing?' *Journal of Higher Education: Academic Matters* Feb.:6–9.

Dua, E. 2000. 'Universities as Racialised Spaces: Women of Colour Experiences within Academia.' Presented at Women in the Academy, HSSFC Congress. Edmonton, AB, May.

Dua, E., and B. Lawrence. 2000. 'Whose Canada Is It? White Hegemony in University Classrooms.' *Atlantis* 24(2 Spring):105–22.

Henry, F. 2006. *Systemic Racism Towards Faculty of Colour and Aboriginal Faculty at Queen's University.* Also known as The Henry Report. http://www.queensu.ca/secretariat/senate/Mar30_06/SEECHenryRpt.pdf.

Henry, F., and C. Tator. 1994. 'Racism and the University.' *Canadian Ethnic Studies/Etudes ethniques au Canada* 26(3):74–90.

Mahtani, M. 2006. 'Challenging the Ivory Tower: Proposing Anti-Racist Geographies within the Academy.' *Gender, Place and Culture* 13(1):21–5.

Peake, L., and A. Kobayashi. 2002. 'Policies and Practices for an Antiracist Geography at the Millennium.' *Professional Geographer* 54(1):50–61.

Smith, M.S., and R. Dhamoon. 2006. *Higher Education Mentoring Program Proposal for People of Colour and Indigenous People.* Edmonton: Faculty of Arts, University of Alberta.

Stalker, J., and S. Prentice., eds. 1998. *The Illusion of Inclusion: Women in Post-Secondary Education.* Halifax: Fernwood.

Thomas, A. 2004. 'Politics, Policies and Practice: Assessing the Impact of Sexual Harassment Policies in UK Universities.' *British Journal of Sociology of Education* 25(2, Ap.):143–60.

University of Alberta, Human Rights Office. 2007. Website 2007.

University of British Columbia. 1998. 'Review of the Equity Office.' Review Committee Report. University of British Columbia, April 8. http://www.equity.ubc.ca/pub/review/index.htm.

Epilogue

FRANCES HENRY AND CAROL TATOR

This book attempts to critically examine some of the historical and contemporary manifestations of racism in Canadian academic institutions. Chapter 1 discusses some of the shared theoretical frameworks that flow through the contributed chapters of Audrey Kobayashi, Patricia Monture, Camille Hernandez-Ramdwar, Carl James, and Enakshi Dua. Their knowledge and experiences and that of many other racialized, Indigenous, and anti-racist Canadian scholars and educators expose the impact of the processes of racialization, Whiteness, Anglo-Eurocentrism, colonization, and hegemony that continue to operate within the academy. Various forms of racism in Canadian universities have been identified and discussed, including everyday racism, institutional racism, systemic racism, epistemological racism, democratic racism, and discursive racism. Within the social spaces of the academy, largely controlled by the dominant White culture, there is a constant moral tension between the lived experiences of racialized and Indigenous students and faculty, juxtaposed against the perceptions and practices of those who have the power within the institution, that is, White educators and administrators. Both the structure of the university and its policies and practices reflect the White and Eurocentric cultural values and norms that define it. In the modern Canadian university there is a deep polarization between how racism is imagined, understood, and acted upon by those with White skin privilege, and those whose life experiences, including their experiences within the academy, are marked by their racialized identities of 'otherness.'

For example, Audrey Kobayashi's deeply nuanced analysis of how Whiteness is experienced by academic women of colour in the Canadian university makes the argument that although racism is produced and reproduced systemically, the attitudes, assumptions, and beliefs that perpetuate racism are held by individuals. Thus, if relations among individuals are to change, that change must involve, to some degree, altering the behaviour of individuals. Without this approach, the policies and programs to combat racism being currently undertaken by many university administrations will be unsuccessful.

Carl James provides further insight into this issue by arguing that race and racial differences must be acknowledged as salient to individual experiences and knowledge. Moreover, the support for the liberal principles and related practices of colour-blindness, individualism, neutrality, objectivity, rationality, meritocracy, and academic freedom reinforce an 'institutional culture of denial' that promotes resistance to equity programs and practices. James argues that the challenge for universities is to ensure equitable and respectful treatment of racialized and Indigenous faculty members. The goal cannot simply be to recruit individual bodies 'representing' the diverse racialized groups that exist in Canadian society, but rather, to employ and engage educators and scholars who offer students new, enriched, and alternative forms of knowledge and pedagogical approaches in their scholarship and teaching. Both Kobayashi and James concur that Whiteness is a set of often unexamined power and privileges that go beyond individual identity but become collectively embedded in the institutional structures, thereby benefiting those with common social and cultural capital.

Patricia Monture moves the analysis forward by describing some of the structural barriers that faced her as an Indigenous scholar in the university. She, along with many other Indigenous faculty and faculty of colour, views the tenure process as one of the most overt manifestations of the continuing power of a White-dominated male culture that persists in the academy. Indigenous systems of knowledge are unknown in traditionally organized universities and, therefore, excluded from criteria used in the tenure decision process. Monture suggests that 'good scholarship,' even within a department such as Native Studies, remains embedded in conventional academic frameworks. The heavy emphasis on peer refereed article publications and books published by university presses further reduces the opportunities for promotion and tenure. The requests of the community for support and assistance in developmental and advocacy work are not seen as relevant to promotion and tenure evaluations, nor are the demands of Indigenous students who want and need support and mentoring from Indigenous faculty.

Among the barriers Monture confronted in her tenure applications was a lack of mentorship in the university. She observes that the absence of a mentor to lend support in clearing a maze of unnecessary obstacles is one of covert exclusion and operates to deny success to anyone who is not a White male. Other barriers and structural processes identified by racialized and Indigenous faculty include the efforts that are made to bring racialized and Aboriginal 'voices' from the community into the classroom, as well as in their research. This often is not valued as a scholarly contribution.

Camille Hernandez-Ramdwar's research findings provide an important window into the experiences of racialized students in the classroom. More specifically, in her interviews with students from the Caribbean, she analyses how both societal and academic racism impact on the academic experiences of these individuals. On a structural level, the students saw and experienced racism in the university in relation to the lack of diversity in the curriculum, faculty, student body, and administration. In her research and interviews, Hernandez-Ramdwar also identifies a number of societal factors that appear to have an impact on the academic performance, health, and well-being of Caribbean students. These include two characteristics commonly found in many Caribbean families: large numbers of single parent female-headed households, and responsibilities and expectations placed on children by their parents regarding financial and other kinds of support. She suggests that both these factors need to be better understood by university faculty, administrators, and bureaucracies in a way that does not result in negative stereotyping when decisions are being made, such as with academic penalties and leaves of absence. Hernandez-Ramdwar also points to the recent studies documenting the impact of poverty and racism on African, Black, and Caribbean ethno-racial groups, which she suggests can have a significant disenabling effect on students in terms of getting into or staying in the university. One of the author's most troubling findings was a correlation between the number of years Black students spent in the university and the greater the accounts of racism in the academy.

These narratives of racism experienced by students link to Carl James's finding that while the actual representation of students in Canadian universities has become increasingly diverse, curricula, courses, texts and content, and pedagogical approaches and assessments continue to be informed by Western European middle-class norms, values, expectations, and traditions. Based on such significant barriers, James argues that diversity can be viewed as little more than a 'public relations enterprise.' The diversity in knowledge needs, interests, and aspirations that minority students bring to the academy continues to be negated or ignored. He further notes that access programs have, in some ways, served to reinscribe the barriers they were expected to eliminate. In many universities with employment equity, affirmative action, and access programs, minority students continually are confronted with the discourse of 'reverse racism,' which is characterized by the assumption that unqualified people are taking places from more qualified applicants primarily on the base of their race, culture, refugee status, and other social factors.

Enakshi Dua's chapter is particularly relevant to the impact of dominant discourse on policies related to affirmative action and employment equity. Dua reviewed thirty-seven university policies that address racism, policies that were not a response to anti-racist initiatives but, rather, a response to feminist activism and legal changes in human rights legislation. In examining these policies, Dua found that the policies are constructed in ways that do not allow for effective implementation. Most exist at the level of general statements and thus lack the procedural requirements that would lead to effective implementation. In her interviews with anti-racist practitioners working in university human rights and equity offices within the universities, most believe that the most significant limitation in implementing current policies and practices was embedded in the various forms of resistance that the policies related to racism invoked among members of senior administration. Some respondents expressed deep concern linked to the resistance of senior administrators to the way in which Whiteness dominated their perceptions of reality and their world-views. Most of those interviewed felt that the policies worked 'as window dressing.' In the same way, employment equity policies at these universities are seen to exist at the level of general statements that lack the procedural requirements that would allow for effective implementation. Thirteen out of fourteen human rights and anti-racism officers interviewed reported that members of senior administration not only failed to have substantive policies that address racism, but also demonstrated that in the case of either individual or systemic complaints of racism there was an unwillingness to act. It is important to note that *all* of the respondents interviewed agreed that racism in their universities is addressed very differently from other forms of discrimination.

Moving towards Change

How then can we explain this lack of responsiveness to the multiplicity of reports that have documented the evidence of racism in the university? Why do we see a whole host of strong and clear recommendations in these studies and reports ignored year after year? How is it that faculty and students who experience the manifestations of racism, sexism, and/or classism are often ignored, criticized, or vilified? Why is it that complaints based on institutional systemic and structural barriers often are reframed as personalized attacks?

As we have argued throughout this book, most of the specific concerns and issues that are experienced by racialized and Indigenous faculty are a function of the dominant institutional culture of the university, that is, the culture of Whiteness. Overriding all their specific concerns, Indigenous faculty and faculty of colour (both men and women) commonly feel detached, alienated, and marginalized from the dominant White male-stream culture that has largely defined the university. The university is seen by racialized faculty as maintaining a culture defined by White power and privilege. The core values, beliefs, and attitudes of many of its individual members reflect patterns of Anglo-Eurocentric dominance. Many of the academics cited in this work argue that the role and function of the academy continues to underpin the structures and ideologies of colonialism and imperialism. The university appears to be an institutional site where dominant everyday discourses continue to reinforce an ethno-racial divide between the majority of White faculty and much smaller numbers of Indigenous and racialized faculty. Faculty of colour recognize and identify issues around interpersonal relationships with colleagues, students, and even administrators; however, the core problem lies with the dominant hegemonic institutional culture of the academy.

While the culture of Whiteness continues to be pervasive and systemic, most universities steadfastly believe that they have demonstrated their commitment to the framework of diversity by mission statements and recruitment strategies. Appadurai (2005) provides some insight into this contradiction by interrogating the meaning and use of the phrase 'culture of diversity' in the modern university (2005, 428–9). He understands the term to mean more than plurality or difference, but 'diversity is a particular organization of difference.' The concern in the university has less to do with what kind of diversity is required and more to do with how it can be 'managed.' The popularity of this notion of 'managing diversity' is found not only in the academy, but as well, across a wide range of organizations, institutions, and systems. 'Managing diversity' may lead to some marginal affirmative action strategies, but in a contested ethos and environment, initiatives are commonly reframed within the dominant discourses of 'quotas, censuses, and entitlements.' However, Appadurai maintains that what is lacking is 'a sustained effort to examine the links between intellectual and cultural diversity' that would lead to a true 'culture of diversity.' If this were accomplished, the 'culture of diversity' would replace the culture of Whiteness as the core mission of any reputable university.

It is against this background that the problems and concerns of racialized minority and Indigenous faculty can be understood. It is indeed paradoxical that one of the defining features of the culture of Whiteness as it manifests in the academy today is its reliance on the values and norms associated with liberalism, which stems from the classical eighteenth-century period of the Enlightenment. Thus, the values of 'liberty,' 'academic freedom,' 'individualism,' and 'universalism' continue to hold ideological supremacy in the Canadian academy. In practice, liberal sentiments often are expressed in coded language such as 'diversity,' 'colour-blindness,' 'neutrality,' 'objectivity,' 'merit,' 'standards,' and 'equal opportunity.' However, these central concepts in a liberal discourse, especially in the context of academic institutions, have immensely flexible meanings, and often become the ideological framework through which racialized beliefs and practices are reinforced and defended. Anti-racism and anti-oppression scholars, in large measure, agree that liberal precepts do not accord significance to the way in which fundamental structural and cultural inequity functions in a racialized, class-driven, gendered, and sexualized society.

For example, it is assumed that individual benefits and opportunities cannot be linked to ascribed personal or group characteristics such as race, sex, and class; and thus, such opportunities must be distributed according to 'individual merit' and 'personal achievement.' Under these terms, the role of the university is to protect individual freedom of choice while supposedly ensuring equality of opportunity. This framework underlies the construct of 'formal' equality. In the academy there continues to be a widespread assumption that ascribed characteristics, such as race and gender, are not supposed to make a difference to any student's or faculty's education or career. Racialized and Indigenous peoples who experience what they believe to be structural or systemic discrimination are perceived by those who support formal equality as being hostile to academic values, ideals, and practices. Within the mainstream culture of Whiteness, complaints by equity-seekers are seen as destructive and dangerous to the academic enterprise. The academy, much like all Canadian institutions (see Henry and Tator 2006), largely rejects the concept of systemic discrimination and mainly recognizes the construct of individual, direct, and intentional sources of bias and discrimination. In this hostile climate and within this culture of White power and privilege, the discourses of domination or democratic racism are employed. The most powerful of these discourses is that of categorical denial that racism or other forms of inequity exist in the university. Thus, the notion and strength of liberalism as a defining ideology in the academy is challenged by those who are stigmatized, marginalized, and excluded. Some of the many critical barriers to inclusion and equity in the academy have been identified in this volume.

A powerful example and one of the central tenets of the culture of Whiteness is that knowledge and its production, on which the university is based, operates in a neutral space. However, as has been maintained throughout this book, the production of knowledge and its evaluation is never neutral and always reflects the values and views of its creators. One of the primary manifestations of racism in the university is that, for the most part, Eurocentrically produced knowledge is privileged over all other forms. Thus, the research and writing of racialized and Indigenous faculty, who often work within non-Eurocentric paradigms, is not seen as having equal value and merit. Other barriers, which reinforce 'Otherness,' discussed at length in this book, include curricular decision making; pedagogical methods and approaches; hiring, promotion, and tenure practices; and research priorities and practices, all of which reinforce the everyday privileges of Whiteness and continue to sustain unequal power relations within the academy.

Within institutions of higher learning, cultural amnesia continues to function in a way that continues to erase the processes of racialization that remain embedded in much of the institutional life within the university. The discourses of denial and of colour-blindness become a defence of everyday norms, values, and practices within the academy, thereby ignoring or dismissing the notion that race/culture exists and has significant material, political, social, intellectual, and academic consequences. The discourses of pluralism and inclusion do not address the tangible, everyday experiences of marginalization and exclusion. The discourse of political correctness attempts to silence those who give voice to their lived experiences of marginalization in the academy. The discourse of academic freedom does not address the issues of 'intellectual homelessness,' 'chilly,' 'unsafe,' and 'hostile' work environments, as described by racialized and Indigenous faculty across this country. The discourse of 'equal opportunity' does not take into account the toll of academic, social, psychological, and physical manifestations of racism in the academy. Each of these discourses represents a profound kind of erasure or amnesia on the part of the White and privileged.

How can this culture of Whiteness begin to be disassembled? Efforts have been made in the last two decades to develop strategies that are supposed to produce change, but the problem with most of these approaches is that they are based on the ideological assumptions of liberalism. Thus, many universities are now committed in some fashion, even if only in mission statements, to a faculty, staff, and student body that reflect the growing ethno-cultural and ethno-racial pluralism in Canadian society. Representation is certainly a desired goal for the academy, but as demonstrated by each of the contributors to this volume, it is not by itself sufficient to effect cultural and structural change. In any event, strategies of recruitment have thus far only functioned to create relatively small numbers of diverse faculty, and many of those are found clustered in physical science areas such as engineering, computer technology, and the like. As this work has also established, there is not only considerable alienation and unhappiness among Indigenous faculty and faculty of colour, especially those relatively newly hired, but also serious barriers to their attaining equitable status with their peers. Real change requires looking beyond representation.

One conclusion that we, our co-authors, and many other scholars on the subject of equity at the university concur with is that the strategies already instituted at most universities do not work effectively or efficiently to produce change. For example, as charges of racism began to surface at some universities, offices designated as 'race and ethnic relations,' or a similar name, were established to deal with them. From the outset, these offices were virtually powerless and often marginalized from the real decision-making structure of the university. In more recent times, and following the best of liberal traditions, these organizations have now morphed into diversity and/or human rights offices in which all types of threats to equality are supposed to be dealt with; however, their powerlessness and the absence of real sanctions has not changed the culture, structures, and systems within the academy. Similarly, some universities still believe that a workshop session in 'anti-racist,' 'diversity,' or 'human rights' training (commonly delivered in as little as three hours) is a useful tool in combating the deep-seated ubiquitous belief systems and practices that pervade the university. Clearly, judging by the results, these measures have done little to bring about changes in either attitudes or structures.

While basic value systems are difficult to change, the everyday policies and practices that maintain the structure and organization of institutions can be more readily influenced, especially as they are frequently subjected to review. This is particularly true in the university, which has instituted review practices at many levels in its efforts to maintain 'quality' and 'standards.' A useful beginning, therefore, might be to reassess the policies and practices that are already in place in most universities with the objective of acknowledging and addressing racism in the academy and incorporating elements of anti-racism education.

For example, most undergraduate departments regularly undertake a review of their curriculum to ensure that all important aspects of their disciplines, or those that they have designated to specialize in, are effectively taught to the student body. This type of review of curriculum should also determine if courses that concentrate on anti-racism, or at least include units on this perspective, are included in the curriculum. (Other areas of inequity might also be included.) At graduate and professional levels, most programs in Canadian universities must meet the requirements established by government ministries in order to train students to become professionals in a discipline. A newly developed program must first pass through an evaluation before it can be accredited. Existing programs are regularly reassessed, some as often as every five years. These assessments are based on traditional academic requirements, such as number and training of existing faculty, research and publications produced, and the general quality and comprehensiveness of the curriculum. Again, as in undergraduate programming, a criterion of assessment could also include an anti-racist perspective. Changing or adding to the criteria of assessment would probably necessitate cooperation between the academy and government ministries; this should not be an insurmountable problem, but one that would depend on a commitment to ensuring greater equity.

It is incumbent on the academy to prepare students entering professions, such as teaching, healthcare, social work, law, journalism, law enforcement, governance, business, and a host of other career paths, with critical analytic skills that include the ability to recognize and critique political, cultural, and economic structures that oppress marginalized peoples. Professional socialization in all of these fields of study should ensure that graduates leave the university prepared with new forms of knowledge, critical perspectives, and tools required to be effective change agents in a culturally pluralistic and racially diverse and divided society.

There are also other equity existing measures, already operating in most universities, whose effectiveness should be evaluated. For example, recruitment advertisements should include a policy statement not just welcoming diverse applicants, but signalling a message that the university is committed to social justice and equity in all areas of its institution. Similarly, the effectiveness of such advertisements, where they already exist, should be examined in terms of their success in broadening the recruitment pool. The placement of advertisements should also be reviewed to ensure that information is dispensed as widely as possible.

Most universities already have an employment equity committee in place largely because they need to comply with government demands. However, it is often alleged that such committees are not functioning effectively and perform their overview task in a perfunctory manner. These committees are usually not seen as critical or central to the university's function and are rarely given real power to scrutinize a department's recruitment and selection practices, nor do they have any real sanctions to dispense against offending departments. At the very least, a review of the performance of these committees and their general effectiveness should be undertaken on a regular basis.

There are undoubtedly other policies and practices in place at different universities, not all of which can be reviewed here. At the very least, however, equity-related strategies should be open, transparent, and subject to regular review. Administrators have a responsibility to avoid forms of tokenism as powerfully described in this book. Certainly, one of the consistent and compelling themes in restructuring the university is the need to accept alternative ways of thinking, knowing, learning, and producing knowledge. We need to provide opportunities for incorporating critical pedagogy and anti-racism perspectives and strategies into our classrooms in order to encourage equity. Teaching environments, curriculum, and pedagogy can more effectively provide tools for emancipation and democratization within the academy and within our society.

As many scholars have noted in this volume, the discourses of equal opportunity, diversity, and inclusiveness may have opened the doors of universities to racialized and Indigenous scholars, women, people living with disabilities, and other social markers of 'different' identities. However, this has not changed the cultural values, norms, and practices of the hegemonic power structures within institutions of higher learning. Nor has that culture of Whiteness been replaced by a 'culture of diversity.' We end this work with the powerful words of Appadurai:

> What is required is a sustained effort to create a climate that is actually hospitable to diversity; one which puts diversity at the center of the curriculum and the demographics of the university, rather than at its statistical or conceptual margins … [it] is not good enough for the university unless it transforms the way in which knowledge is sought and transmitted. That is, without a commitment to the mutual value of intellectual and cultural diversity … the core mission of the university remains insulated from the commitment to diversity. (Appadurai 2005, 429)

REFERENCE

Appadurai, A. 2005. 'Diversity and Disciplinarity as Cultural Artifact.' In C. McCarthy et al., *Race, Identity and Representation in Education*, 427–38. New York and London: Routledge.

Contributors

Enakshi Dua is an associate professor in the School of Women's Studies at York University. She is currently the chair of the CAUT Equity Committee. She teaches critical race theory, anti-racist feminist theory, postcolonial studies, development studies, and globalization. She has extensively published on racism and anti-racism, immigration processes, women and health, equity policies, criminalization and the racialization of masculinity and femininity, globalization, and biodiversity. Her publications include *Scratching the Surface: Canadian Anti-Racist Feminist Thought*. Within the academy, she has held a number of administrative positions that deal with gender, anti-racist, and equity issues.

Professor (Emerita) **Frances Henry** has been actively engaged in research, writing, and teaching in the fields of racism and anti-racism studies in Canadian society. Since the mid-1970s when she published the first study of attitudes towards racialized people, she has consistently pioneered research in this field. Dr. Henry, as a social anthropologist, has also published extensively in Caribbean Studies, including the only ethnographic work so far on Caribbean migration in Canada, *The Caribbean Diaspora in Toronto: Learning to Live with Racism*. She has co-authored many other books, including *The Colour of Democracy: Racism in Canadian Society*; *Racial Profiling in Canada: Challenging the Myth of 'A Few Bad Apples'*; and *Discourses of Domination: Racial Bias in the Canadian English-Language Press*.

Camille Hernandez-Ramdwar is an assistant professor in the Department of Sociology at Ryerson University in Toronto. She teaches in the areas of both sociology and Caribbean studies. Her areas of research include Caribbean cultures and identities, diasporic and second generation identities, and racism and Caribbean peoples in Canada. Dr. Hernandez-Ramdwar is also a writer of short stories, narratives, and poetry dealing with the issues of diasporic, transnational, and multiracial identities.

Professor **Carl E. James** teaches in the Faculty of Education at York University and is currently the director of the York Centre for Education and Community (YCEC). His research and publication interests relate to educational and occupational access and equity for marginalized people and the role of identity/identification pertaining to race, ethnicity, gender, class, and citizenship/immigrant status in the lived experiences of Canadians. He has published several books and contributed to edited texts on racism in Canada.

Audrey Kobayashi is a professor of geography and Queen's research chair at Queen's University. Her research and publication topics include anti-racism, gender, employment equity, and immigration. Her research focuses on how processes of race, class, gender, ability, and national identity emerge in a range of landscapes that include homes, streets, and workplaces. She places a strong emphasis on public policy, and on the legal and legislative frameworks that enable social change.

Patricia Monture is a citizen of the Mohawk Nation, Grand River Territory. Since 1994, she has been employed at the University of Saskatchewan. Completing a term in the dean's office in 2004, she is now a full professor in the Department of Sociology. She teaches in the area of Aboriginal justice and works closely with the students of the Aboriginal Justice and Criminology program. Professor Monture is the author of two books and numerous journal articles.

Carol Tator has worked as an anti-racism advocate, educator, and scholar for over three decades. Her research focuses on an analysis of the impact of racialized ideologies, discourses, policies, and practices across a wide range of institutional sectors. She teaches anti-racism and equity in the Department of Anthropology at York University and has co-authored several books, including *The Colour of Democracy: Racism in Canadian Society*; *Racial Profiling in Canada: Challenging the Myth of 'A Few Bad Apples'*; *Discourses of Domination: Racial Bias in the Canadian English-Language Press*; and *Challenging Racism in the Arts: Case Studies of Controversy and Conflict*.

Index

Aboriginal peoples. *See* Indigenous peoples

Aboriginal studies. *See* Native studies

academic freedom, discourse of, 132, 198, 203

Academic Matters. See *Journal of Higher Education: Academic Matters*

academy, the (general), 4–5; discourse of political correctness, 34; as discursive spaces, 32–3; and dominant discourses of knowledge, 36; goal of, 6, 40; history of, 4–5; liberalism in, 32, 51–2, 132–3; and racial diversity (general), 128–52

Action Travail des Femmes, 61

administrators, university, 29; ethno-racial origins of, 43, 137, 187, 197; and responses to racism, 164, 178–80, 182–91, 200

affirmative action, 16, 66, 78, 131–2, 137, 142–4, 147, 154n16, 200–1; and self-identification, 132, 142–4

Al-Azhar University (Cairo), 4

American universities, 53n3, 85; studies on racial diversity, 128–30

Anglocentric culture, 3, 36, 197, 201.

See also Eurocentrism; White dominant culture

anti-harassment policies, 163–4, 166, 173, 175–91; administrative resistance to, 178–80, 182–91, 200; effectiveness of, 178–82; and grievance process, 176–9, 190–1; and harassment complaints, 62–3, 149, 176–82, 183–91; racism and, 178–82, 183–92, 200; systemic issues in, 181. *See also* human rights and equity offices

anti-oppression. *See* anti-racism

anti-racism: activism and change, 17, 19, 33, 41, 64, 66, 70, 160, 192, 193n1, 202, 204–6; and anti-harassment policies, 178–82, 182–92, 200 (*see also* anti-harassment policies); curriculum and pedagogy, 13, 36, 41, 47–9, 68, 205, 206 (*see also* critical pedagogy); education/workshops, 4, 163, 166, 172–5, 180, 191; and feminism, 68, 163; human rights and equity office (*see* human rights and equity offices); policies in universities, limitations of, 18–19, 160–93, 178–80, 182–92,

www.ingramcontent.com/pod-product-compliance
Lightning Source LLC
Chambersburg PA
CBHW032133020426
42334CB00016B/1149